W9-ANM-111

PAN-AFRICANISM

A short political guide

Also by Colin Legum

ATTITUDE TO AFRICA

MUST WE LOSE AFRICA?

BANDUNG, CAIRO AND ACCRA

CONGO DISASTER

AFRICA

WITHDRAWN
NDSU

P·R·A·E·G·E·R
PAPERBACKS
PPS-82 $1.95

lin Legum

N-AFRICANISM

short political guide

COLIN LEGUM

PAN-AFRICANISM

A SHORT POLITICAL GUIDE

FREDERICK A. PRAEGER, *Publisher*

NEW YORK

160757

DT
30
L39

BOOKS THAT MATTER

Published in the United States of America in 1962
by Frederick A. Praeger, Inc., Publisher
64 University Place, New York 3, N.Y.

Second printing, 1963

All rights reserved

© Copyright: Colin Legum, 1962
Library of Congress Catalog Card Number: 62-13489

Printed in the United States of America

PREFACE

This book is dedicated to the work of the Africa Bureau.

In an abbreviated form it was delivered as the Africa Bureau's 1961 Annual Address. I am grateful to the Chairman, Lord Hemingford, and to the Executive for agreeing that the Address should be published in this expanded form.

The book is in two parts; the first might be more readable, but the second is more useful. In the first part I have tried to trace briefly the origins and growth of Pan-Africanism, and its subsequent impact on Africa after its transplantation in 1958.

In the second part I have provided a documentary guide to Pan-Africanism, the absence of which I personally have felt to be a great handicap in the past. This is only a start; much more work requires to be done by our academic colleagues who have so far largely neglected this field of study.

Although I must accept sole responsibility for the views expressed in this book, I am nevertheless greatly indebted to Dr. George Shepperson of Edinburgh University, and Professor St. Clair Drake of Roosevelt University, Chicago, for having read and criticised this work at various stages; to Mr. Harold R. Isaacs of the Center for International Studies, Massachusetts Institute of Technology, whose studies on Negro literature have been particularly valuable to me in a field in which he has done so much work and of which I know comparatively little. Finally I must mention my wife who has worked almost as hard as I have in revising the manuscript and who wrote the chapter on 'Africa's Divided Workers'.

COLIN LEGUM

London.
November, 1961

ACKNOWLEDGMENTS

The works of all writers quoted have been fully acknowledged. But my special acknowledgment and thanks are due to the following authors and publishers:

Ras Khan, *The Poetry of Dr. R. E. G. Armattoe* (*Présence Africaine*, Paris); Mr. Harold R. Isaacs; *The Langston Hughes Reader* (Braziller, New York); *Selected Poems* (Alfred Knopf, New York); *Tambourines and Glory* (John Day, New York); Olumbe Bassir: *An Anthology of West African Verse* (Ibadan); Miriam Koshland for her translations in Black Orpheus (Ibadan); David Diop, *Le Temps du Martyr* (Presse Universitaires de France, Paris); Aimé Césaire, *Four Poems* and *The Return of the Native* (Black Orpheus, Ibadan, and *Présence Africaine*, Paris); Leopold Senghor, *Anthologie de la Nouville Poesie Negre et Malgache* (Presse Universitaires de France, Paris); Michael Dei-Aneng, *Wayward Lines from Africa*; Claude McKay *Outcast* (Twayne, New York); Leon Dalmas (*Présence Africaine*, Paris).

CONTENTS

A Map, by W. H. Bromage, indicating the present groupings in Africa will be found on pages 70 and 71

ABBREVIATIONS USED IN TEXT

AAPC	All-African Peoples' Conference
AAPO	All-African Peoples' Organisation
AATUF	All-African Trade Union Federation
AEF	Afrique Equatoriale Française
AOF	Afrique Occidentale Française
CGTA	Conféderation Générale des Travailleurs d'Afrique
FLN	National Liberation Front (Algeria)
ICFTU	International Confederation of Free Trade Unions
ICTUF	International Federation of Christian Trade Unions
ILO	International Labour Organisation
NAACP	National Association for the Advancement of Coloured Peoples
NATO	North Atlantic Treaty Organisation
OAC	Organisation for African Community
PAFMECA	Pan-African Movement for East and Central Africa
RDA	Rassemblement Democratique Africain
SEATO	South-East Asia Treaty Organisation
UAR	United Arab Republic
UAS	Union of African States
UGTAN	Union Générale des Travailleurs d'Afrique Noire
UNIA	Universal Negro Improvement Association
UNO	United Nations Organisation
UPA	Union of the Peoples of Angola
UPC	Union of the Peoples of the Cameroons
UPS	Union Progressiste Senegalaise
USSR	*see* Soviet Union
WFTU	World Federation of Trade Unions

APPENDICES

APPENDICES

PAN-AFRICANISM

A short political guide

CHAPTER I

THE ROOTS OF PAN-AFRICANISM

Among the persistent misconceptions of our times is that 'one never knows what goes on in the African's mind'. It is an attitude that unfortunately tells us more about Europeans—especially about those who have lived most of their lives in Africa—than it does about Africans. Europeans have become conditioned to thinking about Africa in European terms; and, of course, in terms of European interests. This is as true of Europeans in the West as of those in the East; a point neatly illustrated at a recent conference in Cairo by Mr. Tom Mboya.

'We find,' he said, 'that both Westerners and Russians look at Africans through the same pair of glasses : the one lens is marked pro-West; the other pro-Communist. It is not surprising that, looking at Africans in this way, most foreigners fail to understand the one great reality about our continent—that Africans are neither pro-West nor pro-Russian; they are pro-African.'

It is a remarkably simple point—once it is grasped. But until then we will continue to read and, no doubt, people who write top-level secret documents, will continue to write, about 'pro-Communist Gizenga'; 'pro-Western Kasavubu', 'anti-British Nasser', 'pro-British Nigeria'; and all the other variations on this theme—the 'moderate' African leaders (meaning those who are for 'us'), or the 'extremists' (those who are against 'us').

There is, of course, nothing new or remarkable about such an egocentric approach, but as applied to contemporary Africa it helps to explain why leaders 'typed' in cold war terms appear to behave inconsistently. What is 'pro-Moscow' Colonel Nasser doing attacking the Russians? Why has 'anti-Western' Sékou Touré asked the Americans to provide dollars for Guinea's new hydro-electric project? Only when we are able to accept that African leaders, for the first time in their history, feel free to shop and trade for imports and exports, as well as for loans and ideas, in any zone of Europe or in any part of the world will we be able to avoid the mistake of attributing ulterior motives to them; and thus avoid acting stupidly for fear that they are going over to the 'wrong side'.

This casting aside by Africans of subservience to foreign masters in all forms, and their confident assertion that African interests are paramount, are expressions—perhaps even the fullest expression—of Pan-Africanism. But although it is possible to talk about the way Pan-Africanism *expresses* itself, it is not so easy to give a concise definition of this relatively new recruit to the world's political vocabulary. Pan-Africanism has come to be used by both its protagonists and its antagonists as if it were a declaration of political principles. It is not.

In its practical expression it can be translated into sets of guiding principles : but these could, and often do, vary greatly—as much, perhaps, as the four Socialist Internationals have varied in proclaiming their understanding of socialism; which does not, of course, invalidate socialist ideas any more than the development of different schools of African thinking invalidates Pan-Africanism.

Emotions of the Black World

It is essentially a *movement of ideas and emotions*; at times it achieves a synthesis; at times it remains at the level of thesis and antithesis. In one sense Pan-Africanism can be likened to socialism; in another sense it can be likened to World Federation, Atlantic Union or Federal Europe; each allows for great scope of interpretation in its practical application. And yet, in its deepest sense, Pan-Africanism is different from all these movements in that it is exclusive. Its closest parallel perhaps is Zionism. In 1919 Dr. duBois wrote '... The African movement means to us what the Zionist movement must mean to the Jews, the centralisation of race effort and the recognition of a racial fount.'[1]

Pan-Africanism began not in the 'homeland' but in the diaspora. Zionism had its origins in Central and Eastern Europe; Pan-Africanism had its in the New World. It developed through what Dr. Shepperson described as 'a complicated Atlantic triangle of influences'[2] between the New World, Europe and Africa. In its early phase—the middle of the nineteenth century up to the turn of the twentieth century—the inhabitants of Africa imbibed these new ideas from their studies mainly in the United States and later in Britain. This seeding process will be described later.

At this point I am not concerned with trying to present either an historical or a comprehensive summary of the numerous political, religious and cultural forces which, in their various ways, were the precursors of the Pan-African movement; my concern is to discover the emotional reactions and drives that produced the nascent ideas of Pan-Africanism. Thus I have felt free to jump from one century to the other and from one continent to another in quoting writers, poets and preachers to illustrate the underlying unity of emotions and ideas in the black world.

The emotional impetus for its concepts flowed from the experiences of a widely-dispersed people—those of African stock—who felt themselves either physically through dispossession or slavery, or socially, economically, politically and *mentally* through colonialism, to have lost their homeland; with this loss came enslavement, persecution, inferiority, discrimination and dependency. It involved a loss of independence, freedom and dignity. *Dignity* : that majestic magical word in the vocabulary of Pan-Africanists; to regain dignity is the mainspring of all their actions.

Alien and Exile

The intellectual superstructure of Pan-Africanism has meaning only if one constantly reminds oneself that at its roots lie these deep feelings of dispossession, oppression, persecution and rejection. This complex of emotions—'the alien and exile' theme[3]—is one of the primary strands in the growth of Pan-Africanist ideas.*

It is typified by Claud McKay's *Outcast* :†

> *For the dim regions whence my fathers came*
> *My spirit, bondaged by the body, longs.*
> *Words felt, but never heard, my lips would frame;*
> *My soul would sing forgotten jungle songs.*
> *I would go back to darkness and to peace.*
> *But the great western world holds me in fee,*
> *And I may never hope for full release*
> *While to its alien gods I bend my knee.*
> *Something in me is lost, forever lost,*
> *Some vital thing has gone out of my heart,*
> *And I must walk the way of life a ghost*
> *Among the sons of earth, a thing apart.*
> *For I was born, far from my native clime,*
> *Under the white man's menace, out of time.*

Ambivalence Towards the West

Claude McKay's deservedly famous sonnet is rich in other emotions which reflected and forecast political ideas. There is the ambivalent struggle with 'the great western world' from whose fee there is no hope of ever obtaining full release. Africa calls, but

* See also the Address by Dr. Edward W. Blyden in Appendix 23.
† Selected poems of McKay (Twayne, New York, 1959–61).

there is no going back; having bent the knee to 'alien gods' he is
an inner exile, forever lost—'a ghost', 'a thing apart'. This spirit of
ambivalence proclaims the inability of Negroes to disengage themselves from the West, even for those who feel their rootlessness
within its society. Here is one of the powerful, romantic internal
conflicts which explains the appeal of Garvey's 'Back to
Africa' movement. It is a potent emotion, but an impotent political
force.

We find the same chord, 'long impotent in me', in Countee
Cullen's work;[4] and much more strongly in Langston Hughes'.
Unlike most Negro writers, Hughes has made a pilgrimage to
Africa. On his return he wrote :

> *We cry among the skyscrapers*
> *As our ancestors*
> *Cried among the palms in Africa*
> *Because we are alone,*
> *It is night,*
> *And we're afraid.*

Black Solidarity

In the poetry of Langston Hughes[5] we find the strong chords of
a third persistent theme—the wish to create a common *identity*
beween all those of Negro stock,[6] to establish a greater sense of
solidarity and security; to achieve a sense of *oneness*,* a political
belonging between the isolated, uprooted communities of the diaspora first with each other and then with Africa.

> *We are related—you and I.*
> *You from the West Indies,*
> *I from Kentucky.*
> *We are related—you and I.*
> *You from Africa,*
> *I from these States.*
> *We are brothers—you and I.*

Langston Hughes, himself of mixed descent, is so light of colour

---

* Later it transpired that this emotional longing for an integral unity
between the Negro of the New World and the African is not always
practicable; an apparently unbridgeable gulf has grown up between the
'uprooted African' and the continental African. But the emotional im-
pulse towards identification and the attempt to bridge the dualism of
being Negro and American and being Negro and African survives powerfully. This is a separate aspect which is discussed in a later chapter.

that he was regarded in Africa as 'a white man'.* But he is deeply colour-conscious.

> I am a Negro:
> Black as the night is black,
> Black like the depths of my Africa.

It it when he writes of his *sense* of colour, of blackness, that he expresses what is undoubtedly the dominant theme in Pan-Africanism : the race-consciousness born of colour.† This is a theme that runs powerfully in its story of growth.

Feelings of Inferiority

> 'Suffer, poor Negro,
> Negro, black like grief. . . .'

In these two lines by the Senegal poet, David Diop, we find all there is to know about the equation between black and grief, suffering and submissiveness. The Jews had, for centuries, kept alive their belief and confidence in themselves by fostering the religious myth of the *Chosen People*; even so, many Jews came to accept the judgment of inferiority passed on them by Gentiles. Negroes, especially those living in the diaspora, had no such biblical myth to sustain them : the extent to which they themselves came to accept the verdict of whites is clearly shown in the extremely valuable studies made by Dr. Harold R. Isaacs[7] and others[8] about the way Negro children see themselves, as in this example :

'In the fourth grade, those pictures of the races of man . . . with a handsome guy to represent the whites, an Indian and then a black, kinky-haired specimen—that was me, a savage, a cannibal, he was just the tail end of the human race . . . he was at the bottom. . . . That picture in the book was the picture of where and what I came from. . . .'‡

Rejection of Inferiority: Pride of Colour

Acceptance of black inferiority in submission to oppression was by no means the only response to a society in which all values were

* Langston Hughes, writing in *The Big Sea* (New York, 1945) says: 'There was one thing that hurt me a lot when I talked with the people. The Africans looked at me and would not believe I was a Negro. You see, unfortunately, I am not black.'

† For a modern political example see Chief Awolowo's Statement, Appendix 24.

‡ A significant historical parallel is provided by an Address delivered by Dr. Edward W. Blyden in 1881 in Liberia. For a fuller text of his Address see Appendix 23. For a brief biographical note see footnote on p. 20.

European values; least of all in the Caribbean territories. There
was both physical and cultural resistance.* The dominant picture,
however, was one of adaptation; this took various forms—sometimes
it was half-hearted, negative and resentful; slowly it became more
creative.

Always there were poets who reflected the bitterness of the black
man as the bottom-dog in a white world. But instead of despising
their own blackness they extolled it; a natural enough reaction to
the idea that all that was black was evil, terrifying and primitive.
Negroes were encouraged to wear their black skins with pride
instead of with shame; this theme finds common expression in both
the New World and in Africa, and it goes back at least to the
middle of the nineteenth century.

We find it in the defiant poetry of the Togo writer Dr. R. A.
Armattoe,[9] who lived for a long time in Europe :

> *Our God is black*
> *Black of eternal blackness*
> *With large voluptuous lips*
> *Matted hair and brown liquid eyes . . .*
> *For in his image are we made.*
> *Our God is black.*

or when he writes in *Negro Heaven* :

> *And angels black as Indian ink*
> *And dark saints blacker still did sing.*

We find it in the poetry of the American writers :[10]

> *Black*
> *As the gentle night,*
> *Black as the kind and quiet night,*
> *Black as the deep and productive earth.*
> *Body*
> *Out of Africa,*
> *Strong and black . . .*
> *Kind*
> *As the black night*
> *My song*
> *From the dark lips*
> *Of Africa . . .*
> *Beautiful*

* According to Shepperson and Price, 'a conservative estimate of the
number of slave risings in the United States would set the figure at over
two hundred and forty' (*Independent African*, page 106).

> *As the black night . . .*
> *Black*
> *Out of Africa,*
> *Me and my song.*

Later in the time-scale, we find it in the poetry of Leopold Senghor, now President of Senegal :

> *Woman nude, woman black*
> *Clad in your colour which is life . . .*
> *Your beauty strikes me to the heart*
> *As lightning strikes the eagle.*[11]

This challenging theme reached its apogee in the works of Aimé Césaire, widely acknowledged to be one of the great contemporary writers of French poetry, a revolutionary, and the unchallenged political leader of Martinique. It was he who introduced the concept of *negritude*, which is discussed presently.

> *My negritude is not a rock, its deafness*
> *hurled against the clamour of the day*
> *My negritude is not a film of dead water on*
> *the dead eye of the earth*
> *My negritude is neither a tower nor a*
> *cathedral.*
> *It plunges into the burning flesh of the earth*
> *It plunges into the burning flesh of the sky*
> *It pierces the opaque prostration*
> *by its upright patience.*[12]

The Sense of a Lost Past

With this acceptance of blackness came a demand to rediscover the lost past of the Negro race—another strand in Pan-Africanism lucidly expressed by the Guyana poet, Leon Dalmas :[13]

> *Give me back my black dolls to play*
> *the simple game of my instincts . . .*
> *to recover my courage*
> *my boldness*
> *to feel myself myself*
> *a new self from the one I was yesterday*
> *yesterday*
> *Without complications*
> *yesterday*
> *when the hour of uprooting came.*

African Personality

In this poem by Dalmas we find the nascent idea of an African personality : *to feel myself myself . . . a new self from the one I was yesterday . . . when the hour of uprooting came.*

'I am a Negro and all Negro. I am black all over, and proud of my beautiful black skin . . ." proclaimed the American negro, John Edward Bruce, in response to Majola Agbebi, a Yoruba Baptist, in 1902 when he inaugurated what was probably the first independent Native African Church in West Africa. It was to Agbebi that the distinguished West Indian, Edward Blyden, first applied the term of 'African Personality', which he explained by saying that 'Africa is struggling for a separate personality'.[14] Agbebi's inaugural address made such a profound impression on John Edward Bruce (1856–1924), a New York journalist and co-founder of the Negro Society for Historical Research, that he led a deputation of New York Negroes to have 11th October observed as 'Majola Agbebe Day' to 'immortalise him an African Personality'. Bruce was much influenced by Blyden's ideas of an emerging distinctive African personality.

Fears that uncritical absorption of Western ideas would in time destroy the distinctive personality of African's was voiced by Edward Blyden's kinsman, Dr Edward W. Blyden,* in his presidential address at the opening of the Liberian College in 1881.

There is little of the latter day sophisticated intellectualisation and political ideology about the African personality in Dr. Blyden's seminal speech which is reproduced as Appendix 23. Its importance lies in the stress he laid on the desirability of controlling the process of acculturation between the West and Africa. For our immediate purpose it is sufficient to quote briefly from Dr. Blyden's address :

'The African must advance by methods of his own. He must possess a power distinct from that of the European. It has been proved that he knows how to take advantage of European culture and that he can be benefited by it. Their proof was perhaps necessary, but it is not sufficient. We must show that we are able to go alone, to carve out our own way.

* Dr. Blyden was born in the West Indies in 1832, the son of two slaves from Togoland. He returned to Liberia as a youngster where he was educated. He became, in turn, teacher, professor, president of the Liberian University, Secretary of State and the Liberian Ambassador to the United Kingdom. He was drawn towards Islam and ended his life as an adviser to the British Government on Islamic education in Sierra Leone where he died in 1912.

We must not be satisfied that, in this nation, European influence shapes our polity, makes our laws, rules in our tribunals
and impregnates our social atmosphere . . .

'It will be our aim to increase the amount of purely disciplinary agencies, and to reduce to its minimum the amount of
those distracting influences to which I have referred as hindering the proper growth of the race. The true principle of mental
culture is perhaps this: *to preserve an accurate balance
between the studies which carry the mind out of itself, and
those which recall it home again* [Author's italics] . . . In
looking over the whole world I see no place where this sort of
culture for the Negro can be better secured than in Africa;
where he may, with less interruption from surrounding
influences, find out his place and his work, develop his peculiar
gifts and powers; and for the training of Negro youth upon
the basis of their own idiosyncracies, with a sense of race
individuality, self-respect, and liberty.'

On another occasion Dr. Blyden said:

'All our traditions are connected with a foreign race. We
have no poetry or philosophy but that of our taskmasters. The
songs that live in our ears and are often on our lips are the
songs which we heard sung by those who shouted while we
groaned and lamented. They sang of their history, which was
the history of our degradation. They recited their triumphs,
which was the history of our humiliation. To our great mis-
fortune, we learned their prejudices and their passions, and
thought we had their aspirations and their power. Now, if we
are to make an independent nation—a strong nation—we must
listen to the songs of our unsophisticated brethren as they sing
of their history, as they tell of their traditions, of the wonderful
and mysterious events of their tribal or national life, of the
achievements of what we call their superstitions; we must lend
a ready ear to the ditties of the Kroomen who pull our boats,
of the Pesseh and Golah men, who till our farms; we must
read the compositions, rude as we may think them, of the
Mandingoes and the Veys.'

The development of the concept of the 'African personality', of
negritude, and of the other ideas that sprang from the emotional
and intellectual reaction of black peoples to their imprisoning world
belongs to a later chapter. In this opening chapter I have been
concerned mainly with trying to discover the roots of the forces
that produced Pan-Africanism. Their common denominator is a
revolt by people of colour against what Aimé Césaire has called
'the influence of the colonial, semi-colonial or para-colonial situation'.[16] The situation existed in the New World and Europe, no less

than in Africa; hence the 'Atlantic triangle of influences' that nurtured Pan-Africanism.

'Africa for the Africans'

Pan-Africanism's slogan is 'Africa for the Africans'. Although Pan-Africanism itself grows out of a sense of racial exclusiveness its slogan has never been so. The origin of the phrase is obscure, but it was almost certainly coined in America; later it gained wide currency as the slogan of Garvey's 'Back to Africa' movement. But its political life began long before then, not in America but in Nyasaland and South Africa. The person who first gave it life and meaning was Joseph Booth who was born in Derby in 1851, emigrated to New Zealand where he became a successful farmer, and came to work in Nyasaland in 1892 as a Baptist missionary. He befriended John Chilembwe and became the political mentor and benefactor of Nyasaland's first nationalist leader. Chilembwe made the slogan his cwn.[17]

Between 1895 and 1896 Booth wrote a book called *Africa for the African*[18] in which he argued not only for African emancipation, but also for Negro colonisation in Africa and against Europe's scramble for Africa. One of his concerns was 'bridging the gulf between the European and the native'. He wrote : 'Whether we look at the Government, mining capitalists or the planter class the spirit is the same. . . . Even missionaries, many of them need teaching that the African is inferior in opportunity only.'

On January 14, 1897, at Blantyre, the African Christian Union was formed by Booth, Chilembwe and others 'to unite together in the name of Jesus Christ such persons as desire to see full justice done to the African race and are resolved to work towards and pray for the day when African people shall become an African Christian Nation'. Its final aim was 'to pursue steadily and un-swervingly the policy "Africa for the African" and look for and hasten by prayer and united effort the forming of a United Christian Nation'.[19]

There was at first support for the Christian Union in Natal. South Africa's first African qualified doctor, Navuma Tembula, as well as Solomon Kumalo and others, were enthusiastically in favour of Booth's idea to raise a fund to enable Africans to be trained to manage their own affairs; and 'to mould and guide the labour of Africa's millions into channels that shall develop the God-given wealth of Africa for the uplifting and commonwealth of the people, rather than for the aggrandisement of a few already rich Europeans'. Africans, with the help of Europeans, were to be encouraged to 'demand by Christian and lawful methods' equal privileges with Europeans. The emphasis was on 'the African to unite and work for his own redemption, political, economic and spiritual'.[20] But when put to the test of African confidence the scheme failed. 'Booth had brought a hundred and twenty educated Africans together (in Natal in 1896), and after a twenty-six-and-a-half hour session they rejected his scheme, but on the simple grounds that no white man was fit to be trusted, not even Booth himself. Bishop Colenso, the last honest white man, was dead. No trust or reliance at all could be placed in any representative of the 'blood-stained white men who had slain scores of thousands of Zulus and their Matabele relations.'[21] Fortunately this bitterness was a phase in the history of the Zulu who, at that moment, were standing at the graveside of their nation as they had known it up to then. Booth saw his 'Africa for the African' movement in terms of racial co-operation 'to stem this tide of prejudice against the white race, pointing out the hopelessness of the African race ever being united and capable of making the best of their noble heritage by their own unaided efforts'.

In a later chapter we will see how this concept of 'Africa for the Africans' works out in its modern setting.

CHAPTER II

GROWTH IN THE DIASPORA, 1900–1958

By no means the first but perhaps the most important link between the 'literary' and political streams of Pan-Africanism is Dr. William E. Burghardt duBois, now in his ninety-third year. For almost half a century he dominated the Pan-African movement. But it outgrew him. Although still treated with reverence as the Grand Old Man, his influence has long since waned; he himself deviated from the mainstream of Pan-Africanism by identifying himself in cold war politics on the side of the Communists. In his autobiography[22] Dr. duBois writes:

'As I face Africa I ask myself : what is it between us that constitutes a tie that I can feel better than I can explain? Africa is of course my fatherland. Yet neither my father nor father's father ever saw Africa or knew its meaning or cared overmuch for it. . . . But the physical bond is least and the badge of colour relatively unimportant save as a badge; the real essence of this kinship is its social heritage of slavery; the discrimination and insult; and this heritage binds together not simply the children of Africa, but extends through yellow Asia and into the South Seas. It is this unity that draws me to Africa.'

So far as the New World is concerned this quotation goes to the heart of the Negro's interest in, and attraction to, Pan-Africanism.

First Pan-African Congress, London, 1900

DuBois was introduced to Pan-Africanism in London in 1900 at the first conference ever held to propagate its ideas. Its sponsor was a Trinidad barrister, H. Sylvester Williams, who, so far as is known, was the first person to talk about Pan-Africanism—although in 1897 duBois had said that 'if the Negro were to be a factor in the world's history it would be through a Pan-Negro movement'.[23] Williams' chief collaborator was Bishop Alexander Walters of the African Methodist Episcopal Zion Church, who provides an important link between this independent religious movement and Pan-Africanism.

At the conclusion of the first conference a Memorial was addressed to Queen Victoria. It is comfortless to recall that at that time they were protesting against the treatment of Africans in South Africa and Rhodesia. By way of reply, Mr. Joseph Chamberlain wrote : 'Her Majesty's Government will not overlook the interests and welfare of the native races.'

It was at that conference that duBois spoke his famous prophetic lines : *'The problem of the twentieth century is the problem of the colour line—the relation of the darker to the lighter races of men in Asia and Africa, in America and the islands of the sea.'*

The Rivals — duBois and Garvey

Although there are many important figures in the early stages of the growth of Pan-African ideas who should claim our attention, the two dominating political figures in the first quarter of this century were Dr. William E. Burghardt duBois[24] and Mr. Marcus Aurelius Garvey.[25] In his *Autobiography* Dr. Nkrumah says he was influenced more by Garvey's ideas than by anything in the United States.

DuBois and Garvey were great rivals.[26] DuBois, a Negro of mixed blood—'tiresomely proud of his own Dutch and French ancestors, and especially of the suggestion of Huguenot nobility';[27] Garvey, a black Jamaican.

DuBois, a vain, prickly, egocentric intellectual, deliberately avoiding mass appeals; Garvey, a rodomontade rabble-rouser, who, at the height of his career, could with some justification, claim the support of millions of Negroes, and command vast sums of their money.

Garvey mocked duBois for his light colour, and refused to co-operate with light-skinned Negroes whom he denounced as 'hybrids'. DuBois dismissed Garvey as a 'little, fat, black man; ugly but with intelligent eyes and a big head'. Although the ideas that divided them are no longer deeply relevant, both men are proto-types of African political leaders; and their attitudes are deeply revealing.

DuBois had co-operated with American liberals in founding the National Association for the Advancement of Coloured Peoples, and for more than twenty years had edited their publication *Crisis* (a valuable source of Pan-African ideas). Three years after attending the London conference, in 1903, he broke with the then hero of Negroes and of white Americans, Booker T. Washington, whose leadership was based on counsels of moderation, patience, education and hard work which he offered as the recipe for Negro advancement. Against these ideas duBois preached the need for an open and vigorous struggle to win equality of rights. All his life his thinking was dominated by his colour. On his ninety-first birthday he said over Peking Radio : 'In my own country for nearly half a century I have been nothing but a nigger.'[28] Observable facts don't justify this statement; but it reflects a deep unhealable wound which, in his latter years, brought him to admire Russian and Chinese communist ideas.

Garvey, on the other hand, wore his colour proudly, even gaily : some would say recklessly. 'I believe,' he wrote, 'in a pure black race just as how all self-respecting whites believe in a pure white race, as far as that can be.' His Universal Negro Improvement Association (UNIA) preached 'Back to Africa' to the Negro masses of the New World.* DuBois fiercely resisted this idea; against it he set his dual objective—regeneration of black peoples in the lands of their adoption, and in association with a freed, independent African Continent. In 1920 Garvey founded his Negro Empire in New York, and summoned a large international convention which he called the first Black Parliament. He proclaimed himself 'Provisional President of a Racial Empire in Africa'. He co-operated with the Ku Klux Klan, who shared his ideas of expatriating all the Negroes. Later when Mussolini came to power, Garvey remonstrated : 'I was the first of the Fascists.' But the money he collected for the Black Star Line,† organised to transport the Negroes 'home', got into a frightful mess. After serving a long prison sentence, Garvey died almost unnoticed in London in 1940 without ever having set foot in Africa.

Seeding of Ideas

One of the results of this bitter and prolonged controversy was a cross-fertilisation of ideas between the West Indies and the United States; these ideas were subsequently carried to Europe and back

* Garvey's 'Back to Africa' movement was by no means the first of its kind, nor the last. As far back as 1788 free Negroes had discussed the possibilities of an exodus to Africa. In 1815 the black captain, Paul Cuffee, took a batch of Negroes to Sierra Leone. In 1816 there was formed the American Colonization Society. In 1877 the Liberian Exodus Joint Stock Company was formed in South Carolina, a ship bought, and a single batch of migrants taken to Liberia. In the West Indies Dr. Albert Thorne formed his African Colonial Enterprise in 1897. And as late as 1961 a West Indian delegation toured Africa to explore possibilities of resettlement.

† Ghana's state shipping service subsequently adopted this name.

to Africa both through Pan-African conferences and through African students. For example, among the twenty or so South African students in America soon after the turn of the century were P. K. Isaka Seme (one of the founders of the first African National Congress in 1912);[29] Sol. T. Plaatje,[30] Prof. J. L. Dube and Prof. D. D. T. Jabavu,[31] and later Dr. A. B. Xuma,[32] all of whom were associated with the growth of African nationalism in South Africa.[33] Still later came the East and West Africans : Dr. Nnamdi Azikiwe,[34] Dr. Hastings K. Banda, Mr. Peter Mbiyu Koinange and Dr. Nkrumah. Two contemporaries who were later to play an important part were the Jamaican, the late George Padmore, and Mr. Otto Makonnen.

The United States provided a stimulating training school for these foreign black students; not only did they get formal education, but they were constantly rubbing up against racial discrimination which made them more receptive to the ideas of the Negro intellectuals and the independent religious movements.[35]

A particularly significant example of cross-fertilisation of ideas between the United States and Africa is the episode of the Nyasaland Rising of 1915 which was led by Mr. John Chilembwe.* He had been a student in America from 1897 to 1900. Chilembwe's story has been brilliantly told in *Independent African* by Shepperson and Price,[36] a rich source book of the early beginnings of Pan-Africanism.

A Commission of Inquiry which reported on the Nyasaland Rising linked it to the American Negro by indicating that one of its causes was 'the political notions imbibed by Chilembwe during his education in the United States in a Negro Baptist seminary', and by claiming that the movement had been affected by a 'class of American Negro publications imported by Chilembwe, the tendency of which was to inflame racial feelings'.[37]

The role of the independent Negro churches—especially the African Methodist Episcopal Zion Church†—cannot be overlooked in any account of the rise of Pan-Africanism. 'For all of them, Negro, Baptist, Methodists and independent "Messianic" groups, the reasons for setting up separate religious organisations were the same : resentment at discrimination in white churches; a direction into a 'neutral' field of energies that lacked appropriate political channels; a desire for corporate ownership; and, through independence, however limited, an advancement of status. If these tendencies

* For earlier reference see p. 22.
† For earlier reference to the African Methodist Episcopal Zion Church see p. 24.

could be expressed in the period after Emancipation in other
than religious fields—and many "advanced" Negroes were sceptical
of the churches—nevertheless religious separatism continued to be
an important part of American Negro reaction to white discrimination.'[38]

They increasingly entered the African missionary field in the
spirit of the Rev. Charles S. Morris, who went to organise the
African Baptists of South Africa and who told the 1900 Ecumenical
Missionary Conference in New York :

> 'I believe that God is going to put into the hearts of these
> black boys and girls in the schools of the South to go with the
> message to South Africa and West Africa, and vindicate
> American slavery as far as it can be vindicated by taking across
> the ocean the stream of life.'

But it was not only in their religious life that the separatist
churches showed signs of independent thinking and action. 'In
Jamaica their connection with the frequent revolts and disturb-
ances there in the first seventy years of the nineteenth century is
clear. In the Denmark Vesey conspiracy of 1822 in South Carolina,
the African Methodist Episcopal Church played no small part. Its
most able leaders were from the local church of this denomination.
. . . Furthermore, in each of the three great risings of nineteenth-
century America, in 1800, 1822, and 1831, scriptural support,
especially from the Old Testament, was used by the leaders to
justify their revolts. They called on the examples of the Jews to
escape from bondage, and on eschatological texts to give a kind of
divine aura or sanction to their movements.'[39]

Second Pan-African Congress, Paris, 1919

The second Pan-African Congress, the first under duBois' leadership, was held contemporaneously with the Peace Conference in
Paris in 1919. DuBois arrived determined 'to have Africa in some
way voice its complaints to the world. . . .' His efforts succeeded
largely through the intervention of Senegal's delegate M. Blaise-
Diagne, at that time the foremost colonial spokesman from the
French territories, and a close friend of Clemenceau. (Later Blaise-
Diagne was much criticised by African nationalists as a French
'stooge'.) 'Don't advertise the Congress,' Clemenceau told Blaise-
Diagne, 'but go ahead'. There were fifty-seven representatives at
that conference; 'Negroes in the trim uniform of American
Army officers . . . coloured men in frock coats or business suits,

polished French Negroes who hold public offices, Senegalese who sit in the French Chamber of Deputies. . . .'[40]

The congress adopted a lengthy resolution which nowhere spoke of the Africans' right to independence.* It proclaimed the need for international laws to protect the natives; for land to be held in trust; for the prevention of exploitation by foreign capital; for the abolition of slavery and capital punishment; for the right of education, and, finally, it insisted that 'the natives of Africa must have the right to participate in the Government as fast as their development permits . . .'

Third Pan-African Congress, London and Brussels, 1921

Nor had these reformist ideas of Pan-Africanism moved much further by the time the Third Congress came to be held in London and Brussels in 1921 when the principal political demand—made on behalf of 'the Negro race through their thinking intelligentsia'— was for 'local self-government for backward groups, deliberately rising as experience and knowledge grew to complete self-government under the limitation of a self-governed world'.

Two sentences from the address of duBois to the Third Congress help to establish another of the emerging themes of Pan-Africanism :

'The beginning of wisdom in inter-racial contact is the establishment of political institutions among suppressed peoples. The habit of democracy must be made to encircle the world.' The emphasis is on inter-racialism and democracy. That, let us recall, was in 1921.

Fourth Pan-African Congress, London and Lisbon, 1923

There were two separate sessions of the Fourth Congress which took place in 1923 in London and Lisbon. The London session was attended by H. G. Wells, Harold Laski and Lord Olivier, and it received a message of encouragement from Ramsay MacDonald. Reiterating earlier resolutions, the most important political demand was still only for Africans to have 'a voice in their own Governments'.

From the Manifesto I choose one paragraph :

'In fine, we ask in all the world, *that black folk be treated as men.* We can see no other road to peace and progress. What more paradoxical figure today confronts the world than the official head of a great South African State [a reference to

* For text of resolutions passed see Appendix 1.

J. C. Smuts] striving blindly to build peace and goodwill in
Europe by standing on the necks and hearts of millions of
Black Africans.'

Fifth Pan-African Congress, New York, 1927

The last in the series of Congresses directly led by Dr. duBois
was held in New York in 1927. It is important at this point to note
the attitude of communists towards the growth of Pan-African
ideas. George Padmore described their 'opportunism' in trying to
discredit both Garvey's and duBois' movements (the UNIA and
the NAACP) and the Pan-African Congress which they regarded
as *petit-bourgeois* black Nationalism . . . blocking the dissemination
of Communist influence among the Negroes. The attitude of most
white Communists towards Negro organisations has been one of
contempt. If they cannot control them, they seek their destruction
by infiltration.'[41]

Pan-Africanism in Britain

The second world war marks the dividing line between the old
and the new Pan-African movements. After 1936—by which time
George Padmore, C. L. R. James[42] and other West Indian and
American intellectuals had broken in disgust with the Communist
International[43]—Britain became the main centre for the promotion
of Pan-African ideas.

In 1944, thirteen active welfare, students' and political organisations came together to form the Pan-African Federation under the
leadership of the International African Service Bureau, formed in
1937 as the successor to the International African Friends of Abys-
sinia. Among its leaders were the late George Padmore, C. L. R.
James, Wallace Johnson, the Sierra Leone trade union leader, and
Jomo Kenyatta.[44] The *gestalt* of Pan-Africanism at that moment in
its growth has been well described by the late George Padmore :[45]

'The years immediately before the outbreak of the second
world war coincided with what is known in left-wing political
circles as the "Anti-Fascist Popular Front Period". This period
was one of the most stimulating and constructive in the history
of Pan-Africanism. It was then that Congress had to meet the
ideological challenge from the *Communist opportunists* on the
one hand and the racist doctrines of the Fascists on the other,
and to defend the programme of Pan-Africanism—namely,
the fundamental right of black men to be free and independent and not be humbugged by those who preached acceptance
of the *status quo* in the interest of power politics. It was also

at this period that many of the Negro intellectuals who were later to emerge as prominent personalities in the colonial nationalist movements began to make a detailed and systematic study of European political theories and systems (Liberalism, Socialism, Communism, Anarchism, Fascism), and to evaluate these doctrines objectively—accepting what might be useful to the cause of Pan-Africanism and rejecting the harmful. In this way the younger leaders of the Congress were able to build upon the pioneering work of Dr. duBois and formulate a programme of dynamic nationalism, which combined African traditional forms of organisation with Western political party methods.'

Sixth Pan-African Congress, Manchester, 1945

The Pan-African Federation, with the blessing of duBois, convened the Sixth Pan-African Congress* in Manchester in October, 1945. The movement had greatly changed through the war years, as the Congress itself shows. Dr. duBois is there : greying, ascetic-looking, at seventy-three very much the Grand Old Man. There are now very few Negroes from the United States. The West Indian contingent is still strong, led by George Padmore, C. L. R. James and Dr. Peter Milliard. But for the first time it is a Congress of Africa's young leaders : they are largely a collection of unknowns, soon to win fame, notoriety and power in their own countries. From the Gold Coast, Kwame Nkrumah; J. Annan, now Ghana's Secretary of Defence E. A. Ayikumi, until recently director of Ghana's large state industrial operations; Edwin J. duPlan, a key figure in the Bureau of African Affairs in Accra; the late Dr. Kurankyi Taylor and Joe Appiah, both of whom later became bitter opponents of Dr. Nkrumah; and Dr. J. C. de Graft Johnson, the historian. From Nigeria, Chief H. O. Davies, Q.C., now chairman of Nigeria's state-sponsored newspapers; Magnus Williams, representing Dr. Azikiwe, who had contributed greatly to the growth of the movement but who could not himself be present. There is a Baptist teacher, Chief S. L. Akintola, now Premier of Nigeria's Western Region. There is Kenya's Jomo Kenyatta; Sierra Leone's redoubtable trade union leader, Wallace Johnson; Togo's poet, Dr. Raphael Armattoe. There is Otto Makonnen who is now director of the African Affairs Centre in Accra. And from South Africa, Peter Abrahams, the South African novelist and poet who, like Padmore and James, had come to turn his back on the

* Padmore calls this the Fifth because he ignores the 1900 conference; dating the Congresses from their start with duBois' first in Paris in 1919. But I can see no good reason for this arbitrary decision.

communists; and Marko Hlubi, representing the African National Congress.

The Manchester Congress offers many clues to the developing ideas of Pan-Africanism.* For the first time we find the forthright challenge : 'We demand for Black Africa autonomy and independence, so far, and no further, than it is possible in this One World for groups and peoples to rule themselves subject to inevitable world unity and federation.'

Also we find the new spirit awakened by Pan-Africanism—a farewell to patience and to the acceptance of suffering : 'We are not ashamed to have been an age-long patient people. We continue willingly to sacrifice and strive. But we are unwilling to starve any longer while doing the world's drudgery, in order to support by our poverty and ignorance a false aristocracy and a discarded imperialism.'

There is the central dilemma of the problem of using violence to back up their challenge—'We are determined to be free.' On the one hand, a threat : '. . . If the Western world is still determined to rule Mankind by force, then Africans, *as a last resort*, may have to appeal to force in the effort to achieve freedom, even if force destroys them and the world.' But pending the 'last resort' Congress opted for *Positive Action*† based on Gandhi's teachings.

There are other signposts in the growth of Pan-African ideas : 'One man, one vote', recognised in a resolution demanding universal franchise. Socialism is not mentioned, but there is an assertion that 'economic democracy is the only real democracy'; and condemnation of 'the rule of private wealth and industry for private profit alone'. Also, there is an acknowledgment of the nascent Bandung spirit : 'Congress expressed the hope that before long the peoples of Asia and Africa would have broken their centuries-old chains of colonialism. Then, as free nations, they would stand united to consolidate and safeguard their liberties and independence from the restoration of Western imperialism, as well as the dangers of Communism.'

West African National Secretariat

In our search for clues to the evolving concepts of Pan-Africanism, we must not overlook the West African National Secretariat organised by Dr. Nkrumah at the Manchester Congress. At its own conference in August, 1946, it pledged itself to promote the concept

* For a text of resolutions passed see Appendix 2.

† *Positive Action* became the slogan of the Convention People's Party in its successful struggle for Ghana's independence.

of a *West African Federation* as an indispensable lever for the ultimate achievement of a *United States of Africa*. The following year Dr. Azikiwe[46] formally endorsed this resolution : it confirmed an idea which, earlier, he had himself put forward.

Emotions into Ideas

We have now almost reached the point where Pan-Africanism was to be finally transplanted *organisationally* to Africa's own soil, and when it ceased to be largely the brainchild of Negro intellectuals and African students in the diaspora. But before we follow the new trail we might conveniently halt for a moment to consider some of the main ideas that have so far emerged from this brief account of the development of Pan-Africanism.

We should begin by distinguishing between the *feelings* that underlie Pan-Africanism, and the political *attitudes* that these feelings have given rise to. *Deep at its quivering, sensitive centre, Pan-Africanism rests on colour-consciousness.* Recognition of the unique historical position of black peoples as the universal bottom-dog led to a revolt against passive submission to this situation. The emotions associated with blackness were intellectualised; and so Pan-Africanism became a vehicle for the struggle of black people to regain their pride, their strength and their independence. But although black skins were made into a shield for the battle, Pan-Africanism became a *race-conscious* movement, not a *racialist* one. I would postulate this as one of its most significant characteristics. The distinction is a valid one, and indeed a vital one. It is a pity that it is not more widely recognised. What is the distinction?

Race-Consciousness and Racialism

Race-consciousness is the assertion by a people with recognisable ethnical similarities of their own uniqueness; a belief in their own special qualities, distinctions and rights. It is a positive statement in defence of one's race; but it does not seek to elevate that race above other races. When *race-consciousness* elevates itself above other races, discriminates and attacks other races, it becomes *racialism*. What we are dealing with is the difference between positive and negative attitudes; between defensive attitudes and persecuting attitudes. One can be *for* one's own race, without being ill-disposed to another. Antisemitism is a form of *racialism*—an expression against Jews; whereas Zionism is *race-consciousness*—a statement in favour of the rights and needs of Jews.

There is, of course, always the danger that race-consciousness will turn into racialism; the balance is often very fine. Equally great is the danger of its becoming chauvinistic.* The chronicles and literature of Pan-Africanism are full of examples of both racialism and chauvinism : nevertheless the mainstream of ideas is remarkably unpolluted by either.

To see Pan-Africanism, or its modern agent African nationalism, as simply another version of racialism—to equate it, for example, with white nationalism (the cardinal error committed by the Capricorn Society in Central Africa)—is to misunderstand its purpose and functions, which is to regenerate black peoples and to inspire them with a belief and a confidence in themselves *as peoples*.

A notable example, among many, that black nationalism is not to be equated automatically with racialism is that provided by South Africa, where for forty-nine years the African National Congress has actively worked with South Africans of other races; even the Pan-Africanist Congress of South Africa, sharply race-conscious as they are, and while believing in the separate organisation of each race for the liberation of South Africa, nevertheless oppose (at least in their philosophy) ideas of racialism.

Attitudes to Whites

We cannot leave this question without considering some of its other aspects. Since Pan-Africanism asserts the rights of *blacks* against the claims of *white supremacy* it postulates a clash. Why, then, has Pan-Africanism not developed into anti-whiteism? It seems to me there are two reasons. Firstly, blacks are characteristically less racialistic than Teutonic-speaking peoples. As Prof. Toynbee has pointed out : 'race-feeling is an exceptional failing'.[47] Secondly, because blacks are in a hopelessly ambivalent love-hatred relationship with whites. Their rejection of the white men and all his works is never wholehearted; criticism of Europe or America is seldom undiluted. If we look closer at this *ambivalence* (as we will when I come to deal with *negritude*) we will find it to be an outstanding characteristic of Pan-Africanist feelings.

There is, as one might expect, a feeling of deep racial bitterness in Pan-Africanism. And, indeed, why not? These feelings of bitterness, however, are often matched by a remarkable quality of for-

---

* Dr. Azikiwe wrote in *The Future of Pan-Africanism* (Note 34): 'It would be useless to define "Pan-Africanism" exclusively in racial or linguistic terms, since the obvious solution would be parochial. And chauvinism, by whatever name it is identified, has always been a disintegrating factor in human society at all known times of human history.'

giveness once the dignity of independence and equality has been respected. This is shown by the change of attitudes of nationalist leadership in newly-independent states. But there are also nearly everywhere in Africa, the United States, the Caribbean territories and in Europe individuals whose race-consciousness has soured into racialism. They are generally to be found among middle-aged or elderly intellectuals—people who found more satisfaction in being the victims of persecution in the emancipation struggle than in the creative tasks of the post-liberation situation—and among very young and militant nationalist leaders who themselves played little or no part in the independence struggle, and who are already dis-satisfied with the Old Guard now in power. These pockets of racialism—not important in their numbers, and nowhere outside of the New World constituting an organised group—are nevertheless a significant reminder of the bitterness of old feelings as well as of the possibility of racial feeling being whipped up in times of great tension; as for example when Patrice Lumumba was murdered, and at the time of the Hola disaster that befell Mau Mau detainees in Kenya. When nationalists feel that their independence is being threatened or that the 'Western (i.e. white) world' is 'ganging up' against them, the smouldering fires of *blackism* flare up as strongly as ever. One has only to read the speeches[48] in the Nigerian Parliament when it was debating the threat of the first French nuclear tests in the Sahara to be reminded of the strength of this feeling. Here is one typical statement made by Mr. R. A. Fani-Kayode, the Member for Ife :

> 'This is the opportunity we have been looking for to show that black men all over Africa must stand or fall together. I have said it often and often in this House that *blackism* is the answer to our problems.'

And another Nigerian example—the land of misleadingly labelled 'moderates'—to show that independence does not *automatically* end old memories. On his return from the United Nations where he was the much-lauded representative of his country, the Hon. Jaja Wachuku said at a Press conference that African people would be deceiving themselves 'to think that European and Asian countries accept the black man as their equal'.[49]

Feelings of Vengeance

Pan-African teaching does not, however, inculcate the desire for vengeance against yesterday's oppressors. This is perhaps one of the most remarkable of modern Africa's phenomena; especially if

one recalls the feelings of anger and bitterness that have been
welling up inside the continent for centuries.

> *The white man killed my father*
> *My father was proud*
> *The white man seduced my mother*
> *My mother was beautiful*
> *The white man burnt my brother*
>   *beneath the noonday sun*
> *My brother was strong.*
> *His hands red with black blood*
> *The white man turned to me*
> *And in the Conqueror's voice said*
> *'Hey, boy! a chair, a napkin, a drink.'*[50]

What has happened to the natural desires for vengeance found in
all people, as shown, for example, in Europe after the defeat of
the Nazis? Is it that the vengeance is still to come in those parts of
the continent where white oppression has been most vicious?

There has, so far, been remarkably little vengeance. No anti-
white violence in any of the independent African states (other than
the Congo), and only a few exceptional situations in the various independence struggles. Some French *colons* were murdered in
Morocco; Algeria is untypical because it is primarily a colonial
war, not a race war. Angola has, so far, been the worst. It is pro-
bable that 1,400 white Portuguese were killed and wounded in the
single week of the start of the rebellion there in 1961, while upward
of 20,000 Africans were killed or wounded. The extent of the atrocities in the Congo after the revolt of the *Force Publique* were
greatly exaggerated at the time. Out of a total of 80,000 Belgians in
the Congo fewer than one per cent complained of any kind of ill-
treatment; many of these complaints have subsequently turned out
to have been either inventions, due to panic, or at least over-
drawn.[51] The total European and Asian civilian casualties in the
Mau Mau revolt in Kenya were fifty-eight killed and sixty-two
wounded—a tiny fraction of Mau Mau's black victims which came
to almost 3,000. There has been one major case of white
casualties in Central Africa when Mrs. Buxton was burnt to death.
Apart from three incidents in South Africa there have been no race
killings by Africans of whites. There have been other isolated instances, in the Cameroun Republic and elsewhere.

The vengeance sought by the intellectuals of Pan-Africanism is
not physical. There is an element of desire to enjoy 'Black power'
over the whites as shown in Paul Robeson's thinking:[52]

'I think a good deal in terms of the power of the black people in the world. That's why Africa means so much to me. As an American Negro, I'm as proud of Africa as one of those West Coast Chinese is proud of China. Now that doesn't mean I'm going back to Africa, but spiritually I've been a part of Africa for a long time. *Yes, this black power moves me.* Look at Jamaica. In a few years the white minority will be there on the sufferance of black men. If they're nice decent fellows they can stay. Yes, I look at Senator Eastland and say, "So you think you are powerful here. If only I could get you across the border." Although I may stay here the rest of my life, *spiritually I'll always be part* of that world where the black man can say to these crackers, "Get the hell out of here by morning." If I could get a passport, I'd just like to go to Ghana or Jamaica just to sit there for a few days and observe this black power.'

The *instinct* for vengeance exists, but Jean-Paul Sartre is wrong, I think, when he describes it as a *desire*.[53] The evidence he quotes— Aimé Césaire's work—proves the opposite. Listen to Césaire :

> *... preserve me, heart, from all hatred*
> *do not turn me into a man of hate whom I shall hate*
> *for in order to emerge into this unique race,*
> *you know my world-wide love,*
> *know it is not hatred against other races*
> *that turns me into the cultivator of this one race*
> *for what I want*
> *arises from infinite hunger*
> *from infinite thirst*
> *finally to demand them to be free*
> *freely in their secluded soul*
> *to create the ripening fruit.*[54]

But no discussion of the characteristics of black attitudes and thinking is adequate except in the framework of the Pan-Africanists' ambivalence towards the West : these attitudes will be more fully considered when we come to consider the concepts of *negritude* and 'the African personality'.

CHAPTER III

BACK TO AFRICA, 1958–1962

The Pan-African political movement came home in 1958; but its cultural wing remained in Europe and the New World. At the time of its transplantation Pan-Africanism possessed a programme of ideas and action which can be summed up in nine points.*

1. 'Africa for the Africans' : complete independence of the whole of Africa. Total rejection of colonialism in all its forms, including white domination.

2. United States of Africa : the ideal of a wholly unified continent through a series of inter-linking regional federations within which there would be a limitation on national sovereignty.

3. African renaissance of morale and culture : a quest for the 'African personality'; a determination to recast African society into its own forms, drawing from its own past what is valuable and desirable, and marrying it to modern ideas. Modernism is heavily accentuated.

4. African nationalism to replace the tribalism of the past : a concept of African loyalty wider than 'the nation' to transcend tribal and territorial affiliations.

5. African regeneration of economic enterprise to replace colonial economic methods : belief in a non-exploiting socialist or *communalistic* type of socialism; International Communism is rejected outright.

6. Belief in democracy as the most desirable method of government based on the principle of 'one man one vote'.

7. Rejection of violence as a method of struggle, unless peaceful methods of struggle—*Positive Action*—are met with military repression.

8. Solidarity of black peoples everywhere, and a fraternal alliance of coloured peoples based on a mutual history of struggle against white domination and colonialism.

* Padmore, in *Pan-Africanism or Communism,* offers a useful comparison for this summary.

9. Positive neutrality (as it was then called): non-involvement as partisans in power politics, but 'neutral in nothing that affects African interests'.*

The Afro-Arab-Asian Front

Two important events intervened between the last Pan-African Congress (1945) and the first Conference of Independent African States (1958). The first was Egypt's February 23 Revolution (1952) which marks the breakthrough of modern Arab nationalism; the second was the Bandung Conference (1955) which was symptomatic of Asia's arrival on the world scene.

The Pan-Africans played no real part in the Bandung Conference. Ethiopia was the only non-Arab independent African state represented; the then Gold Coast sent observers. Nevertheless, the Bandung Declaration† quickly became absorbed into Pan-African thinking.[55]

Col. Nasser's ideas about Egypt's and the Arabs' role in Africa are described in his important brief work on *The Philosophy of the Revolution*.[56] He sees The Revolution linked to three circles—the Arab circle, the African continent circle, and the circle of 'our brethren-in-Islam'. Of the African circle he writes:

'... We cannot under any condition, even if we wanted to, stand aloof from the terrible and terrifying battle now raging in the heart of that continent between five million whites and two hundred million Africans. We cannot stand aloof for one important and obvious reason—we ourselves are in Africa. Surely the people of Africa will continue to look to us—we who are the guardians of the continent's northern gate, we who constitute the connecting link between the continent and the outer world. We certainly cannot, under any condition, relinquish our responsibility to help to our utmost in spreading the light of knowledge and civilisation up (*sic*) to the very depth of the virgin jungles of the continent.'

Col. Nasser thus clearly saw Egypt playing a leadership role in the continent; a view that he still strongly holds. Cairo became a home for African exiles; Radio Cairo developed special programmes to encourage the liberation struggle; and the city put itself forward as a political capital for African independence movements. Islamic teaching was used to expand the 'African circle' but it is much less of a political factor than is often thought. It has been more of a factor in, say, Somalia, than in Nigeria.

* Dr. Nnamdi Azikiwe's phrase.
† See Appendix 3.

Cairo's political links were mainly organised through the Afro-Asian Solidarity Movement whose first conference was held in Cairo in the closing days of 1957. This conference deviated strongly from the tradition of the Pan-African movement and from the canons of the Bandung Declaration by inviting to full participation —both in the conference itself and in the movement's subsequent work—one of the two sides involved in the cold war. Seeking to justify the participation of the Russians* and the Chinese, an official Egyptian statement listed four factors.[57] First, that the effectiveness of the policy of positive neutrality had become more evident. Second, that the socialist bloc had given proof of great superiority in the strategic and scientific fields, thus doubling the chances for peace and freedom in the world. Third, that the struggle between the powers of imperialism and the people of Asia and Africa had crystallised. And fourth, that the fortunes of colonialism had suffered a sharp decline.

But the Afro-Asian Solidarity Movement never became either a successful movement or a happy one, despite some excellent Egyptians on its staff. Few African countries have contributed to the working of the organisation notwithstanding promises to do so. The Egyptians themselves have been concerned, from the start, to isolate the influence of the Russians and the Chinese whose participation (tenuous as it has been) has been a source of weakness and embarrassment to them. Egyptian agreement to this heterodox partnership must be explained, not by the rather naïve reasons already quoted, but by the sense of obligation felt at the time for Russia's agreement to build the Aswan dam. Significantly, Col. Nasser did not himself open the first conference. His spokesman was Anwar el-Sadat whose keynote address made a mockery of the structure of the movement :

'We in Egypt believe in neutralism and non-alignment. This principle has been adopted by many of our friends in Asia and Africa. We believe that by adopting this attitude we ward off the shadow of war, narrow the area facing conflicting blocs and establish a wide area of peace which will impose its existence gradually on the whole world. The neutralism in which we believe means that *we should keep aloof from international blocs* and at the same time make efforts to bring about a rapprochement between those blocs.' [Author's italics.]

How does one explain the relationship between Pan-Africanism —with its *black consciousness*—and the Arabs and Asians? The

* The Russians were not regarded as being 'Asians' qualifying for Bandung membership.

answer, I think, is that although blacks identified themselves emotionally with their skins, they were always intellectually willing and able to identify themselves with peoples of other colours who were in the same boat as themselves—victims of white superiority, of colonialism, of imperialism, and of discrimination. Black regeneration was one aspect of the struggle for emancipation; the wider struggle against colonialism and injustice demanded wider alliances. That is why, in his famous statement, Dr. duBois spoke of 'the problem of the Twentieth Century' as 'the problem of the colour-line—the relation of the darker to the lighter races of men in Asia and Africa. . . .' He explored this question fully in his prolific writings.* In the earlier stages of Pan-Africanism, Duse Mohammed Ali, editor of the anti-imperialist *African Times and Orient Review*, identified himself with the struggles of Marcus Garvey and other Pan-Africanists. He was an Egyptian nationalist of Sudanese descent and an ardent supporter of Zaghloul Pasha, the Wafd leader.[58]

The practical expression of the colour struggle also led quite naturally to the Sixth Pan-African Congress (1945) expressing the hope 'that before long the people of Asia and Africa would have broken their centuries-old chains of colonialism. Then, as free nations, they would stand united to consolidate and safeguard their liberties and independence from the restoration of Western imperialism, as well as the danger of Communism.'[59]

However much, therefore, blacks feel as *blacks*, their colour-consciousness has found political expression in associations with peoples of other colours and, indeed, also with Europeans who have been willing to identify themselves with their struggle for emancipation. 'Anti-imperialism knows no colour,' Mr. Kofi Baako, Ghana's Minister of Defence, has said in discussing Nkrumahism. In its wider political context, therefore, Pan-Africanism has not remained racially exclusive, even if the emotional feelings associated with blackness have not necessarily altered in quality.

First Conference of Independent African States, Accra, 1958

The formal launching of the pan-African movement was auspicious. Except for South Africa, all eight independent States met in Accra in April, 1958.[60] Only two—Ghana and Liberia—belonged to Black Africa; five were predominantly Arab and Muslim— Egypt, Tunisia, Libya, Sudan and Morocco; the eighth, Ethiopia, was making its official debut in the wider stream of African

* For an earlier reference to this subject by duBois see p. 24.

politics; the Emperor could no longer afford to maintain his policy of isolation in an Africa that was discovering itself.

The Accra conference immediately proved the validity of one of the concepts of Pan-Africanism : a bond of colour did exist between former colonial peoples. It proved that neither Islam nor the Sahara constituted an insuperable barrier.* In fact, at the first conference and since, it has emerged that some black African States have much more in common, politically, with some Arab States, than either have with their own immediate neighbours. The only divisive factor between the Arab and non-Arab African states has been the question of Israel : but even on this point the Islamic black States have refused, in their practical affairs to be drawn into the Arabs' war against Israel.

The Accra conference† committed the Independent African States to direct involvement in securing the emancipation of the continent : they declared war on colonialism and on South Africa and gave full support to the FLN struggle in Algeria. Henceforth, the colonial struggle was to obtain direct support and encouragement from within Africa. In foreign affairs there was the beginning, too, of a new policy of non-alignment as between 'the two antagonistic blocs' in the world; and a determination to establish 'an African Personality' in world affairs by working for 'a fundamental unity' between African States on foreign questions. This unity was to be based on the Bandung Declaration, the Charter of the UN, and on loyalty to UN decisions. The resolution on racialism not only condemned its practice by others but recommended to African States that they themselves 'should take vigorous measures to eradicate, where they arise, vestiges of racial discrimination in their own countries'. All the members agreed to observe each other's political and territorial integrity, and to settle their differences, if any, by conciliation and mediation within the African community.

The All African Peoples Organisation (Accra, 1958; Tunis, 1960; Cairo, 1961)

There was no mention at the first Accra conference of the United States of Africa, nor of regional federations. It is when we come to the first All African Peoples Conference‡ a non-governmental conference of political parties, which was held in Accra in

* This view is not apparently accepted by Chief Awolowo. See Appendix 24.
† For a text of its resolutions see Appendix 4.
‡ For the constitution and standing orders of the AAPO see Appendix 22, A, B and C.

December, 1958 that we find a resolution in support of the ultimate objective of a Commonwealth of free African States.* It is worth noting in passing that this concept has never been endorsed by any of the several conferences of Independent African States (Accra, 1958; Addis Ababa, 1960; Brazzaville, 1961; Casablanca, 1961; Monrovia, 1961). But it usually found a place in the resolutions passed by conferences of non-governmental organisations such as the AAPO.

The first AAPO conference[61] illustrated three other elements in Pan-Africanism. The question of violence was raised, mainly on the insistence of the FLN. After serious debate the conference rejected violence as a means of struggle : it recognised that national independence could be gained by peaceful means 'in territories where democratic means are available'; but it pledged support equally to those who 'in order to meet the violent means by which they are subjected and exploited, are obliged to retaliate'.†

The second element relates to inter-racial co-operation. White delegates from South Africa were fully accredited as delegates; these included the Rev. Michael Scott representing Chief Hosea of the Hereros, Mr. Patrick Duncan of the South African Liberal Party, and Mrs. Louise Hooper as a representative of the South African National Congress. This practice was also followed at the second AAPO conference in Tunis in 1960;‡ but at its third conference in Cairo in 1961§ neither Indians nor whites managed to get full accreditation. This, it was said, was due to local organisational factors and was not attributable to a change of policy. Accreditation is in the hands of both a Steering Committee and an Accreditation Committee; which did not work very well at the Cairo meeting.

In his welcoming address to the first AAPO conference Dr. Nkrumah declared :

'... We are not racialists or chauvinists. We welcome into our midst peoples of all other races, other nations, other communities, who desire to live among us in peace and equality. But they must

* For a full text of the resolutions passed see Appendix 22 D.

† Ghana sponsored a conference on Positive Action and Security in Accra in April, 1960 to discuss methods of non-violent resistance. The Rev. Michael Scott and other *Satyagraha* exponents were prominently identified with this conference. In opening it Dr. Nkrumah said: 'By our concerted non-violent positive action, we can help to ensure that this march forward is a swift and peaceful one....'

‡ For a text of the resolutions passed at the Tunis conference see Appendix 22 E.

§ For a text of the resolutions passed at the Cairo conference see Appendix 22 F.

respect us and our rights, our right as the majority to rule. That, as our Western friends have taught us to understand it, is the essence of democracy.'

At this conference, the question of the Pan-Africanist slogan 'Africa for the Africans' was raised. The Accra conference chairman, Mr. Tom Mboya, announced from the platform, 'Once the principle of "one man, one vote" is established, we will not practice racism in reverse'. Dr. Nkrumah went further : 'When I speak of Africa for the Africans this should be interpreted in the light of my emphatic declaration that I do not believe in racialism and colonialism. The concept—"Africa for the Africans"—does not mean that other races are excluded from it. No. It only means that Africans, who naturally are in the majority in Africa, shall and must govern themselves in their own countries.'[62]

Mr. Julius Nyerere and other leaders have since spoken along the same lines.

Dr. Azikiwe has said :[63] '. . . it should be obvious that unless we accept a broad definition of terms there can be no worthy future for Africanism. That being the case I would like to speak of the peoples of Africa in general terms to include all the races inhabiting that continent and embracing all the linguistic and cultural groups who are domiciled therein.'

A third element peeped out briefly at the Accra conference. 'The independence of Ghana,' Dr. Nkrumah said, 'will be meaningless unless it is linked up with the total liberation of Africa.' At one time many believed this was not to be taken seriously; but it has recently become quite clear that Ghana's President is in earnest when he says he will commit all the resources and energies of Ghana towards achieving Africa's independence and unity. We will return to this point.

Among the little-known delegates who made their bow at this conference were Mr. Patrice Lumumba and Mr. Joseph Gilmore, better known as Roberto Holden. Mr. Lumumba returned from the Accra meeting to address a mass meeting in Leopoldville which was followed by an outbreak of serious rioting in the city that helped precipitate the decision to give the Belgian Congo its independence. Mr. Holden, the leader of the Union of the Peoples of Angola (UPA), launched his violent liberation campaign just two years later after having 'done the rounds' of the African capitals to obtain moral and financial support for his movement. Another delegate who did not accept the non-violent philosophy of the conference was Dr. Felix Moumie, the colourful and loquacious leader of the *Union of the Peoples of the Camerouns* (UPC) who, until he was poisoned in Zürich in 1960, was one of the most active of Africa's itinerant politicians, travelling tirelessly from one African capital to the other and putting in frequent appearances in Moscow and Peking as well. He symbolised the left-wing revolutionary young African leader for whom national independence means more than an exchange of black government for white administration. Leaders who share these feelings are often driven towards alignment with the communists.

The Conakry Declaration

The next important event to be noted is the Conakry Declaration of May 1, 1959,* when Guinea and Ghana 'solemnly agreed to seal the Ghana-Guinea Union in practice'. But the Conakry Declaration went further : it envisaged the Ghana-Guinea Union as the beginning of a *Union* of Independent African States. The use of the term *Union* as opposed to regional federation or association, alarmed Liberia's President Tubman.

The Sanniquellie Declaration

Dr. Tubman took the initiative in calling a meeting with M. Sékou Touré and Dr. Nkrumah at Sanniquellie, a small Liberian village, where they produced the Sanniquellie Declaration of July 19, 1959.† It formulates six principles for the achievement of *The Community of Independent African States* : no longer any mention of *Union*. The crucial point is the third principle :

> Each state and federation, which is a member of the Community, shall maintain its own national identity and constitutional structure. The Community is being formed with a view to achieving unity among independent African States. It is not designed to prejudice the present or future international policies, relations and obligations of the States involved.

The Sanniquellie Declaration marks a new phase in the argument between Pan-Africanists about the best way of developing African unity.

Second Conference of Independent African States, Addis Ababa, 1960

This division came into the open when the Sanniquellie Declaration was raised at the Second Conference of Independent African

* For text see Appendix 6.   † For text see Appendix 7.

States in Addis Ababa in 1960.* Its membership, meanwhile, had increased from eight at the first meeting to fifteen : Algeria Provisional Government,† Cameroun, Ethiopia, Ghana, Guinea, Libya, Liberia, Morocco, Nigeria, Somalia, Sudan, Tunisia, United Arab Republic. (Togo and Congo Leopoldville failed to attend.)

Ghana's Foreign Minister, Mr. Ako Adjei, was at great pains to spell out in detail the ideas which Dr. Nkrumah had been advocating with increasing urgency in the latter part of 1959 and early 1960. Commending the Sanniquellie Declaration for adoption he said :‡

'It is clear from this declaration of principles that the Union of African States which the three leaders discussed and agreed upon is intended to be a political Union. Such a political Union in their view, will provide the framework within which any plans for economic, social and cultural co-operation can, in fact, operate to the best advantage of all. To us in Ghana the concept of African Unity is an article of faith. It is a cardinal objective in our policy. We sincerely believe that the Independent African States can, and may some day, form a real political Union—the Union of African States . . . It does not matter whether you start with an Association of African States or whether with economic or cultural co-operation . . . we must start from somewhere, but certainly the Union can be achieved in the end.§

Apart from Guinea this view received little support; the main opposition to it came from the leader of the Nigerian delegation, Mr. Yussuf Maitima Sule. His speech‖ is important for several reasons : firstly because of its disagreement with the Ghana approach; secondly, because of its unveiled attack on Dr. Nkrumah —something new to African assemblies; and thirdly because it demonstrates that Nigeria is no stranger to Pan-Africanist ideas :

'Pan-Africanism,' said Mr. Sule, 'is the only solution to our problems in Africa. . . . No one in Africa doubts the need to promote Pan-Africanism. . . . But we must not be sentimental; we must be realistic. It is for this reason that we would like to point out that at this moment the idea of forming a Union

* For text of resolutions passed see Appendix 5.

† The admission of the Algerians as full members marks the growing success of their effective pressure at Pan-African conferences for unqualified support for their struggle.

‡ Mr. Adjei's speech is given in greater detail in Appendix 10.

§ For those who wish to refer to the original documents it is important to note that the speech of Ghana's Foreign Minister as circulated was altered in some important respects at the time of its delivery.

‖ It is given in greater detail in Appendix 11.

of African States is premature. On the other hand, we do not dispute the sincerity and indeed the good intentions of those people who advocate it. But we feel such a move is too radical —perhaps too ambitious—to be of lasting benefit. Gradual development of ideas and thoughts is more lasting . . . it is essential to remember that whatever ideas we may have about Pan-Africanism it will not materialise, or at least it will not materialise as quickly as we would like it to if we start building from the top downwards. We must first prepare the minds of the different African countries—we must start from the known to the unknown. At the moment we in Nigeria cannot afford to form union by government with any African States by surrendering our sovereignty . . . President Tubman's idea of the association of states is therefore more acceptable for it is as yet premature to form a Union of States under one sovereignty.'

He then went on to make his much-publicised warning that 'if anybody makes the mistake of feeling that he is a Messiah who has got a mission to lead Africa the whole purpose of Pan-Africanism will, I fear, be defeated'.

In this exchange between Mr. Ako Adjei and Mr. Sule we have the crystallised views of two sides contesting the right way towards unity : Nigeria played the rôle of the Fabian, arguing from the standpoint of the federalist seeking to build from the bottom upwards; Ghana, the revolutionary unafraid to impel change from the top—a spirit in consonance with ideas of centralist democracy and unitarianism.

These attitudes have become two poles in the Pan-Africanist world; they divide the unitarians from the federalists (this was the tragic argument between Lumumba and Kasavubu in the Congo); the revolutionaries from the reformists, in economic as well as in social questions; and the promoters of a 'political union' from those who favour a slower, functional approach.

The Conference of Independent African States did not endorse the Sanniquellie Declaration. In the end they merely requested the President of the conference to address Heads of African States to initiate consultations through diplomatic channels with a view to promoting African unity, and to consider the item at their next meeting in 1962.

Quarrels and Rivals

But this issue was not the only divisive factor between the Independent States. At the Addis Ababa Conference the Cameroun Republic—the first former French territory to join the Conference of Independent African States—mounted a bitter attack on Guinea for harbouring the rebel headquarters of Mr. Moumie's UPC at Conakry. Somalia and Ethiopia are unreconciled over 'the Somali lands'. Tunisia and Egypt have grown steadily apart. For a time their relations were completely ruptured following an unsuccessful attempt to assassinate M. Habib Bourguiba, which he blamed on Cairo. Togo and Ghana quarrelled over the question of Ewe reunification and despite attempts at conciliation have remained on bad terms. Relations between Nigeria and Ghana have remained at the level of polite restraint.

What is as significant as the disagreements is that despite them, until roughly October 1960, the Independent African States continued to share a common platform through the Conference of Independent African States, through the Secretariat of the African Group at the United Nations, and even through the AAPO. As late as August 1960, the 'Little Summit' conference of thirteen African States was able to reach agreement in Leopoldville (with only Guinea dissenting) on their policy of support for the United Nations in the Congo.*

Then everything changed. The five main events associated with this change are : the independence of Nigeria; the sudden independence of the thirteen French territories; the quarrel between Morocco and Mauritania which led to a rift between Morocco and Tunisia because of the latter's support for Mauritania's separate independence; the breakdown in the Central Government of the Congo; and the role of the International Confederation of Free Trade Unions in Africa.

The limited scope of this survey does not allow for a full discussion of all these factors. The serious divisions over the ICFTU, are discussed later. Before their independence, many of the leaders of the French-speaking territories had come to be looked upon by the African States in control of the Pan-African organisation as 'stooges'. It was alleged against them that they had failed to stand

---

* The countries attending this conference in Leopoldville at the request of the late Mr. Lumumba were Algeria, Congo, Ethiopia, Ghana, Guinea, Libya, Liberia, Morocco, Sudan, Togo, Tanganyika, Tunisia and the U.A.R. The conference disagreed with Mr. Lumumba in his attack on the policies of the U.N. and especially against Dr. Ralph Bunche, who had been Mr. Hammarskjöld's personal representative. They praised the work of the U.N. and unanimously agreed to send a message of appreciation to Dr. Bunche. They emphasised the importance of 'harmonising' all aid in the Congo within the U.N. programme. While condemning the 'secession and colonialist manoeuvres' of Katanga, and pledging support for the integrity of the Congo, they did not agree on a policy for dealing with Mr. Tshombe.

against French policy in Algeria—some were even supplying troops
to help fight the FLN; that they had not come out against French
atomic tests in the Sahara; that they had openly sided with
Western policies in contravention of the Pan-Africanist convention
of non-commitment; that several states, such as the Cameroun and
Togo, had signed treaties for the supply of French troops to defend
their governments. As a result, Accra, Rabat, Conakry and Cairo
gave open support to exile groups from the French-speaking territories, so that Pan-African organisations (especially the AAPO)
had become committed to the opponents of some of the governments in the pre-independent French territories, notably the
Cameroun and Niger. In the affairs of the former Belgian Congo,
the French territories—led by Congo (Brazzaville)—had openly
worked against the Lumumbaists in support of Mr. Tshombe and
President Kasavubu. Here, in a nutshell, were the elements making
for strong antagonisms against leaders of the emerging French-
speaking states.

The second event was the belated arrival of an independent
Nigeria on the African—and especially West African—scene. By
the time of her independence there was, as we have already seen,
a division between herself and Ghana on the right approach to
African unity. Many of the Nigerian leaders had also come to resent
the dominant rôle assumed by their dynamic neighbour.

The third event was the Congo disaster.[64] Until the fissure
opened in the Central Government between Lumumba and
Kasavubu, the African states in the United Nations enjoyed their
finest hour. They worked in unison, compelling the Security
Council to operate effectively; they staved off the incipient 'cold
war' threat in the Congo. The presence of Africa as a force in the
councils of the world had been made real for the first time in
history. There is a great deal still to be written about that period :
about Ghana's rôle as mediator and moderator; about Guinea's
rôle as irritant and militant, outflanking Ghana on the left; about
the French African leaders' negotiations with Mr. Tshombe and
President Kasavubu; and about Nigeria's incursion through Mr.
Jaja Wachuku's chairmanship of the UN Conciliation Commission.
But for our purposes it is enough to record that faced with its first
major test in an African crisis, the African states were disunited.
Nor was it the French-speaking Africans against the rest; the
divisions were much more fundamental. In the end one group of
African states recognised the Gizenga Government in Stanleyville;*
another recognised the Kasavubu Government in Leopoldville. And

* These included Ghana, Guinea, Mali, the U.A.R. and Morocco.

around this division—but for a wider variety of reasons—there grew up two groups, the Casablanca Powers and the Monrovia States.

It is against this background that one must examine the rival groupings that emerged towards the end of 1960.

The Brazzaville Group

The Brazzaville Group[65]—or to give it its official title, *The Union of African States and Madagascar*—grew out of a meeting summoned by the Ivory Coast in Abidjan in October 1960 primarily to discuss the possibility of the French African territories mediating between France and Algeria. The need for such an initiative had become urgent in view of their approaching application for membership of the United Nations. At a subsequent meeting in Brazzaville in December 1960 the decision was taken to form a more permanent association, and this decision was implemented at a meeting in Dakar in January 1961.

The Brazzaville Powers are Congo (Brazzaville), Ivory Coast, Senegal, Mauritania, Upper Volta, Niger, Dahomey, Chad, Gabon, the Central African Republic, Cameroun and Madagascar. Not all the members have agreed to join the French Community; and Togo has not joined the group.

The Brazzaville Declaration* called for peace in Algeria by 1961; favoured mediation in the Congo; and upheld Mauritania's independence. While opposing political union in the sense of establishing integrated institutions, it nevertheless accepted a permanent Inter-State Economic Secretariat.†

This development introduced two new elements into African politics : for the first time invitations were extended to a restricted list of independent states, and a deliberate attempt was made to create a bloc of African states (as opposed to regional groupings).[66]

The Casablanca Powers

Brazzaville led to Casablanca. The group of African states which had adopted a clear-cut Lumumbaist line in the Congo had for some time felt the need to co-ordinate their policies. They had become a minority in the African Group at the United Nations and they were anxious to reassert the initiative taken by them in the earlier stages of Pan-African developments, Morocco, reacting to

* For French and English texts of the Brazzaville Declaration see Appendix 13.

† Decision taken at Yaounde in March 1961 where Madagascar's President Tsiranana was elected first president of the organisation.

the Brazzaville Group's sponsorship of Mauritania, took the initiative in calling the Casablanca Conference in January 1961.[67] The list of invitations was again a restricted one. Although more states were invited than finally came, the sponsors have kept their original list of invitations secret. Seven African delegations—Morocco, Ghana, Guinea, Mali, the UAR, Libya, and the Algerian Provisional Government—as well as Ceylon—were represented.

Apart from discussions on a constitutional framework for the Casablanca Powers, four issues dominated the conference: Mauritania, Congo, Israel and the concept of political union. This last point is taken up more fully later in this chapter.

Libya, Ghana and the Algerians had not at first supported Morocco's attitude to Mauritania. Ghana had, in fact, favoured her admission to membership of the United Nations. But for the sake of 'greater unity' they subsequently reversed their previous stand. (Libya once again changed her position at the subsequent Monrovia Conference.)

On the Congo question the argument was mainly between Ghana and the rest. Only Ghana had refused to withdraw her troops from the UN Command in the Congo (a position she has steadily maintained). On this point she was notably out of step not only with the Casablanca Powers but with her own allies in the Ghana-Guinea-Mali Union. Nor did Dr. Nkrumah favour the suggestion that direct military aid should be given to Mr. Gizenga's Stanleyville régime. He argued at great length against a military adventure because, as he insisted, the 'logistics' of keeping Stanleyville supplied would ensure its failure. By all accounts he took a tremendous hammering from many of the other delegations because of this attitude. But in the end his view prevailed.*

Ghana was the only member which could have resisted the UAR's demand for branding Israel as an 'imperialist base', as it had done at other conferences. But after the Congo debate, Dr. Nkrumah was unwilling to isolate himself on yet another point. Casablanca was the first occasion where a group of African States agreed to the UAR resolution on Israel.†

The broad principles of agreement reached at the Casablanca Conference were subsequently incorporated into the Casablanca Charter‡; its Protocol was signed at a meeting of Foreign Ministers

* For the text of resolutions passed at the conference see Appendix 15.
† Col. Nasser tried to get support for the Casablanca resolution at the Belgrade Conference of Non-aligned States in September 1961, but failed.
‡ For text of the Casablanca Charter and Protocol see Appendices 15 and 16.

in Cairo in May 1961. Libya did not sign the Protocol. The nineteen articles of the Protocol regulate the executive machinery of the Charter and provide for four permanent committees to be established—political, economic, cultural and a Defence Supreme Command. The Political Committee consists of the Heads of State, or their representatives, and is scheduled to meet 'periodically' to co-ordinate policies. The Economic Committee is composed of the Ministers of Finance of member-states, and the Cultural Committee of the Ministers of Education. The Supreme Command consists of the Chiefs of Staff of the various Armed Forces. Bamako, Mali's capital, is designated as the headquarters for the secretariat, with a Moroccan as Secretary-General.

The Charter prohibits accession to foreign military pacts and lays down that all signatories shall strictly adhere to policies of non-alignment. Any independent African state can accede to the Charter.

The Monrovia States

In the same way as Brazzaville had led to Casablanca, so Casablanca in its turn led to Monrovia. The Conference of twenty states that opened in the Liberian capital on May 8, 1961, included the twelve Brazzaville States; as well as Liberia, Nigeria, Somalia, Sierra Leone, Togo, Ethiopia, and the Casablanca deviate, Libya. Tunisia came but chose observer status. The Sudan stayed away as she had from Casablanca. Her official objection was to Mauritania's presence. Neither Congo (Leopoldville) nor the Stanleyville régime of Gizenga was invited to either of the two Conferences.

The Monrovia Conference was originally initiated by Dr. Leopold Senghor, Senegal's President, who had become increasingly concerned about his own country's isolation. Although Senegal belongs to the Brazzaville Powers it is not altogether secure in this association. Not wishing to take the lead himself Dr. Senghor approached Togo's President, Mr. Sylvanus Olympio. After consultation with Liberia's President Tubman and Nigeria's Premier, Sir Abubakar Tafawa Balewa, the three agreed together to act as sponsors, and persuaded the Ivory Coast and Cameroun to join as co-sponsors. At one stage they persuaded Guinea and Mali to act as co-sponsors as well, but under pressure from Ghana these two withdrew on the grounds that the meeting was inopportune and that it should consist only of Heads of State.

In his welcome address to delegates President Tubman indicated some of the aims of the Conference as well as the anxieties that had led up to its being convened :

'It should be crystal clear to every leader that Africans cannot live in isolation if they expect to allay suspicion, fear and tension. The idea of *primus inter pares,* first among equals, is destructive of African Unity and Peace.... The sense of oneness should be deeply rooted in the breast of every African. But the whirls of circumstances and ambition can make it difficult for us to fit ourselves into the picture of a unified Africa, the foundation for which we hope will be laid before this Conference closes. I come now to the question of leadership of Africa.... In this connection I have observed that there seems to be three schools of thought on this subject. There are those who feel that Liberia should assume leadership based on the fact that she is the oldest African Republic and is riper in political experience; but it will require more than age and political experience to assume leadership of Africa. There are others who assume that Ghana should assume that rôle because she is physically more developed and embraces larger territories. It will require more than development and larger territory to assume leadership of Africa. And there are yet those who opine that Egypt with its rich traditions dating back to the remotest antiquity should do so. It will require more than rich traditions of antiquity. It will require, in my opinion, the aggregate of the best that is in all compounded in such a manner as to represent the divisibility of Africa indivisible.'

The Monrovia Conference has so far been the largest single gathering of African states. For the first time the whole of the French-speaking states joined with a majority of the English-speaking states. On questions affecting the principles of colonialism* it spoke with the same sharp voice as the AAPO and other militant Pan-Africanist groupings. It faltered, however, on the atomic tests in the Sahara; its resolution condemning tests in general took note of French assurances that tests in the Sahara would cease. And on Algeria, it accepted a tepid compromise expressing goodwill for the negotiations between the two sides that were about to take place. It backed economic sanctions against South Africa, and promised material support for the Angolans. It expressed full support for the Congo Central Government, but deleted a resolution condemning the assassination of Mr. Lumumba.

The Monrovia approach to the question of co-operation and unity is discussed in the next section. The Conference regretted the absence of the Casablanca Powers and left open the door for them to join at a follow-up conference to be held in Lagos where the machinery of co-operation was to be discussed in greater detail.

* For text of resolutions see Appendix 17.

By the end of the Conference Togo's President, Sylvanus Olympio, was able to say[68] : 'At last we are beginning to think of ourselves as Africans and not simply *as extensions* of the European Powers.'

No event did more to flutter the dovecotes in Africa's capitals than the Monrovia Conference. Ghana's Press was livid. Having published nothing about the Conference, except to refer to the absence of this or that Head of State, the pro-government papers opened a campaign to show how 'bogus' the Conference was. 'The very moment the BBC and other imperialist broadcasting brass-bands began their phoney adulation of the so-called virtues of the Monrovia slave-mentality operated slogan (*sic*) of "unity without unification", students of African history suspected with considerable concern the genesis of this new brand of His Master's Voice, just to discover that it was only the hand that was of Esau.' This article in the Ghana *Evening News* went on to suggest that 'the imperialists chose Monrovia because they believed that Liberia is still pulling the economic apron-strings'. Liberia is referred to as being 'in the economic mess-pot with her split, deformed and distorted personality'; and President Tubman is called upon to admit that he is 'an American first, African second'.

The Nigerian Press was incensed by this language. The *West African Pilot* (the paper started by Dr. Azikiwe and which has always expressed his policies) wrote on May 18, 1961 :

> 'One single parliament for all Africa would be the ideal thing but, unlike Dr. Nkrumah, we would not strive to attain the unattainable. The Ghanaian leader talks sense most of the time but when he goes amiss he does so in a big way. We know that he is a great advocate of African unity but that does not mean that he is always right in his approach to African affairs. Dr. Nkrumah launched a blistering attack on the Monrovia Conference the other day. He was not there and yet this was an opportunity for all leaders of Africa to get together. Dr. Nkrumah is an advocate of unity. He was not there because he and his minority group could not, as they planned, impose their will on the conference. Dr. Nkrumah says Pan-Africanism means nothing unless it transcends the artificial barriers and boundaries imposed by colonialism. Ghana is in union with Guinea. They do not yet have one parliament or currency. Ghana is a very different country indeed, from Guinea, and the so-called union remains a scrap of paper. The Ghanaian Messiah has not yet succeeded in removing "artificial barriers imposed by colonialism".

> 'As an advocate of unity, Dr. Nkrumah has failed to rally the Ashanti region of Ghana behind him. The lash of the

Preventive Detention Act has created an artificial unity. Without his police and para-military groups such as the Builders' Brigades and the Young Pioneers, Dr. Nkrumah knows he will be facing a revolt any day. Yet this is the man who goes before the world, preaching unity. Dr. Nkrumah chooses to believe that the Monrovia powers do not represent the majority of African States. Twenty-one [sic] States were represented at Monrovia. There are only five countries in the Casablanca bloc. THE TRUTH IS THAT DR. NKRUMAH MUST BE AT THE HEAD OF ANYTHING OR OUTSIDE IT because he must always lead. He is the Messiah and no camp follower, this man. Dr. Nkrumah must be told that his reckless pursuit of his ambitions for expansion will lead him nowhere. His real aim is to swallow up little Togo and chew off parts of Ivory Coast. This talk of an African parliament and an Africa without boundaries is merely a cloak to conceal his aims. No matter how much we may admire the Ghanaian leader, it is our duty to warn him to desist from the pursuit of false principles.'

In another editorial attack[69] the *West African Pilot* said that in pursuance of 'cold war tactics' in Africa a struggle for leadership has already developed. 'Until recently it was a tournament between Nasser and Nkrumah but Africa today contains many stars and meteorites, all of them seeking positions of eminence.'

Politicians joined in the Press war; the NCNC issued a special Press statement appealing to Ghana, Guinea and Mali to join in the discussions with the Monrovia States. In the end, Dr. Nkrumah himself ordered that the Ghana Press should 'unilaterally' end its campaign. The importance of this spilling of ink was that for the first time many of the things that had previously only been said in private were now a matter of public discussion with the benefits that go with open disagreements openly discussed.

Pan-African Unity: The Crucial Question

Brazzaville, Casablanca and Monrovia have broken the charmed circle of Pan-African unity. But nobody who has closely followed the interplay of African forces can believe that the present divisions are permanent. Alliances and relationships are still extremely fluid in the Continent. As recently as 1959, Ghana and Guinea signed the Sanniquellie Declaration with Liberia; yet less than two years later the Ghana Press was busy denouncing the Liberians as 'western agents of America'. But Liberia had not changed. The Tubman of the Monrovia Conference was the same Tubman of

Sanniquellie. It is a feature of the contemporary game that friend-ships and enmities change fast. Nowhere in the Continent have politics or alliances had sufficient time to solidify.

It is not yet possible to make a confident assessment of the funda-mental differences that divide the Casablanca Powers from the Monrovia States. Casablanca was for Gizenga's régime; now (like the Monrovians) they are for the Congo Central Government. They support Morocco's claim on Mauritania; Monrovia is opposed to it. On the other hand both groups have declared themselves em-phatically against the remnants of colonialism and against *apar-theid*. Casablanca is on record for non-commitment; Monrovia is silent on this point. But it would be misleading to tag all the Mon-rovians as 'pro-Western' : they represent many different attitudes, ranging from Somalia's strict non-alignment to Madagascar's Francophilism. Is there a clear-cut division then between the two groups on the crucial question of how best to achieve African unity?

The Monrovia declaration on promoting better understanding and co-operation among African states defines five principles : re-cognition of each state's equality and sovereignty; freedom from annexation; the right for any state freely and voluntarily to join with another without hindrance; respect for the principle of non-interference in each other's internal affairs; respect for territorial integrity, and condemnation of any state harbouring dissident elements who might wish to carry on subversive activities against another state.

Monrovia accepted the idea of promoting co-operation through-out Africa, conditioned by *'non-acceptance of any leadership'*. The key to their attitude on Pan-African unity reads : 'The unity that it is aimed to achieve at the moment is not the political integration of sovereign African States, but unity of aspirations and of action considered from the point of view of African social solidarity and political identity'. Also, they accept, in principle, that an inter-African and Malagasy *Advisory* Organisation shall be created. Committees of technicians have been set up to plan co-operation in the economic, educational, cultural, scientific, technical and com-munications field.

How does all this compare with Casablanca's proposals for African unity? The Casablanca Charter goes only so far as to 'affirm our will to intensify our efforts for the creation of an *effective form of co-operation* among the African States in the economic, social and cultural domains'. While it provides for the immediate establishment of four Joint Committees—political, economic, cultural and a military command—these are purely con-

sultative and have no power of any kind. It is completely vague on
the crucial question of what is intended by 'an effective form of
co-operation'. There is no mention of abandoning sovereignty, nor
of political union. In fact, although Dr. Nkrumah argued strongly
at the Casablanca Conference for political union, his proposal was
not accepted. In its closing stages Dr. Nkrumah made his own
position admirably clear : 'The future of Africa lies in a political
union—a political union in which the economic, military and cultural activities will be co-ordinated for the security of our Continent'. But he spoke for himself; Casablanca was silent on political
union.

   Political union is an idea of which Dr. Nkrumah has become
the leading and, indeed, virtually the only prominent exponent in
Africa; even Guinea and Mali are less specific, except in their
approach to the Union of West African States. Dr. Nkrumah's
latest book, *I Speak of Freedom*,[70] is, significantly, dedicated to
'Patrice Lumumba, late Prime Minister of the Republic of the
Congo, and *all those who are engaged in the struggle for the political unification of Africa.*' [Author's italics.] To all the disturbing
problems in Africa—poverty, neo-colonialism, balkanisation, disunity, cultural and language differences—Dr. Nkrumah offers one
recipe : 'strong political unity' and 'the African race united under
one federal government'.

   'The emergence of such a mighty stabilising force in this strife-
worn world should be regarded,' he writes,[71] 'not as the shadowy
dream of a visionary, but as a practical proposition which the
peoples of Africa can and should translate into reality. There is a
tide in the affairs of every people when the moment strikes for
political action. We must act now. Tomorrow may be too late. . . ."

   The debate over *political union* (or as it is sometimes called
organic union) and *regional association* (or *functional co-operation*)
has become a lively issue not only in the higher spheres of Pan-
African politics but in national parliaments and on the political
hustings as well. Nigeria's official Opposition, the Action Group
which is led by Chief Obafemi Awolowo[72] introduced a motion
into parliament in September 1961, to promote the idea of a Union
of West African States. Opening for the Opposition, Chief Tony
Enaharo attacked government policy for advocating 'functional
co-operation among African States at a time when the climate of
progressive opinion throughout Africa is overwhelmingly in favour
of organic union.'[73]

   But neither he nor his leader, Mr. Awolowo, appear to subscribe
to the idea of political union as advocated by Dr. Nkrumah. This

emerges clearly from a Press Statement made by Chief Awolowo on behalf of the Action Group in June 1961.* It is in many ways a remarkable document, coming as it does from a great and influential party which has always been counted in the past among the reformers and traditionalists. It illuminates the strength of feeling about blackness. 'The first principle which I advocate is that, in the present context of the world, the black man *qua* the colour of his skin, is confronted with certain knotty and intractable problems which are peculiar to him.'

It calls for the creation of an Organisation for the African Community which must be 'first and last a revolutionary body ... it must openly advocate the overthrow of all white rule in Africa, whether such rule is by white settlers or by white colonial powers.'

But while it makes a number of concrete proposals to achieve African unity, these do not amount to *political union*. It concedes that *confederation* might be considered.

I am not here concerned with the charges levelled against Mr. Awolowo that his plan is only intended to make 'political propaganda'. The significant fact is that the idea of unity is considered to be sufficiently important to encourage an influential political party to adopt it as its platform in opposition to the Nigerian Government's foreign policy.

What do other Nigerian leaders think? The Governor-General, Dr. Nnamdi Azikiwe, is of course the doyen of the Pan-African leaders in West Africa. In an address delivered in London in August 1961† he put forward his idea for what he called 'a concert of African States'.

> 'Granted that political union is desirable,' he said, 'the question arises whether it should be in the form of a federation or a confederation. If the former, should it be a tight or a loose one, in which case it will be desirable to know whether it is intended to surrender internal or external sovereignty, or both? In this context we cannot overlook the struggle for hegemony as indeed has been the case in the last few years. Hand in glove with the struggle for hegemony goes the manoeuvre for the control of the armed forces for the effective implementation of policy.'

Dr. Azikiwe's successor as Premier of the Eastern Region of Nigeria, Dr. M. I. Okpara, was even more concrete in the proposals he outlined for an African Union in London in August 1961 at the end of an extensive tour through Asia and Europe.[74] His proposals

---

* Extracts from this statement are reproduced as Appendix 24.
† For a summary of this speech see Appendix 25.

envisage : firstly, that Africa should be organised into five Economic Regions (North, East, Central, South and West) with common customs, currency, transport and research organisations; secondly that these economic regions should be welded into political unions; and thirdly, that the five political units should form either a Federation or a Confederation, or even a Common Market.

'My contacts during my journeys through Asia and Europe have confirmed my view that the Union of African States will make for rapid economic advance on this Continent. Its political advantages will be enormous, as the Continent will be completely liberated, and a source of constant temptation to the Imperialist will be removed. . . . Unless there is a rapid and complete change of policy such as we have seen on the West Coast [of Africa], the West will definitely lose Africa. To hasten this change Africans must band themselves together into a Union. . . . It is important that we should carry all along with us if we are to arrive at the goal of a United Africa in peace and not in pieces. Only by the fullest discussion and persuasion is this possible. Coercion or precipitate action will achieve nothing; indeed it might imperil this vital objective of African unity. This is the lesson of Nigerian unity.'

But this argument is not confined only to West Africa; it is going on everywhere in the Continent. In an invaluable pamphlet[75], Mr. Dunduza K. Chisiza, Parliamentary Secretary to the Minister of Finance in Nyasaland and one of Dr. Hastings K. Banda's most effective lieutenants, writes :

'Pan-Africanism, as a strategy for emancipation, is unquestionably effective, but we must build from down upwards, not from up downwards : the fabric of the regions must be knitted together not merely tacked. As a unifying agent for regional co-operation Pan-Africanism is superficial; it is an 'operation roof-top'. This is not a counsel for gradualism in the attainment of independence, which must come quickly, but of realism after it. Ideas about stages vary with writers not only in politics but also in other disciplines such as economics. The writer suggests the following : 1. Attainment of independence. 2. Vigorous modernisation of economies. 3. Encouragement of regional economic co-operation and regional consciousness. 4. Political regrouping of neighbouring countries.'

Non-alignment and Belgrade (1961)

Non-alignment has become a second major divisive factor between the African states. All believe in non-alignment, or at least

profess to do so. There is, however, a wide difference between the
positive neutrality of Bandung or the *non-commitment* of the first
Conference of Independent African States in 1958, and the policy
demanded by the Conference of Non-aligned Countries in Belgrade
in 1961.

Of Africa's twenty-eight independent states, only ten went to
Belgrade : Congo (Leopoldville), Ethiopia, Ghana, Guinea, Mali,
Morocco, Somalia, Sudan, Tunisia and the UAR.* And of these
only two—Somalia and Ethiopia—are members of the Monrovia
States. Two others—Tunisia and the Congo—lean towards Mon-
rovia. On the other hand, all the Casablanca Powers were at
Belgrade. They had played a leading part in the earlier work of
the preparatory committee which met in Cairo in June 1961 to
plan the non-aligned conference. Only three non-Casablanca
Powers attended this meeting from among the African States :
Sudan, Ethiopia and Somalia.

The Cairo preliminary meeting[76] decided two important questions. It defined for the first time what was meant by non-alignment; and, in the light of its definition, it recommended which
states should be invited. To be non-aligned a country must : 1.
Pursue an independent policy based on peaceful co-existence. 2.
Not participate in multilateral military alliances (e.g. NATO, the
Warsaw Pact, SEATO or CENTO). 3. Support liberation and independence movements. 4. Not participate in bilateral military
alliances with Great Powers; nor should they have foreign military
bases on their territory, set up with their agreement.

What is a military alliance? Does it rule out, for example,
defence agreements for training local armies? No precise definitions
were agreed; this led to bitter controversies both about Latin
American and African membership. The Brazzaville Powers were
not even seriously considered, but Nigeria was—and it was decided
not to invite her (or Tunisia), despite strong protests from such
countries as India, the Sudan and Ethiopia. After 'the battle of
Bizerta' Tunisia was invited; and as a result of a special initiative
by Ethiopia a belated invitation went to Nigeria. Her government
angrily rejected it, not without bad blood.

'It is a matter of prestige,' Nigeria's Foreign Minister, Mr. Jaja
Wachuku told Parliament when questioned why the Government
had not accepted the invitation.[77] 'An African country spent all
its time fighting against Nigeria attending this conference. . . .

* Algeria's Provisional Government attended the Belgrade Conference
as a full member; it was accorded *de jure* recognition by a number of the
other countries attending the Conference.

Nigeria is not going to beg for a thing that she is entitled to. . . . If we had the same time as these people have had, perhaps twelve months from today, it may be that all those who have been making the noise will find themselves very backward in international affairs.'

Until nearly the end of 1960 the newly-independent African states were, generally-speaking, 'neutral on the side of the West'. (Two exceptions were Guinea and the UAR; each had good reasons for its attitude.) Even though criticisms of Western policies were voiced everywhere in the Continent, the African leaders continued to shop for aid and ideas almost exclusively in the West. By the end of 1961 this picture had largely changed : no African countries were pro-Communist; none was overtly anti-West; but fewer were 'neutral on the side of the West'; and a great number were genuinely non-aligned.

These attitudes are not only reflected in the policies of governments; they are even more strongly shown in the attitudes of political leaders, and especially among the African youth.

Even if Western policies were attuned to the real feelings and needs of Africa it is doubtful whether the drift into non-alignment could have been stopped. Indeed, it is questionable whether Western policies would have been well served by trying to stop it— but that is another question. Nevertheless, Western mistakes contributed greatly to its changing fortunes in Africa. The tragedy of the Congo, and Western pressures in the United Nations (both in the Security Council and in the lobbies) probably did more than anything else to harden sentiment in favour of a more strict application of non-alignment :[78] for one thing it helped to produce the Casablanca Conference with its rigid insistence on members being genuinely non-aligned. But French policy in Africa—the Sahara bomb-tests, the method of surrendering power in some of the French-speaking territories, the Algeria war and Bizerta, as well as her voting record at the United Nations on such questions as South-West Africa and South Africa—also played its part. France's allies in NATO could not escape sharing responsibility for her policies once they refused to disassociate themselves publicly from the French nuclear tests (which were carried out in defiance of the moratorium on testing); and when they tacitly agreed to NATO arms being shipped to Algeria. Once rebellion broke out in Angola, anti-NATO (hence anti-Western) feelings became further hardened, although the uncompromising position adopted by the United States towards the Salazar régime possibly made things less bad than might otherwise have been the case.

These developments occurred at a time when independence was bringing both frustration and fresh opportunities to African states. For the first time many of them had political freedom to negotiate for economic aid where and with whom they chose. At the same time they needed vastly increased technical and financial aid to carry forward the impetus independence gave to development. For these reasons alone the period 1960-62 would unquestionably have witnessed a 'breakthrough' of the Communists' economic and technical aid programme into Africa; and this must inevitably have led to some change of attitudes. The Communists' 'arrival' as a competitor in Africa should not be connected with Western policies, even if their apparent strength in one or two countries is almost certainly due to Western reluctance to help.

This coincidence of a period of disillusionment with the West and the appearance of the Communists fresh on the African scene, gave a much sharper edge to African attitudes on non-alignment. While this impact was strongest on militant elements in the Pan-African movement, it had its effect also on such countries as the Sudan, Ethiopia, Tunisia and Somalia.

Reformers and Revolutionaries

On the question of political union the majority of the Casablanca Powers have, as we have seen, less in common with Dr. Nkrumah than they have with the Monrovia States. And yet in their general attitudes the two groups are clearly distinctive. Where, then, lies the difference?

When one comes to examine the most active protagonists in both groups one is struck by certain fundamental differences of attitude. There is, for example, a similarity between Ghana, Guinea, Mali and the UAR* on the one hand; and, say, Nigeria, Liberia, Senegal and the Ivory Coast on the other.

The first category is militant in a revolutionary sense.† Although there are differences between them, they all subscribe, in one form or another, to the concept of the State and the Party being one and the same : an idea presented as 'democratic centralism'. They are

* But not Morocco, their Casablanca partner.
† Sir Charles Arden-Clarke, speaking on 'The West and Africa's Challenge' on the occasion of the Royal African Society's sixtieth anniversary in London, said of Africa's post-colonial governments: 'These new governments are not the result of a slow process of evolution. They are revolutionary in character, have revolutionary tasks to perform, and are obsessed with the idea that their task of carrying out extensive economic and social changes must be made with speed.' (Quoted in *East Africa and Rhodesia*, June 8, 1961.)

willing to force the pace of change by direct state pressure from above. They are not afraid to risk drastic economic experiments.

None of this is true in equal measure of the second category. That is not to say there are no 'democratic centralists' among the Monrovia States, for there are. But the general attitude of the Monrovians is reformist and radical rather than revolutionary. Their radicalism lies in their nationalist struggle; but once having achieved independence they are not anxious for too rapid or widespread social and economic changes. Their chief preoccupation is with their own affairs; they are not champions of a particular political concept which they would like to persuade *all* the African states to adopt. But the triumph of the militant Pan-Africanists (or is it the dynamics of Pan-Africanism?) is that the reluctant reformers and radicals have been compelled to compete for authority and influence, either by creating their own organisations in self-defence, or by joining in the organisations started by the revolutionaries. It is not accidental that when one thinks of the *political capitals* of Africa one thinks automatically of Accra, Cairo, Conakry and latterly of Bamako. Among the 'Monrovians' the nearest one gets to the idea of a political capital is Brazzaville, but this has largely to do with the regional aspirations of M. Fulbert Youlou.

Another important distinction we have noted is that while both believe in 'non-alignment', the revolutionaries believe in an aggressive assertion of this policy. It is not enough that their own foreign bases should go; they are pledged to see that everybody else's should go as well. The majority of the 'Monrovians', e.g. the 'Brazzaville Twelve', Liberia, Sierra Leone and Togo—that is three-quarters of the Monrovia States—assert this belief in non-alignment (if they do so at all) as a theoretical concept rather than as a practical policy.

But while these distinctions have validity at the present time it is possible to misconstrue the dynamic forces of Africa if one regards them as either rigid distinctions or constants. In the rapid changes of a society—not only in transition from colonialism to independence, but from a society unadapted to modern statehood to a future nowhere yet clearly defined—there is a strong interplay between radical and revolutionary ideas. Neither the reformers with their cautious attachment to traditions and slow change, nor the revolutionaries with their belief in rapid modernisation are sufficiently sure of themselves to resist each other's arguments. Both forces are present in every African society, and there is hardly a government that does not include representatives of both. Thus far the radicals have tempered the revolutionaries rather than the other

way around. But recent developments in Egypt and Ghana show
that the swing may now be going the other way. There is no logical
reason why the revolutionaries should not in time establish themselves as the stronger force in Pan-Africanism; if such a development should come it would dramatically change the whole picture
in Africa.

CHAPTER IV

AFRICAN REGROUPINGS

Africa is a jig-saw in fifty-six parts. Contemporary nationalists who ascribe this condition to 'balkanisation by the imperialists', ignore that there were hundreds of separate parts to the jigsaw before colonialism. To give the old devil his due, colonialism contributed greatly towards regrouping different ethnic units and laying the foundations for nation-states, even if it did so for its own reasons, and in doing so created artificial boundaries which have been bequeathed to the new African leaders in the shape of lively irredentisms. Nobody imagines that a Continent with a population of perhaps only 230 millions, and with a widely disparate distribution of resources, can be expected to produce either effective or stable states within its present higgledy-piggledy boundaries. Pan-Africanism's answer is to create large regional organisations.

The importance of regional grouping is not an issue in dispute; its importance is accepted by the Casablanca Powers no less than by the Brazzaville States and the Monrovia States. What is in dispute is the best way of going about it. 'The basis of regional government,' writes Nyasaland's Dunduza Chisiza,[79] 'is regional consciousness ... those who would regroup countries must first address themselves to the problem of encouraging a regional outlook among their countrymen. So far, infinitesimally little has been done in this direction. On the other hand, there is a lot of activity on the Pan-African level. It is not clear whether the belief is that by fostering a Pan-African spirit the foundations for regional political federations are being laid. If this is so, some rethinking is urgently required here'. He goes on to suggest that regional government should be built up from the bottom.*

Kenya's Jomo Kenyatta says: 'I want to see first East Africa united and federated, and then the whole of Africa as one.'[80] Eastern Nigeria's Premier, Dr. Okpara, advocates the functional approach to regional organisations through interlinking Customs Unions†; this is the view, too, of the Brazzaville and the Monrovia States. Ghana's Dr. Nkrumah rejects this view; the need for unity,

* See page 59.   † See page 59.

he argues, is too urgent to allow of gradualism. 'The solution is to find a form of political organisation which gives full expression to all ethnic groups and yet maintains that essential unity which is a prerequisite of true independence.... I mean an African Continental government—*a single Continent* which would develop a feeling of one community among the peoples of Africa.... I firmly believe that such an African Continental Government is essential.'[81]

A single Continent? Chief Awolowo, Nigeria's Opposition leader does not agree. He wishes to see 'one large *black African community*'. In an interview in Accra he said he felt only black African countries should be admitted to the community because many North Africans 'including President Nasser' were more Pan-Arabist than Pan-African in their outlook.[82]

Dr. Nkrumah's associates, M. Sékou Touré and M. Modeiba Keita, wish to set different criteria. The former believes : 'If the laws of development lead to the regrouping of societies, and in consequence to the enlargement of existing entities and their transformation into multi-national entities, it is still necessary that each element should find itself in identical conditions, should have similar means available, and should use these means to the same ends.'[83] This Marxist 'means and ends' viewpoint is stated with more directness by Mali's President : 'We are convinced that the States of Africa will never be independent, in the full sense of the word, if they remain small States, more or less opposed to one another, each having its own policy, each taking no account of the policy of the other. Our Constitution therefore provides for a total or partial abandonment of sovereignty* in favour of a grouping of African States, but such an abandonment of sovereignty demands an identity of views with our fellow-States. One cannot build a complete whole without contradictions. Certain common viewpoints on international policy and on economic policy are absolutely necessary, together with an understanding of the contradictions contained in economic planning, and the necessity for each State to consider its economy within the framework of one large African economy, if it is to constitute an entity with other States. For this reason we recognise that this abandonment of sovereignty necessitates an identity of views with our partners, both in foreign and domestic policy. Nevertheless the Republic of Mali has decided to co-operate in all fields with all the African States, whatever may be their political, economic or social set-up. This means however that we envisage *a political organisation* in co-operation with the

* Ghana, Guinea, Tunisia and Egypt have also provided for limitation of their sovereignty in their constitutions.

other African States only in so far as they have identity of views with us in the field of international policy and also in the field of internal economic policy. But this does not preclude us from *co-operation* with all the African States, whatever their alignment in international policy, and whatever may be their political or economic system.'[84] [Author's italics.]

It is against this background of conflicting ideas that one can most usefully look at the attempts made so far to achieve wider regroupings in Africa.

The Idea of a Maghreb Federation

Geographically, the Maghreb (Arabic for 'the West') covers North West Africa north of 26° N. and east as far as 25° E.[85] Politically it embraces Algeria, Tunisia, Libya, Morocco, Mauritania, and the French Sahara and Spanish North Africa : total population 25 million. The idea of the unity of the Maghreb goes back to the dawn of the Islamic conquests in North West Africa. As a modern political concept it derives from the nationalist political movements of Tunisia (neo-Destour), Morocco (Istiqlal and the *Mouvement pour le Triomphe des Libertés Démocratiques*) and Algeria (now represented by the National Liberation Front—FLN).

The preamble to Tunisia's constitution commits her to adherence to 'the unity of the Greater Maghreb'. The Constitution's general provisions (Article 2) formally affirms the Tunisian Republic to be an integral part of the Greater Maghreb, and lays it as a duty on the state to make it a reality.

The first Maghrebin Charter was signed by the three independence parties of Tunisia and Morocco in May 1945. But while the idea remained alive no effective follow-up occurred until April 1958 when the FLN joined with the Tunisians and the Moroccans at a Conference in Tangiers[86] to prepare a Convention which declared :

   1. That achievement of Maghreb unity was the goal of all.
   2. That federation was the best means of achieving it.
   3. That a Consultative Assembly made up of the three National Assemblies should be convoked to consider matters of federal and common interest during the transition period.
   4. That the three Governments should refrain from making basic international agreements on matters of foreign policy or defence until the federal institutions could be made effective.

A permanent secretariat was established by each of the three governments. But effective implementation of these resolutions was delayed largely, though not only, on account of the Algerian war.[87] There has also been some notable feet-dragging on the part of Morocco. Egypt has always strongly opposed the establishment of this exclusive North West African Arab federation. Nor have the notoriously bad relations between Cairo and Tunis made the task any easier. Tunisia's President, Habib Bourguíba, in a speech[88] in which he bitterly attacked 'Pharaonic Imperialism', said : 'The Arab League's intention is to draw us nearer to one another; it can become the instrument of unity. All depends on how it is used and how patient we are. As far as we are concerned we shall go on with the task that faces us within the framework of the Arab Maghreb. We are trying to narrow divergences of opinion, to co-operate with the others, and to work together for the kind of unity which we consider best. Only if that unity is freely accepted by all the interested parties can it be valid and lasting. Such is our position where the Arab world is concerned. I am convinced that all the Arab countries desire a policy of this sort (Egypt excepted, of course). I am also convinced that all thinking people in the Arab countries, and all governments even, are united on this point.'

In October, 1960, President Bourguiba boldly proposed in a new initiative that the Algerian problem should be solved by an immediate union between Tunisia and Algeria pending their association with the other Maghreb countries. 'The idea is in the air. We have launched it to let it grow, and we would like it to be a contribution to peace. . . .'[89]

The independence of Algeria is certain to create a new condition in which the Maghreb Federation will, at last, become practicable politics. It is a cause to which the 'revolutionary parties' of the Maghreb have committed themselves. 'A common wish for unity exists in Tunisia, Morocco, Algeria, Mauritania and even Libya,' wrote El Mehdi Ben Barka, Secretary-General of the Moroccan *Union Nationale des Forces Populaires.*[90] 'A united Maghreb will surely therefore come, and its people alone will decide its political and economic institutions. It will not be a historical restoration, an attempt to recapture the past splendours of the Almoravid and Almohad Empires. It will turn to the future, fully conscious of its historical inheritance and of the rôle it should play in the Mediterranean area and on the African Continent.'

Union of the Nile States

Egypt's most immediate African objective has been to forge a union between itself and the Sudan (total population 37 million), and perhaps eventually with Uganda (5½ million), to create a single region of the users of the Nile river. While the Uganda idea has never advanced outside the drawing-rooms of Cairo, a union between Egypt and the Sudan was destroyed in 1955 only by Egypt's insensitive interference in the Sudan's internal affairs as soon as she achieved independence.[91] The Independence Government was formed by the then pro-Egyptian National Unionist Party, led by Mr. El Azhari. A subsequent attempt by Egypt to make good a territorial claim on the Sudan by military force made matters much worse in 1958.

Although the idea of a union between the two states is not practical politics at this juncture, relations between them improved sufficiently to allow for an agreement to be reached on the use of the Nile Waters to enable Egypt to build the Aswan Dam. Khartoum is not likely quickly to forget the insult it feels Cairo handed out in 1955; nevertheless different leaders and different times could very well produce a climate of opinion in which closer association might become possible.

Greater Somalia

A third Islamic federation movement exists in the Horn of Africa where the idea of a Greater Somalia (total population between four and five million) is pursued with varying degrees of enthusiasm by all the Somali political parties.[92] The aim is to use the Somalia Republic (itself a successful regrouping of the former British and Italian Somali protectorates) as a nucleus to unite all those Somalis now living in French Somaliland, the Ogaden and other Somali-inhabited areas of Ethiopia, and in the Northern Territories of Kenya.

The pursuit of this policy, allied to the unfortunate history of the transfer of the Somali's traditional grazing grounds in the Haud and Reserved Areas to Ethiopia, has produced seriously strained relations between Somalia and Ethiopia. The situation is somewhat different in Kenya, where the local Somalis demand the withdrawal of the Northern Territories from Kenya, before it achieves independence to enable them to accede to Somalia. This demand is not impelled by external forces but expresses purely local feelings. The government of Somalia has not wished to get itself involved in a quarrel with the African nationalist leaders of Kenya, who strongly oppose surrendering any of their territory. On the other hand Somalia has not been able to ignore altogether the aspirations of their kinsmen in Kenya who are themselves using the movement of

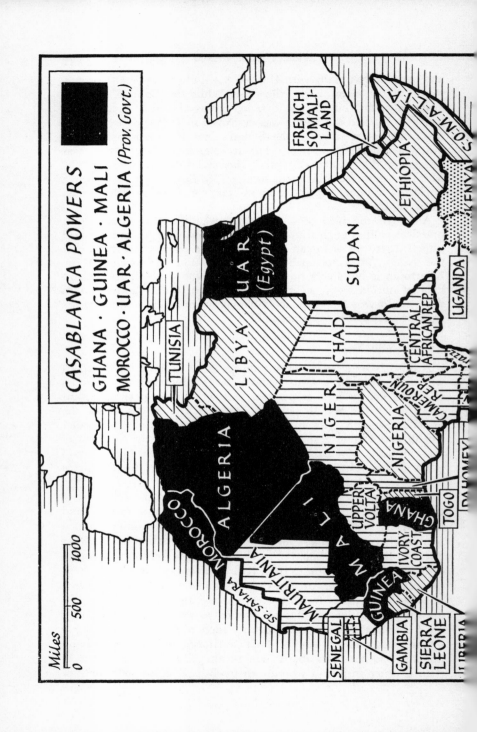

CASABLANCA POWERS
GHANA · GUINEA · MALI
MOROCCO · UAR · ALGERIA (Prov. Govt.)

Miles
0   500   1000

FRENCH SOMALI-LAND

SOMALIA

ETHIOPIA

KENYA

UGANDA

SUDAN

UAR (Egypt)

TUNISIA

LIBYA

CHAD

CENTRAL AFRICAN REP.

ALGERIA

NIGER

NIGERIA

CAMEROUN

RÉP.

SP. SAHARA

MOROCCO

MAURITANIA

MALI

UPPER VOLTA

GHANA

TOGO

DAHOMEY

IVORY COAST

GUINEA

SENEGAL

GAMBIA

SIERRA LEONE

LIBERIA

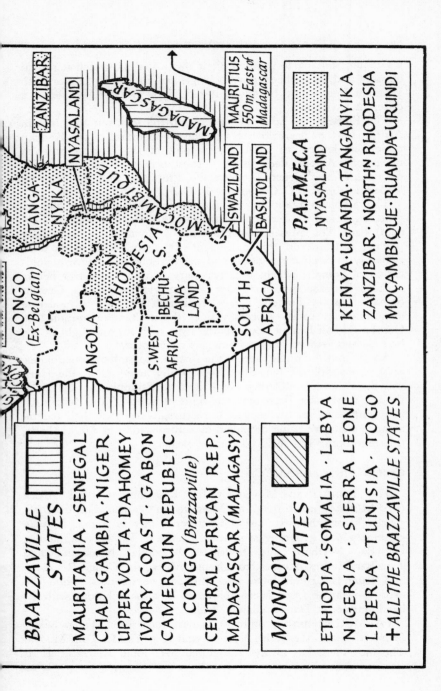

ZANZIBAR

NYASALAND

TANGA
NYIKA

MOÇAMBIQUE

MADAGASCAR

MAURITIUS
550 m. East of
Madagascar

SWAZILAND

BASUTOLAND

CONGO
(Ex-Belgian)

N.
RHODESIA

S.
RHODESIA

ANGOLA

BECHU-
ANA-
LAND

S.WEST
AFRICA

SOUTH
AFRICA

P.A.F.M.E.C.A
NYASALAND

KENYA · UGANDA · TANGANYIKA

ZANZIBAR · NORTH RHODESIA

MOÇAMBIQUE · RUANDA-URUNDI

BRAZZAVILLE
STATES

MAURITANIA · SENEGAL

CHAD · GAMBIA · NIGER

UPPER VOLTA · DAHOMEY

IVORY COAST · GABON

CAMEROUN REPUBLIC

CONGO (*Brazzaville*)

CENTRAL AFRICAN REP.

MADAGASCAR (MALAGASY)

MONROVIA
STATES

ETHIOPIA · SOMALIA · LIBYA

NIGERIA · SIERRA LEONE

LIBERIA · TUNISIA · TOGO

+ ALL THE BRAZZAVILLE STATES

a Greater Somalia to promote their own interests, which it should be admitted, have been gravely neglected in Kenya in the past. Whether they would be any better off in a Greater Somalia is a different question.

The Emperor of Ethiopia—always on the look out for allies in Africa—has not been slow to seek the co-operation of the Kenyan nationalist leaders to resist the impetus of the Greater Somalia movement. A joint declaration of resistance to Somali 'territorial' nationalism was signed between the Ethiopian and the Kenyan leaders at the AAPO Conference in Cairo in 1961.

The problems raised by the pan-Somali movement for the re-grouping of several territories can lead to difficulties unless wisely controlled. The present Government of Somalia is successfully placing restraint on this movement. Its own policy is to work patiently through conciliation and negotiations to achieve a unifi-cation of Somalis which, it is necessary to add, has never before existed. But the emotional appeal the grandeur of a Greater Somalia has for Somalis makes it difficult for even a moderate government to resist—especially since the militant opposition (the Greater Somali League) exploits the issue with little thought of the bad feelings aroused among Somalia's neighbours.

Apart from the unification of the British and Italian Somalilands, another example of federation successfully achieved in the Horn was the voluntary adherence of Eritrea to Ethiopia in 1952[93]. Al-though there have been ominous signs of stress in this federation in recent years, mainly because the Eritreans feel that their federal arrangements are being despoiled by centralization in Addis Ababa, this regrouping has survived for ten years.

Central Africa: PAFMECA

The Pan-African Movement for East and Central Africa (PAFMECA) was formed at Mwanza in Tanganyika in 1958, shortly before the first AAPO Conference met in Accra. It is an extremely loose grouping of political parties in Tanganyika, Kenya, Uganda, Northern and Southern Rhodesia, Nyasaland and Zanzibar. Representatives from South Africa, the Congo Republic, and Ruanda-Urundi have also attended conferences, while the exile movement from Mozambique is in close relations with its headquarters at Dar-es-Salaam.

PAFMECA's most prominent leaders have been Tanganyika's Prime Minister, Mr. Julius Nyerere, and Kenya's Mr. Tom Mboya. The movement has always recognised Mr. Jomo Kenyatta as its natural leader, even when he was in detention. It is the only effective regional political organisation in the continent and acts as a co-ordinating body rather than as a unifying organisation[94]. Despite sharp divisions between its component parties (rival parties from each territory are admitted to membership), it has achieved a remarkable degree of unanimity on major questions; for example on the need for a regional federation in East and Central Africa. Although not bound by a caucus, its members have constituted an almost natural alliance at AAPO and other Pan-African Conferences. At the Tunis meeting of the AAPO (1960) they strongly disagreed with the platform which they felt was being unduly dominated by the Ghana-Guinea leadership. In the argument over membership of the ICFTU (see next chapter) they have almost unitedly stood against those advocating secession.

When Mr. Tom Mboya, the first chairman of the AAPO, was denounced by Accra in 1959 (because of his divergence of view on the ICFTU and his insistence on more effective regional representation and consultation at AAPO headquarters), he received considerable support from PAFMECA's leaders. Their feeling (as shown in resolutions) is that the AAPO and other Pan-African movements are too rigidly controlled by the Accra-Conakry wing of Pan-Africanism. PAFMECA has tried to redress this balance, but they have been careful not to let their private disagreements develop into a break with Accra and Conakry.

PAFMECA's policy on promoting continental unity emphasises the need to avoid hasty proposals and supports the idea that it should be constructed by stages. It suggests that the first stage should be to achieve a consolidation of regional associations. In their own region they are officially committed to the idea of an East African Federation of Tanganyika, Kenya, Uganda and Zanzibar. (Total population—22 million people in an area of nearly 700,000 square miles, the size of Europe west of the Oder River.) This plan also envisages the possibility of a wider federation to include Nyasaland, Northern Rhodesia, Mauritius, Ruanda-Urundi and eventually Mozambique as well. (Total population of this larger federation would be 40 million.)

It is totally opposed, however, to the continuation of the present Central African Federation on the grounds that it is an 'imposed constitution'.

The idea of an East African Federation goes back to the 1920's when it was supported by the white settlers.[95] Successive British governments explored the proposal but beyond creating an East African High Commission nothing ever came of it.[96] Africans had all along been suspicious of the federation because of its origins. The first sign of a change of African opinion was given by Mr. Nyerere in a policy statement made to the Conference of Independent African States in Addis Ababa (1960). 'Many of us agree without argument,' said Mr. Nyerere, 'that a Federation of the East African States would be a good thing. In our struggle against imperialism we have emphasised that our strength lies in our unity. We have warned ourselves against the dangers of divide and rule. We have said, and rightly so, that the boundaries which divide our countries were made by the imperialists, not by us, and that we must not allow them to be used against our unity.... The weak and divided can never hope to maintain a *dignified independence* how ever much they may proclaim their desire to be strong and united; for the desire to unite is a very different thing from actual unity.... It is really not necessary to argue with any intelligent African nationalist that a *dignified African personality* requires actual unity and not a sentimental desire to be united.' [Author's italics.]

Mr. Nyerere developed his ideas in a memorandum which, with few changes, was adopted as the official policy of PAFMECA at a meeting held in Nairobi in January 1961. 'In the struggle against Colonialism,' says the statement, 'the fundamental unity of the people of Africa is evident and is deeply felt. It is, however, a unity forged in adversity in a battle against an outside Government. If the triumph in this battle is to be followed by an equal triumph against the forces of neo-imperialism and also against poverty, ignorance and disease, then this unity must be strengthened and maintained.' At that time the hope was that federation might be achieved before all the territories had achieved their separate independence, an aspiration that failed.

Until Tanganyika's independence (December 1961) regional services were provided by a colonial-administered East Africa High Commission with a partly-representative Central Legislative Assembly. This has been replaced by the East African Common Services Organisation. Tanganyika, Kenya and Uganda participate as equal partners in its control; and Zanzibar has been offered the right to join in the association. Ultimate responsibility for the Organisation rests with the three Prime Ministers of Kenya, Uganda and Tanganyika, who will function collectively as the East African Common Services Authority. A Central Legislative Assembly will in future be composed of Ministers and elected representatives from the three Legislatures. The Common Services include higher education, transport and communications, posts and telegraphs, currency, research, statistics. Thus at least the framework of a federal organisation exists.

The Kenya African National Union was not, however, satisfied with these arrangements. They insisted in a memorandum (June 28, 1961) that the new Organisation should have 'guaranteed the presence of a popularly elected and fully representative government drawing its authority from the people instead of the Colonial Office'. Their objections to the new proposals for the Central Legislative Assembly was that it should have become 'the nucleus for a future Federal Assembly'. A few months later, in August 1961, the Kenya Legislature appointed an all-party Select Committee to consider the practical aspects of achieving federation.

What of the much wider East and Central African Federation? Until the fate of the crumbling Central African Federation is finally decided not much progress can be expected in regrouping its components. But a sentiment in favour of this wider association continues to develop. Northern Rhodesia's major nationalist movement, the United National Independence Party, led by Mr. Kenneth Kaunda, has come out in favour of the proposal which, however, is opposed by the smaller African National Congress. In Nyasaland, the Malawi Congress leader, Dr. H. K. Banda, has expressed the hope 'to see the day when Dar-es-Salaam is the capital of the United States of Central Africa, or the Federation of East and Central Africa—whichever is decided upon.'[97] A delegation of the Mauritius government has visited East Africa to discuss the possibility of their 650,000 islanders becoming associated with a future federation.

Although East Africa contains all the parochial, tribal and particularist factors common to other regions it appears to offer a surer basis for co-operation than any other African region. Its leaders have similar attitudes; their policies are not disharmonious; their economies are complementary; they share many of their services; and the rough framework of federal institutions already exists.

West Africa

The only concrete step taken towards fulfilment of the proposal for a United West African Federation made at the sixth Pan-African Congress in 1945, is the Ghana-Guinea-Mali Union.* Its possible extension to include Upper Volta (one of the Brazzaville States) has been mentioned following the Paga Agreement (June 27, 1961) when the Voltaic President, Maurice Yameogo, and Dr.

* See Appendices 6 and 14.

Nkrumah 'determined by concrete measures quickly to achieve the total independence and *effective unity* of Africa....' [Author's italics.] As a first step they agreed to knock down a wall (specially erected for this purpose) to symbolise their agreement that 'freedom of movement for persons and goods shall be the rule and the equitable refund of customs dues collected on re-exports from Ghana shall be paid into the Upper Volta Treasury'.[98]

What is the reality behind this Union? In the first place it is not a *union* in the proper political sense. It is, at best, a loose political association. The Ghana-Guinea Union was born in the desperate days of Guinea's traumatic birth when she was allowed to cut adrift from the French community with the prospect of immediate economic disaster. Ghana rushed to her aid with a sisterly offer of a £10 million loan (of which less than half has been utilised), and the two countries decided on a closer association.* Neither this Union of the two states, nor the enlarged one with Mali which, in July 1961, was formally established as the Union of African States (UAS)†, has produced a political organisation with common institutions. Proposals for a common currency have to date come to nought. The practical proposal that each country should have a Resident Minister serving in each other's cabinet has never properly worked. Each has pursued its own internal, economic and social policies with little reference to the other. The three Presidents have, however, consulted frequently on wider issues of African and international affairs. This co-operation has been seen to its best advantage in the events leading up to the Casablanca Charter, in the preparatory committee work of the Belgrade Conference of Non-alignment, and in the Afro-Asian Group at the United Nations. But they have not always been united even in these affairs. As already shown,‡ Dr. Nkrumah found himself isolated at the Casablanca Conference when he opposed military aid to the Stanleyville régime. Guinea and Mali both withdrew their troops from the UN Command in the Congo, Ghana did not. Nor is it much of a secret that Ghana and Guinea were giving contrary advice to the late Mr. Patrice Lumumba when he was still Prime Minister. In the end the Guineans were in fact more certain of getting their militant advice listened to than was Dr. Nkrumah, whose counsels of moderation accorded ill with Mr. Lumumba's mood at that time.

The episode of Ghana's treaty with Upper Volta did not improve relations between Dr. Nkrumah and his two fellow-Presidents. They felt (and said at the time) that he was making more fuss over his

* See Appendix 6.   † See Appendix 13.   ‡ See page 51.

economic agreement with the Voltains (which cost Ghana £3½ million) than was justified by its actual terms. Nothing in the agreement itself justified the view that Upper Volta might be willing to join the Ghana-Guinea-Mali Union; but Dr. Nkrumah was not to be dissuaded. The Presidents of Guinea and Mali pointedly stayed away from the ceremony of 'knocking down the Wall'. Subsequent events have proved Nkrumah wrong. Ougoudougou, the capital of Upper Volta, was chosen as the headquarters for the Joint Defence Command of the Brazzaville States. In a joint statement with the Presidents of Ivory Coast and Niger, the Voltaic President agreed in October 1961 to avoid 'vigorously any action that will weaken the solidarity of the *Conseil de l'Entente*,'[99] which associates Upper Volta with the Ivory Coast, Niger and Dahomey.* Subsequently, too, M. Yameogo insisted that the agreement was purely economic and had no political significance at all. This episode illustrates an important facet in Dr. Nkrumah's political thinking; for him form matters more than performance. He has often repeated that what matters is that the 'right spirit' should exist; this, he insists, is the prelude to effective action. It is this belief that has led him to exaggerate the importance of some of his achievements. This attitude finds little favour with M. Sékou Touré and M. Modeiba Keita who are both much more realistic and hardheaded in their policies. For them performance matters more than an outward display of agreement.

Does this mean that the Ghana-Guinea-Mali Union is without any importance? Surely not; for despite difficulties and the differences between its leaders, the association exists. It is a pointer towards closer association. As such it has had a considerable influence on African politics. Speaking in a wider context about the differences that exist among African countries, M. Sékou Touré commented : 'Some peoples call this the fragility of the forces of our union, but these are really only technical secondary differences.'

It is as wrong, in my view, to minimise the importance of the Ghana-Guinea-Mali Union as it is to exaggerate its effectiveness. Whatever its future, it should be seen as an important milestone in the growth of the idea of a regional association between three African countries of widely different cultures and policies.

French-speaking Africa

French colonial rule produced two vast federations—*Afrique Occidentale Française* (AOF) with 25 million people, and *Afrique*

* See page 78.

Equatoriale Française (AEF) with $5\frac{1}{4}$ million people. These broke up partly under the strains and rivalries of independence, and partly because of General de Gaulle's active discouragement of regional unification—a policy hard to understand and impossible to justify.[100] The long years of practical experience of federalism—and notably the history of the inter-territorial political party, the *Rassemblement Democratique Africain* (RDA), and of the trade union movement—have left their mark on these states. If the recent experiments in closer association have not so far worked out very well, that is no reason for believing that future attempts will be equally unsuccessful.

The Mali Federation—as originally conceived at a conference in Dakar in January 1959—was intended to regroup Senegal, the Sudan, Dahomey and Upper Volta. The sixty-two articles of its constitution provided for integrated political and economic institutions—an Executive with a President and two Ministers from each State; a Legislature with twelve members nominated from each of the four Territorial Legislatures. Of the four sponsor members, only Senegal and the Sudan entered into the Federation; referendums in the other two Republics defeated the proposals. France had openly expressed opposition to this idea; by unsubtle economic pressures she had encouraged Upper Volta, and especially Dahomey (which stood to lose a new harbour at Cotonou built by the French) to withdraw. But the greatest pressure came from the Ivory Coast, whose leader, M. Houphouet-Boigny, has traditionally set his ideas and his capital, Abidjan, against those of M. Senghor and his capital, Dakar. Wealthier than Senegal and able to exercise more direct pressure on Upper Volta, Abidjan was able to counter with a proposal of its own. The results were twofold. Mali was reduced to two members—Senegal and the Sudan—which broke up within a few months. And there was created the *Conseil de l'Entente*, or as it is sometimes called, the *Sahel-Benin Union*.

The *Entente* originated from an agreement in April 1959 between the Ivory Coast and Upper Volta. It provided for the harbour of Abidjan to become a common establishment; the Abidjan-Niger railway to be communally used; road transport to be co-ordinated; a customs union with provision for the equitable distribution of duties and taxes; a common Court of Appeal; and eventual common postal services. The *Entente* would regulate all inter-governmental affairs, and an inter-state convention was to be adopted to create a *Fonds de Solidarité*. Both Niger and Dahomey subsequently joined the *Entente* which thus regrouped four territories with 10 million people into a functional association, dominated by the wealth of the Ivory Coast and the personality of M. Houphouet-Boigny. But while the framework of the *Entente* has survived, its unity has remained fragile largely because of the Ivory Coast's reluctance to implement fully the financial terms of the agreement. M. Houphouet-Boigny is no champion of federations.

Little progress has been made in regrouping the former members of French Equatorial Africa despite many attempts to do so. These efforts continue to be made and despite the reluctance of the Gabon, the other three Republics in the region—Chad, Congo (Brazzaville) and the Central African Republic—have never abandoned the hope that their efforts might yet succeed.

To date, the only effective regrouping that has taken place in West and Equatorial Africa is that of the Cameroonians. The inhabitants of the southern part of the former British Cameroons have joined in a federation with the Cameroun Republic, and those of the northern part with the Northern Region of the Nigerian Federation. Less successful has been the movement towards reunification of the Ewe tribe in the Togo Republic and in the Trans-Volta region of Ghana; though it still remains a lively issue, the borders between the two territories have become rigidified because of disputes arising from the contrary pulls exercised by Accra and Lome.

If regional regrouping and territorial federations have so far eluded the French-speaking states there is some encouragement to be found in the growth of the functional organisations either planned or already created by the Union of African States and Madagascar (the Brazzaville Powers). They have agreed to co-ordinate their defence through a Joint Defence Council and have created a single Airline. Various proposals have been worked out to provide for inter-territorial economic, transport, research and educational co-operation. Promising as some of these proposals look, their implementation cannot yet be taken for granted.

Several conclusions can be drawn from these attempts to recreate the older unity of the AOF and the AEF, and from the failures of the Mali Federation and the *Entente*. First one must acknowledge France's unfortunate rôle in her attempts to discourage the rebirth of federations which at one time she had striven so valiantly to create. If Pan-Africanists cite French policy as an example of the wish by former imperialists to 'balkanise' Africa, it is hard to know how to answer.

Thomas Hodgkin and Ruth Schachter in their valuable pamphlet[101] list among the reasons for Mali's failure, the 'deep-seated conflict between the policies of the UPS (*Union Progressiste*

Senegalaise, Dr. Senghor's governing party) and the *Union Souda-naise* (M. Modeiba Keita's governing party); between gradualism and radicalism in matters of economic and social policy; between a broadly pro-French and a strongly Pan-African orientation; between the conception of Mali as a loose federal system and as a centralised unitary State'.

All these factors have already been referred to as sources of friction and division between the different attitudes that produced the Casablanca Powers and the Monrovia States.

In the case of the *Entente,* Hodgkin and Schachter rightly identify its lack of any clear economic, geographic or historic bases. The governing parties in the territories other than the Ivory Coast lacked stability with the result that the *Entente's* unity was 'liable to be disturbed by domestic political changes'. This is an important factor since rival parties competing for power inevitably attack the wider alliances of the government party. Another important factor in the *Entente* is its domination by one rich country—the Ivory Coast—which is determined to use its own wealth for itself. Little altruism is shown towards poorer neighbours. The same factor explains the failure of the former members of French Equatorial Africa (AEF) to establish a regional association; in their case the wealthiest country, Gabon, with a meagre population of half a million has been unwilling to weaken itself economically in support of its poorer neighbours. In the absence of a strongly-developed Pan-African consciousness, the natural wish of a government is to look after the interests of its own people first. The 'you have never had it so good' attitude is not confined to any one country. In Africa it is the poorer states who are most willing to combine with others, or those which are governed by revolutionary governments such as in Ghana, Guinea, Mali and Egypt.

CHAPTER V

AFRICA'S DIVIDED WORKERS

The first AAPO Conference in 1958 spurred the desire for Pan-African trade unionism by, unanimously, calling for the establishment of a single All-African Trade Union Federation (AATUF). This was strongly endorsed by the second AAPO Conference.* Subsequent attempts to implement this resolution have produced perhaps the angriest of all divisions in the Pan-African front. Although an AATUF has been established it is by no means what the 1958 decision had in mind; and it represents only a fraction of the organised workers of the continent.

The Birth of UGTAN

The disengagement of Africa's working-class movements from the pressures exercised through the three Labour Internationals—the International Confederation of Free Trade Unions (ICFTU), the World Federation of Trade Unions (WFTU) and the International Federation of Christian Trade Unions (ICTUF)—during the colonial period originally came from M. Sékou Touré in 1956. Until then three separate trade union centres existed in the French-speaking territories; these reflected the divisions of the French trade union movement between the CGT (communist), *Force Ouvrier* (socialist) and the CETC (catholic). The strongest was the CGT (communist) which was affiliated to the WFTU. It was of this group that M. Sékou Touré was secretary-general when in 1955 the communists decided that a Pan-African trade union conference should be formed through the WFTU. Sékou Touré, long resentful of the importation of Europe's labour divisions into Africa, resisted. In April 1956 he led the Guinea and Senegal trade unions into a new affiliation, the *Confédération Général des Travailleurs d'Afrique* (CGTA) which broke both its French and its WFTU affiliations. This action was the first successful blow struck in French West Africa for independence from French institutions. Hitherto the trade unions—like so much else—were simply 'an

* See Appendix 22 III.

extension of Europe into Africa'. The appeal of Sékou Touré's action was dramatic. It spread throughout French-speaking Africa, and within a few months a representative conference at Cotonou decided to launch a unified *Union Générale des Travailleurs d'Afrique Noire* (UGTAN) free of all affiliation, metropolitan or international. Its aim was 'to unite and organise the workers of black Africa, to co-ordinate their trade union activities in the struggle against the colonial régime and all other forms of exploitation . . . and to affirm the personality of African trade unionism.'[102] At about the same time the Egyptian leaders took a similar initiative in forming a Pan-Arab trade union movement.

Sékou Touré's ambitions for UGTAN as the nucleus of a Pan-African labour movement were frustrated by the development of separate autonomies in the French-speaking territories which weakened their old affiliations. Nevertheless, the majority of French-speaking trade union centres continued at first to maintain their links with UGTAN. But after Guinea chose complete independence in 1958, its UGTAN affiliates began to play an active political rôle in the other territories which had not immediately followed Guinea's lead in claiming their immediate independence. The various territorial governments took action against the trade union political activities. Soon the UGTAN affiliates were suppressed in most of the territories or they were squeezed out through the creation of state-sponsored rival trade union centres. By the end of 1959 Guinea stood alone in defending UGTAN; later she was joined by Ghana and Mali.

WFTU Bows Out—ICFTU Comes Forward

The WFTU, meanwhile, had read the sign of the times. Weakened by the disaffiliation of the French-speaking unions (from which it had previously drawn virtually all its African support) it ceased to canvass for new members in the continent. But the ICTUF and the ICFTU followed a different policy. The latter, especially, began to campaign intensively to win Africa to its side. With the enthusiastic support of the Ghana Government the ICFTU held its first African regional conference in Accra in 1957 under the chairmanship of Mr. John Tettegah, Secretary-General of the Ghana TUC. It was attended by delegates from seventeen African territories who agreed to establish three ICFTU Area Committees.

This was the situation when the AAPO Conference decision was taken in 1958 to establish the AATUF. The WFTU, with nothing to lose, could welcome it; the ICTUF and especially the ICFTU were obviously deeply concerned with the manner in which this new movement would develop.

Clash of Policies, 1959–1960

But by the time the second ICFTU Regional Conference came to be held in Lagos in November 1959, a basic conflict had emerged between the Pan-African labour leaders. It was not over the formation of AATUF itself; but over the question of its individual affiliates being allowed to retain their membership of other internationals. This clash reflects two emerging trends. Firstly, it was an extension of the growing struggle for ascendancy between the different political capitals of Africa, into which struggle subsidiary issues were drawn. Secondly, the clash reflects fundamental differences of approach by Pan-African leaders, not so much on matters of principle as on methods of co-operation.

Related specifically to trade unionism the conflict is over different interpretations of non-alignment. The militants see the WFTU as communist dominated; and, by the same token, they see the ICFTU as inseparably linked to Western interests.[103] In their view non-alignment demands that links be broken with both. Once AATUF has been established they are willing that it should be impartially affiliated to all the Internationals, while still proscribing national affiliations. Those who oppose this view are no less committed to a policy of non-alignment. But they point to the fact that the ICFTU has never supported the West on colonial issues—that, on the contrary, it has been in the vanguard of the forces struggling to put an end to colonialism in all its forms. Its attacks on France over Algeria; on Belgium over the Congo; on Portugal over Angola; on South Africa over apartheid; and on Britain over the Central African Federation have been completely in line with the views of Pan-African Conferences.[104] This being so, the ICFTU affiliates claim that membership is not in conflict with a policy of non-alignment: on the contrary the ICFTU is a sympathetic channel 'through which the African Personality may be projected and become effective in world forums'.[105]

This conflict between the two wings of Pan-African labour thinking was brought sharply to a head by the Ghana TUC. Knowing of the venue and timing of the second ICFTU Conference in Lagos, they announced their resignation from the ICFTU and a decision to inaugurate AATUF in Accra to coincide with the Lagos meeting. The decision to launch AATUF was taken without consulting the

Committee of the AAPO (or even its Chairman, Mr. Mboya) which had originally decided to sponsor the new movement.

The Accra decision represented a direct challenge to the ICFTU-affiliated centres to choose between the two conferences. In the end only Ghana, Guinea, the UAR, Morocco and one of the two Nigerian trade union centres sent delegates to Accra. The great majority went to Lagos; but many sent observers to Accra to support the AATUF in principle, while condemning the proposal that membership should involve resignation from the ICFTU.

The Accra Conference produced no immediate result beyond setting up a Steering Committee to pursue the aims of AATUF, while the Lagos Conference agreed to establish at its next meeting an autonomous ICFTU Regional Organisation, with a Secretariat in Africa and control over its own funds.[106] It also demanded more effective African representation and control in the Brussels headquarters.

The stage was now set for a trial of strength. Both sides campaigned hard preparatory to the second AAPO conference in Tunis in 1960; but there the disagreements were papered over with a compromise resolution welcoming the AATUF while leaving open the question of affiliation. The reason for this compromise was that the trade union leaders had insisted that a final decision should be made by themselves at a separate conference to be held in Casablanca in May 1960. That conference never took place.

Nineteen-sixty was a year of intense public lobbying and private negotiations. ICFTU affiliates—led by Mr. Mboya of Kenya, Mr. Tlili of Tunisia and Mr. Borha of Nigeria—continued publicly to support the ICFTU. Their opponents were equally busy. Mr. Diallo Abdoulaye, Secretary-General of the AAPO, said at a Press Conference in Accra on August 4 :[107] 'The [African] workers should have relations with all the world's workers, and should not consider a portion of them as antagonists. . . . We cannot equally be members of two organisations at the same time. It is for this reason that we reject [both] affiliations'. President Nkrumah sent Mr. Tettegah on a tour of Africa with the dictum : 'Africa should have her own trade union federation. It should owe allegiance to neither the WFTU nor the ICFTU. . . .'

November 1960 saw an apparent victory for the ICFTU affiliates. A joint declaration[108] signed in Nairobi by Mr. Tettegah and Mr. Mboya on behalf of their trade union centres concluded : 'Both organisations subscribe to the policy of positive independence and non-alignment as between the power blocs—East and West—and warn against any country, political party or trade union being used as pawns in this struggle. The establishment of AATUF will help to guard against this possibility. It is agreed that AATUF should not be affiliated to any of the international trade union centres—ICFTU, WFTU or Christian International. The Kenya Federation of Labour and the Ghana TUC *both recognise the right of each national centre to decide on its international relations.* [Author's italics.] We find nothing in the present position that would make it difficult for both centres to participate fully in the formation of the AATUF.' Thus Mr. Tettegah clearly appears to have recognised the right of each constituent centre of the AATUF to decide its own international affiliations. But it was not a position that he maintained for long.

ICFTU in Tunis, 1960

Two weeks before that agreement was signed, the ICFTU held its third Regional conference in Tunis (November 1960). In accordance with its previous decision, the conference established a Regional Organisation (AFRO) with a Secretariat in Lagos. The only national centres not represented were Ghana, Guinea and the UAR. Even the Moroccans and Algerians came. The conference's resolutions on colonialism and neo-colonialism in general, and on specific issues like South Africa, Algeria and Central Africa, were as militant as any passed by the AAPO.[109] Only the welcome accorded to the independence of Mauritania was controversial. But on the question of the AATUF, the final statement issued on behalf of the conference was guarded. It starts with a warning :

'In this great process of change [in Africa], the African trade union movement is being pressured and infiltrated by State-operated trade unions from inside and outside Africa. . . . A clear understanding of the objectives of these trends . . . is needed so as to be ready at all times to give effective leadership in the choice that has to be made eventually between totalitarian trade union practices and beliefs on the one hand and free democratic trade unionism on the other.'

And it continues :

'It is against this background that [we] consider as a relevant question . . . the new trend which has given vocality to the demand for the formation of an AATUF. . . . [We] recognise the natural desire of African workers to work in co-operation among themselves, and to share their hopes and aspirations with workers of other Continents in the true spirit of brotherhood and international solidarity. . . . [We] hold that the idea of a Pan-African Trade Union Federation is not basically inconsistent with the free trade union movement of Africa, and that it would be injudicious to ignore the spiritual and emotional appeal which Pan-Africanism generates in the political and social institutions of twentieth century Africa. And there is reason to be concerned that unless the free trade unions participate in its creation and direction, it may quite easily fall into the hands of other forces and be used for political ends by certain African States, and thereby cause a split in the African Labour front. With this consideration in view [we] recommend that the free trade unions should not take a back seat in the projection, direction and policy-making of the proposed Pan-African trade union federation; provided that vital principles of free trade unions are not compromised.'

On the point of what these principles should be the conference aimed an even sharper shaft at the Steering Committee of AATUF.

There is already unmistakable evidence that certain African States . . . have embarked upon arrangements as a matter of policy to convert the trade unions into an arm of Government administration. . . . This . . . is a particularly dangerous threat to free and democratic trade unionism. . . . [We] note that the Governments of the African States concerned are also vigorously employing money and questionable forms of inducements to force similiar arrangements upon other African States in a manner which totally disregards the territorial integrity of neighbouring African States.'

To sum up, the ICFTU (AFRO) clearly took issue with the AATUF Steering Committee on three points.

1. The belief that individual trade union centres should be allowed to 'unite with workers of other Continents in the spirit of . . . international solidarity'.
2. The belief that trade unions ought to remain independent of governing parties, and that the militants in AATUF were trying to undermine this principle.
3. The accusation that the militants were trying to interfere with, and subvert, trade union organisations affiliated to the ICFTU.

The Line-up of Forces

Where do the various trade union centres stand in these conflicts? Ghana, Guinea, Mali and the UAR—each with a single trade union centre associated with the governing party—stand foursquare behind a totally non-aligned AATUF and disaffiliation of all constituent centres from the ICFTU and the WFTU. The

Algerians tend to back this group, though they are still affiliated to the ICFTU. The Moroccans are divided : the *Union des Travailleurs Marocains* (which forms part of the opposition to the Moroccan government) adopts the same position as the Algerians; but the government-sponsored rival trade union centre is accredited to neither of the Internationals. In Tunisia the *Union Générale des Travailleurs Tunisiens*, led by Ahmed Tlili, is a staunch ICFTU supporter. It has no rival in Tunisia; and President Bourguiba makes no bones about its association with his Neo-Destour Party. 'Tunisia,' he says, 'has chosen the path of complete cohesion and . . . unity between the trade union movement and national policies.'

The Nigerian trade unions are deeply divided between Lawrence Borha's official TUC of Nigeria (TUCN) which strongly supports the ICFTU, and Michael Imoudu's break-away Nigerian TUC, supported—and allegedly financed—by Ghana.* Tom Mboya's Kenya Federation of Labour is firmly committed to the ICFTU; it recently overcame the tiny breakaway anti-ICFTU group led by Arthur Ochwada which has rejoined the main body. All the other East and Central African union centres are ICFTU supporters, although Uganda and Nyasaland both have small splinter movements (allegedly financed by Accra, and scarcely existent except on paper) opposed to international affiliation. The *Federation Générale des Travailleurs du Kongo* of the Congo (Leopoldville)—formerly led by the Premier, Mr. Cyrille Adoula—is affiliated to the ICFTU. So is the militant Somali trade union centre, though not with any real enthusiasm. The same applies to the Zanzibar union.

In South Africa, the African trade union movement is split between supporters of the two political Congresses. The South African Congress of Trade Unions—supporters of the African National Congress—is affiliated to the ICFTU, but recently attended a WFTU meeting in Accra.† The Federation of Free African Trade Unions of South Africa, supporters of the Pan-African Congress, is not affiliated to the ICFTU; it failed to be accredited to the 1961 Casablanca conference of AATUF.

The Gambia TUC is affiliated to the ICFTU, but its leader, Mr. Jallow, is known to favour the Accra point of view. The Sierra Leone TUC, by contrast, is firmly committed to the ICFTU. In

* These two groups have recently agreed to come together, but their unity is by no means assured yet.

† This WFTU conference which met in Accra early in 1961 was its first reappearance in Africa since 1958. Although maintaining its opposition to both the ICFTU and the WFTU the Ghana TUC nevertheless agreed to play host to this conference—but its delegation participated only as observers.

the French-speaking African states, except for Guinea and Mali, the unions are affiliated to the ICFTU. Most of them are also either closely associated with or controlled by the governing parties.

One thing emerges clearly. By no means all the ICFTU affiliated unions are able to live up to the principle of freedom and independence from governing parties which they extol at their conferences. Although the Tanganyika Federation of Labour, for example, has declared for continuation of its ICFTU affiliation, Mr. Nyerere often refers to the unions as 'the industrial wing' of the Tanganyika African National Union.[110] Nor have Tanganyika's unions—or indeed those of Tunisia or the French-speaking states—taken exception to statements like these.

The Casablanca Conference: Birth of AATUF

The conflict finally came to a climax at a conference to launch AATUF in Casablanca in May 1961. Both sides had previously agreed to wipe the slate of all previous decisions and to make a completely fresh start. But the immediate effect of the conference was to deepen and perpetuate old quarrels. By the time the final decisions came to be taken—by acclamation, not by vote—about a third of the delegations had left. They included the Tunisians, most of the East and Central Africans, and Mr. Borha's section of the Nigerians.

The chief complaint against the organisers of the conference was that no attempt was made to reach agreement or even fully to debate controversial issues; that they tried by irregular methods to force their own point of view on the conference. No credentials committee was established. The organisers were accused of inviting unrepresentative splinter centres as delegates; ignoring, or giving only observer status to centres which support ICFTU affiliation. Trade union centres represented on the Steering Committee were allegedly allowed six delegates each, while the others had to be content with two. A further accusation was that 'the public'—in the form of individuals hired to acclaim the militant point of view— were admitted to the conference hall.[111]

The conference issued a declaration of purposes, passed 'by acclamation' :*

> 1. Each African State should have only one trade union centre.
> 2. Trade unions should be independent of governments and political parties.

* See Appendix 21.

3. Trade union centres affiliated to other Internationals should within ten months break their affiliations and join AATUF.

4. Trade unions must participate fully in the work of economic planning.

As a result of these decisions AATUF was established with head-quarters in Casablanca, with a secretariat comprising a president and seven secretaries. The first president is Mahjub Ben Seddik (Morocco), and the secretaries are drawn from Ghana, Guinea, Algeria, Mali, Kenya and the UAR. Among the secretaries listed is Mr. Mboya. But neither his national centre, nor any of the ICFTU affiliates who comprise the great majority of African trade union centres, have accepted membership of AATUF. On the contrary. Reaction to what happened at the Casablanca conference has been unrestrainedly hostile, except by the trade union leaders orientated towards the Casablanca Powers.

Repudiation of the Casablanca AATUF

On his return to Tunisia, Mr. Tlili rejected the conference as unrepresentative :[112] 'We left the conference having rejected all proposals that at this first congress the principle of disaffiliation should be accepted, and we have proposed that this question should be referred to a later meeting which would be more valid and more representative.' He went on to say that delegates invited to the conference were 'mainly fellow-travellers', among whom were 'Africans who have lost all touch with African workers, and who for the most part live in Eastern countries'. Others, he said, 'have no independence at all, and are rather leaders imposed by their governments'.

In Nigeria, the TUCN was no less angry. Its acting General Secretary, Mr. Henshaw, said that the conference had been a complete failure;[113] that the decisions had been taken not by the representatives of African trade unions but by splinter groups, individuals representing nobody and 'hired hooligans'.

Tom Mboya issued a firm but careful statement on his return to Kenya :[114] 'In the first place, I am an African nationalist, who supports Pan-Africanism and believes that it is the logical approach to unity and understanding in Africa. However, I am firmly of the opinion that Pan-Africanism cannot succeed . . . unless it is based on the recognition of the need for sound . . . national unity. This means recognising and respecting the wishes of the people in the various countries. . . . For the time being at any rate this calls for the guaranteeing of national autonomy and sovereignty of our various States, national trade union organisations, political parties, etc. . . . It is conceded that African trade unions are still in their formative . . . stage. Consequently the Pan-African Trade Union Federation cannot be rigid. It must be flexible enough to allow for growth and evolutionary problems of the various African unions, and must avoid the emerging political splits at the Pan-African level. . . .'

He goes on to criticise the conduct of the conference and concludes : 'In this kind of atmosphere no decisions could be reached. . . . This issue of disaffiliation from international organisations became a bone of contention because our plea for national autonomy was ignored. Those who allege that we deliberately wrecked the conference are wrong. We have some basic principles . . . and we are not willing to be bullied or coerced out of them. We support and continue to support an AATUF. . . . One point that we must pose and many leaders still ask is—who will finance the AATUF, especially now that two political blocs are emerging among the African States; and whether, if financed by either bloc, AATUF will be used as a political weapon against some States in Africa?'

Nowhere in his statement did Mr. Mboya mention the ICFTU. He was concerned throughout with variations of the accusation that the steering committee had tried to 'rig' the conference, and would continue to 'manage' AATUF to further sectional Pan-African ambitions.

A "Declaration of War"

The answer to Mr. Mboya's questions were given with unmistakable clearness by Mr. Tettegah. At a Press conference in Accra he declared that AATUF would wage 'total war' on African unions refusing to disaffiliate from other international organisations. 'We shall isolate them,' he said, 'and enter their countries and form AATUF unions there. It is as simple as that—total war.' He said that AATUF planned to fill the vacuum regarding assistance received by some unions when they disaffiliated from international bodies, adding that the Ghana TUC was already active in various independent countries helping to create trade unions. He concluded by describing the Tunisian labour leader, Mr. Tlili, as 'an imperialist puppet'.[115]

The Casablanca labour conference led to a demand by those dissatisfied with its outcome for another attempt to reach agreement on AATUF. A number of delegates to the ILO conference which met in Geneva in June 1961 agreed to convene a conference at Dakar, which was chosen as not being too closely associated with the ICFTU. In the end the conference was postponed because of the Bizerta crisis. The initiative for a new conference was enough, however, to arouse the strongest reaction yet from the Ghana TUC. Its official publication[116] declared in a leading article : 'Stern, stubborn and desperate like a dying tiger, imperialism at bay grasps everything that it could lay hands on, for the last breath. . . . For the true African trade unionist, the . . . tiger which imperialism has unleashed against him at this decisive hour of victory is the ICFTU . . . ravenous monster of subversion, sabotage and vicious propaganda. . . . The quack actors on this fake stage of African trade unionism have been briefed and indoctrinated in Brussels, in mastering the various characters in which they are to pose as "authentic African trade unionists" in order to woo the African working masses against the Casablanca AATUF.'

But one should not be too misled by such fierce language. No sooner was it written than Mr. Tettegah was again proposing to meet Mr. Mboya to clear up 'misunderstandings'. On the principle of establishing such a Federation everybody is agreed. On the principle of African trade unions upholding the policy of non-alignment everybody is also agreed. The difference lies in the narrow question of whether national trade union centres should continue to enjoy their autonomous right to affiliate to both the AATUF and to *any other* Labour International of their choice, or whether such affiliation should be debarment to membership of the AATUF. But even this is not the real issue : the causes of the friction are the methods that have been used by some groups to try and secure their political domination over AATUF.

African Trade Union Confederation

Finally, as we go to press, there is a report of a conference in Dakar (January 9–14, 1962) where the decision was taken to create a new organisation, the African Trade Union Confederation. The prime movers of this rival to AATUF were the labour leaders of Senegal, Tunisia and Kenya. The first president is Ahmed Tlili (Tunisia); David Soumah (Senegal) is the administrative secretary; and Tom Mboya (Kenya), who was not at the conference, was elected as one of seven vice-presidents. The headquarters will be in Dakar.

CHAPTER VI

CULTURE AND POLITICS: THE RIFT IN THE LYRE OF BLACK ORPHEUS

Paris became the centre of a dynamic Pan-African literary movement in the early 1930's, just about the same time as London was becoming the political centre of Pan-Africanism. This shift in the organised life of Pan-Africanism from its birthplace in the New World to the capitals of Europe brought with it many changes. The most important was that the movement developed in two different milieux which further helped divide the English-speaking and the French-speaking black world. The ideas of the Paris circle, which later came to be known as the *negritude* movement, had a much greater influence on French-speaking African political leaders than did the political ideas emanating from London.

Negritude—which has become identified with the cultural journal *Présence Africaine*—has its earlier beginnings in *Légitime Défense*, a literary journal founded in the early 1930's by the Martiniquan poet Etienne Léro in association with Jules Monnerot and René Menil. 'More than a review, *Légitime Défense* was a cultural movement. Beginning with a Marxist analysis of the society of the West Indies, it discovered in the Caribbean the descendants of the Negro-African slaves held for three centuries in the stultifying conditions of the proletariat. Léro affirmed that only surrealism could deliver them from their taboos and express them in their integrity.'[117]

Marxism and surrealism were distinctive strands in the early pattern of *negritude* : its dialectics were Marxist; its poetic imagery, surrealist. Later, these strands were to fray and weaken. The Marxists were reduced to a minority group in *Présence Africaine*; and surrealism came to be regarded more and more as an irrelevant theory of the French surrealists to recapture their own failing powers of revolutionary inventiveness.

The Return of the Native

Léro's heir was another Martiniquan, Aimé Césaire, who came to Paris as an eighteen-year-old student in 1931. He was happy at first to become assimilated and to earn his living as a lecturer in literature; after a time he grew discontented. A Yugoslav student (now Professor Petar Guberina of Zaghreb, a distinguished writer on African culture) persuaded Césaire to spend a holiday with him on the Dalmatian coast. There he wrote *Cahier d'un Retour au Pays Natale*, a poem of seventy pages, which started a new literary movement, based on his concept of *negritude*.

> *Listen to the white world*
> *how it resents its great efforts*
> *how their protest is broken under the rigid stars*
> *how their steel blue speed is paralysed in the mystery*
> *   of the flesh.*
> *Listen how their defeats sound from their victories.*
> *Listen to the lamentable stumbling in the great alibis.*
> *Mercy! mercy for our omniscient, naïve conquerors.*
> *Hurray for those who never invented anything*
> *hurray for those who never explored anything*
> *hurray for those who never conquered anything*
> *hurray for joy*
> *hurray for love*
> *hurray for the pain of incarnate tears.*

Césaire's poem is about his return to his native home and about his return to himself.[118] It is about his coming to terms with both. He accepts the squalid town where he grew up, and its squalid people. He accepts what all his life he has tried to escape from— his own origins and his own true being. He rejects finally from himself his own resentment at being black. This is a profound and, essentially, a universal theme, the achievement of personal integrity and wholeness. It is connected in the poem with being black, because the Negro is despised by the rest of the world for his black skin, and so may come to despise himself for it. The only escape is for him to affirm his blackness, so that what was the symbol of rejection becomes the centre of his pride. In Césaire, the concept of *negritude* emerges from intense personal experience, and from the expression of this in the poetry itself. It is not a matter of self-justification but of defiant self acceptance. It scorns the self-confidence based on the glories of a real or imagined past.

When Césaire's poem first appeared in 1939 it made little impact. During the war, André Breton, the 'pope' of the surrealist movement, discovered Césaire and his poetry in Martinique. When Breton published a new edition of Césaire's great poem in 1947 it created an immediate sensation. Breton claimed him for the surrealist movement; but by then Césaire had inspired his own movement with poets like Rabemananjara from Madagascar; Senghor, Birago and David Diop from Senegal; Roumain from Haiti; Tirolien and Paul Niger from Guadeloupe; and Leon Dalmas from Guiana. 'What they all had in common was the same protest against colonial rule, and they all met in Paris where they came under the spell of Césaire and Senghor. They became conscious of their African heritage which they tried to revaluate, and they developed a new race consciousness, culture consciousness, an attitude they called by Césaire's term *negritude*.'[119]

Césaire was not only a poet : like Senghor, Rabemananjara and others he was both poet and politician. He represented Martinique in the French National Assembly; he was mayor of Martinique's capital; and in 1957 he won thirty-four of the thirty-seven seats in the island's legislature. Césaire is a Marxist and until 1956 he was a member of the French Communist Party and a supporter of International Communism.

The Concept of Negritude

Described in straightforward terms *negritude* 'denotes a certain quality which is common to the thoughts and behaviour of Negroes. It stands for the new consciousness of the Negro, for his newly-gained self confidence, and for his distinctive outlook on life, with which he distinguished himself from non-Negroes'.[120] But in the hands of Gallic and Marxist-trained dialecticians it becomes a much more complex ism.

Jean-Paul Sartre—the white apostle of *negritude*—gives it a romantic twist. 'Black poetry . . . is functional, it answers a need which exactly defines it. . . . From Haiti to Cayenne it is a sole idea . . . to make manifest the black soul. Negro poetry is evangelic, it comes bearing glad tidings—*negritude* is found again.'[121]

The American writer, Stanley Allen, defining it dialectically says : 'It represents in one sense the Negro African poet's endeavour to recover for his race a normal self-pride, a lost confidence in himself, a world in which he again has a sense of identity and a significant rôle. It is in Sartre's figure from classic mythology, his Eurydice recovered by Orpheus from Pluto, his lost beloved, his ultimate identity, his vision of the world and not that of a culture holding him in derision and in contempt. It is not a goal to be accomplished, but rather, more basically, an affective disposition. In Heidegger's existentialist term, the Negro's 'being-in-the-world' . . . Sartre has used Hegelian terms. . . . *Negritude* in African poetry is an anti-racist racism; it is the moment of negativity as reaction to the thesis of white supremacy. It is the antithesis in a dialectical progression which leads to an ultimate synthesis of a common humanity without racism . . .'.[122]

Is it possible for racism in any form—even 'anti-racist racism'—to find an 'ultimate synthesis of a common humanity without racism'? That it *is* possible has been shown by two of the leading apostles of *negritude*. Césaire, in a poem quoted earlier, writes :*

> . . . *you know my world-wide love,*
> *know it is not hatred against other races*
> *that turns me into the cultivator of this one race* . . .

Césaire's 'world-wide love'—his concern, for instance about anti-semitism—appears later in this chapter. His fellow-poet Senghor told a Press conference in London in October 1961 : 'I am not really a Pan-Africanist. I am a humanist.' It is shown, too, by the manifesto of *Présence Africaine* setting out its own ideas.†

As expressed by the French-speaking school, *negritude* finds little sympathy among English-speaking Africans. In an attack on 'The Cult of *Negritude*' Ezekiel Mphahlele,[123] the South African writer, says : 'Our music, dancing, writing and other arts reveal the cultural cross-impacts that have so much influenced our lives over the last three hundred years; and *negritude* to us is just so much airy intellectual talk either in terms of artistic activity or as a fighting faith. It is exciting, if often excruciating, to be the meeting-point of different cultural streams. If my writing shows any African-ness, it is as it should be, if my note and tone has an authenticity. I take my negro-ness for granted, and it is no matter for slogans. Imagine a Chinaman waking up one morning and shouting in the streets that he has discovered something Chinese in his sculpture or painting or music.'[124]

Mr. Mphahlele's views are refreshing, but his criticism does not accurately represent *negritude*. The Chinese never were cut off from their cultural roots, dispersed or dominated by an imposed foreign culture. The apostles of *negritude* explicitly deny that they wish to reject all their acquired European culture. They say that even if that were possible it would still be undesirable to do so. But they feel that until they have 'recovered' their own roots it is not possible to achieve what Senghor calls Africanity : 'a synthesis or rather a symbiosis of Negro-African, Berber and European contri-butions'. They are indulging, therefore, in an intellectual exercise of sloughing off (at least emotionally) their European acquired

* See page 37. † See page 96.

habits and methods, while at the same time seeking out their 'lost' habits and traditions in order to achieve a new synthesis. This intellectual and emotional experience is perfectly comprehensible. But it is natural, too, that those who have grown up furthest from their own roots (as is the case with Césaire himself) should be fiercest in their attacks on Western traditions and more strongly emotional in their search for something they (unlike Mphahlele) had never really known.

What we are up against in trying to analyse the conflicts and contradictions of *negritude* is its embedded ambivalence : acceptance and rejection of Western culture, as well as acceptance and rejection of African culture. Ambivalence more than anything else characterises the 'dialogues' and writings of Negro intellectuals—and especially those who do not live, and never have lived, in Africa. It is not surprising that the cult of *negritude* is primarily the cult of the 'exiles'.

Congress of Negro Writers and Artists

The first Congress of Negro Writers and Artists was held at the Sorbonne in September 1956, and the second in Rome in March 1959.* Both were held under the auspices of *Présence Africaine*, 'a cultural journal of the Negro world', which was started in Paris in 1947 by Mr. Alioun Diop 'to affirm the presence, or ethos, of the black communities of the world, and to defend the originality of their way of life and the dignity of their culture'. Those associated with this venture (who include both Africans and French intellectuals) affirm in a manifesto that 'the problem is not only one of assuring the theoretical equality of individuals between black and white. They know that the question goes back far beyond the problem of the concession of certain rights or the limitation of certain privileges. They know it concerns a fundamental recasting of the structure of European civilisation and of African life, and the links which bind us should spring from the cultural level. In short, it involves an emergence of the African personality from the accretion of Western culture, which colonisation has thrown into disequilibrium and servitude'.

This manifesto expresses both the desire for a new synthesis between Europe and the Negro world, and the elements of its conflicts. The opening statement by the distinguished Haitian academic figure and Ambassador, Dr. Price-Mars, at the first Congress set its theme : 'There are some sixty of us, from every

* For the text of resolutions passed at these two Congresses see Appendices 19 and 20.

clime of Africa, America and Europe. . . . We claim to represent an immense multitude of human beings spread over a great part of the world's surface, especially in Africa. We are all, or nearly all, distinguished by an indelible peculiarity, the more or less dark colour of our skin. . . . It was this peculiarity which the hateful commercial system of the sixteenth and seventeenth centuries took advantage of to lead millions of our ancestors into servitude across the Atlantic. Very well, and now by a magnificent reversal of the things of the world and a supreme revenge of the spirit, it is this distinctive sign which we rely upon in the twentieth century to confirm, exalt and glorify the culture of the Negro peoples.'

My outstanding impression of both the Paris and the Rome Congresses was the great gulf between the French-speaking and the English-speaking delegates. There was indisputably fundamental unity: but both in attitudes and methods the delegates divided largely along the language culture-line. The French speakers were dialectical to a degree; the English speakers almost ridiculously pragmatic. Nothing could have pointed the contrast more strongly than the speeches of the French West Indian Aimé Césaire (undoubtedly the dominating figure at both Congresses) and the British West Indian George Lamming;[125] the former subtle, involved and analytical; the latter robust, straightforward and confident.

The large American Negro contingent was clearly unhappy: Césaire provoked them strongly. 'I ask myself,' Dr. Mercer Cook intervened at one point, 'what am I doing in this outfit? Mr. Césaire has certainly said that we American Negroes have a semi-colonial status; but since 7 o'clock I feel myself less and less at one with my African compatriots. And that troubles and hurts me greatly.' To which Césaire presently replied: 'Quite sincerely, I was very pained to learn what emotions my words had aroused . . . particularly among the American delegation. . . . If you are not in a colonial situation you are in a situation which . . . is a sequel to slavery—and therefore, in the last analysis, a sequel to the colonial régime. And I think that this is undeniable, and it is not passing a derogatory judgment on American democracy to say that slavery has left its traces—which those [sic] people are trying to eradicate —but has nevertheless left traces which still persist today in the history of the United States.' I will return presently to the place of American Negroes in the African 'outfit'.

The theme of the first Congress was *The Crisis of Negro Culture*; that of the second, *The Unity and Responsibilities of African Negro Culture*. The second Congress was a less happy affair than the first.

Its venue was the *Instituto Italiano per l'Africa*. Unhappily, the Italians did not think of locking the doors to the great halls in the Institute which are filled with the guns and flags and trophies of their colonial wars in Africa. The Marxist elements clearly felt their growing isolation; when the body of the conference was received in audience by his Holiness the Pope they stayed away and produced their own declaration.* But the venue apart, there was not much opportunity for effective discussion, and the Congress never had much of a chance of coming to life. Nevertheless its committees produced a series of interesting conclusions and recommendations.†

It is not my purpose to discuss either of the Congresses at any length; what I am concerned with are some of the more important themes that illustrate the growth and divergences of Pan-African thinking.

Attitudes to the West

Negro intellectuals—especially those educated outside Africa, or living outside it—often face two separate problems : the colour line that divides them from fully participating in Western society, and the line that divides them (usually intellectually) from African society. These divisions sometimes make 'exiles' of intellectuals who live in Africa as much as of those who do not. Where do these 'exiles', the intellectuals, belong? They are 'in the West' but not wholly of it; and they are 'in the black world' but yet separated from the lives and culture of the mass of the ordinary people. It is a situation—vigorously denied by many negro intellectuals, but nevertheless a real one—that calls for a great effort of adjustment. The editor of *Présence Africaine*, Mr. Alioun Diop, has spoken of it in moral terms as a crisis of conscience.

'However much we may admire and love Western civilisation,' he said,[126] 'we do not think any the less about what distinguishes us both from the Europeans and from the (African) populations which have remained attached to the soil and to their own traditions. . . . It is important to emphasise here that believers and atheists, Christians, Moslems and Communists alike, we all share the feeling of being frustrated by Western culture. Jean-Paul Sartre pointed out some years ago that the French language veiled the thought of the Negro poet. The truth is that the personality of the Negro intellectual or artist cannot be divorced from the personality of the people. And that the personality of these people could not have been conceived or foreseen, and cannot be truly embodied and

* See Appendix 20.   † See Appendix 20.

expressed by European culture and civilisation. Neither the political parties nor the churches, neither the literary chapels nor the codes of good form give adequate recognition to the original, but by no means inhuman, stature of the Negro personality. And the intellectual has a sense of frustration . . . because his own people themselves have been misunderstood and history has been falsified. . . . Let us be under no illusion. We live in an age in which the artists bear witness and are all more or less committed. We are bound to take sides; every major work by an African writer or artist bears witness against Western racism and imperialism.'

The late Richard Wright,[127] speaking as 'a Western man of colour', posed the problems of his own conflicts. '. . . My position is a split one. I'm black. I'm a man of the West. . . . I see and understand the West; but I also see and understand the non- or anti-Western point of view. How is this possible? This double-vision of mine stems from my being a product of Western civilisation and from my racial identity which is organically born of my being a product of that civilisation. Being a Negro living in a White Christian society, I've never been allowed to blend in a natural and healthy manner with the culture and civilisation of the West. This contradiction of being both Western and a man of colour creates a distance, so to speak, between me and my environment. I'm self-conscious. I admit it. Yet I feel no need to apologise for it. Hence, though Western, I'm inevitably critical of the West. My attitude of criticism and detachment is born of my position. Me and my environment are one, but that oneness has in it, at its very heart, a schism. . . . Yet, I'm not non-Western. I'm no enemy of the West. Neither am I an Easterner. When I look out upon these vast stretches of this earth inhabited by brown, black and yellow men . . . my reactions and attitudes are those of the West. I see both worlds from another and third point of view.'[128]

If Richard Wright's feelings can be described as love-hatred, the exile poet-politician from Madagascar, Jacques Rabemananjara[129], expresses feelings of hatred-love; this is not just a play on words; the distinction is an important one, because the weight of the one over the other fundamentally shapes action.

'The primacy of European values was . . . a thing which was taken for granted; one of the most remarkable consequences of the second world war was that it shook confidence in the stability of this dogma, and forced Europe to question itself on the legitimacy of this Article of Faith. . . . Whence came the awakening? From a shock. The narcotic lost its effects once the duplicity of the West was made obvious to us, the contradiction between principle and

conduct, between theory and practice, between words and deeds.
We began to be uneasy. And we began to doubt. The major
revelation was this : Europe has inherited the privilege of Janus;
she has two faces. On one side, a face of stone, of death, a
grimacing Gorgon's face of unequalled cruelty, cynicism, rascality
and self-satisfaction, the face incarnated by our inventors of Negro
barbarism, of the experts in supplying human flesh for the
cremation furnace. On the other side, a face of lilies—one kingdom
has even made them the symbol of its arms—a face of purity, of
spring water and dawn, the marvellous imprint of the mask of
Venus, so beautiful that she seems to have embodied in herself the
sum of all human perfection, in being the first to call forth from
the limbo of our consciousness all the luminous principles of the
Rights of Man. . . . It is true that there exists a Europe which we
do not love, which we cannot love, which we shall never love;
there are too many lies, too many injustices, too much blood and
dirt between her and us. . . . But in our hearts the cult of the other
Europe is not dead.'[130]

Finally, there is a third dominant attitude born out of the
sublimation of conflict, which is fairly common in the English-
speaking parts of West Africa. The Sierra Leonean scientist and
writer, Davidson Nicol[131] explains it in these terms : In West
African writing there is a lack of the motive power of burning racial
injustice which carries through in the writing of other peoples of
African descent. This driving force will be noticed in most of the
literature by modern Negro writers. The nineteenth-century attitude of easy social inter-racial mixing and the current British post-
war colonial policy of rapid advance towards self-government has
outstripped extreme nationalism, Communism, and racial bitterness
in British West Africa. The distressing but stimulating convenience
of a setting of Afro-European conflict is thus fortunately or unfortunately denied them.'

Two Cultures or One?

Is there any future for Negroes in cultural assimilation? This
question is closely tied in with ambivalence to the West; in fact it
is prompted by it. Negroes in the New World, by and large, accept
the necessity and even the desirability of an assimilation of cultures.
'I came to this Congress as an American and as a Negro,' Mr.
John A. Davis told the first Congress of Negro Writers and Artists.
'*As an American* I am a builder. We are pragmatic people. . . .'[132]

Mr. Richard Wright's forthright American assimilation views have already been quoted.

Aimé Césaire dissents from this view. In Martinique and in Europe he will borrow from Western culture; but he denies that 'borrowing' by one civilisation from another leads to assimilation. 'The truth is quite otherwise; the borrowing is only valid when it is counter-balanced by an interior state of mind that *calls* for it and integrates it within the body which then assimilates it so that both become one—what was external becomes internal. Hegel's view applies here. When a society borrows it takes possession. It acts, it does not suffer action. . . . For our part, and as regards our particular societies, we believe that in the African culture yet to be born, or in the para-African culture yet to be born, there will be many new elements, modern elements, elements, let us face it, borrowed from Europe. But we also believe that many traditional elements will persist in these cultures. We refuse to yield to the temptation of the *tabula rasa*. I refuse to believe that the future African culture can totally and brutally reject the former African culture. . . . In the culture yet to be born, there will be without any doubt both old and new. Which new elements? Which old? Here alone our ignorance begins.'[133]

Leopold Senghor is a bridge-person between Africa, Europe and the New World. He stands closer to Césaire than to many of his fellow Africans : 'Césaire is right when he says—and I said it myself twenty years ago—that we must not be assimilated, we must assimilate; that is, there must be freedom of choice, there must be freedom of assimilation . . . even when we have solved this problem [of colonialism], there will still be another problem—that of the choice between civilisations in contact; we shall have to see what we shall take from Western civilisation and what we shall keep from Negro African civilisation.'[134]

Assimilation is rejected by Alioun Diop as a type of relationship inspired by colonialism. 'Its aim is to make the individual (it is never concerned with anything but individuals), torn from the background natural to him and which brought out his personality, agree to replace his habits of thinking, feeling and acting by others, which he could only share with an alien community . . . our peoples reject assimilation without at the same time wishing to isolate themselves in their own cultures. The straight choice between isolation and assimilation has during the last ten years been the trap in which the malice of the coloniser has cunningly tried to catch the conscience of the Africans. But life is not simple. It is true that there is another trap, which consists of innocently putting you to the challenge of choosing which African values to preserve and which European values to adopt . . . the men of culture of the Negro world do not disguise from themselves the magnitude of their responsibilities as the link between the Western world and the universe of their peoples. They have certain responsibilities in purifying the morals and language of that culture which the West tends to impose upon the whole planet. . . . In the face of that culture our rôle in the immediate future must be to redress all the errors and false values introduced and turned into institutions in Europe by a unilaterally creative subjectivity, whose passionate urge was given tenfold strength by the whole weight of European imperialism.'[135]

Away from all the intellectualising, the Ghanaian poet Mr. Michael Dei-Aneng (who is also head of his country's Ministry of External Affairs) proclaims :[136]

> *Here we stand*
> *Poised between two civilisations*
> *Backward? To days of drum*
> *And festal dances in the shade*
> *Of sun-kist palms.*
> *Or forward?*
> *Forward!*
> *Toward?*
> *The slums, where man is dumped upon man?*
>
> *   *   *
>
> *The factory*
> *To grind hard hours*
> *In an inhuman mill*
> *In one long ceaseless spell?*

No better attempt has been made to understand and explain these arguments and themes than Janheinz Jahn's *Muntu*.[137] Whatever its failings, it offers a comprehensive and a comprehensible analysis of the effects of the culture conflict between Europe and the black world. He already sees a new culture emerging which suggests synthesis rather than antithesis :

'. . . African intelligence wants to integrate into modern life only what seems valuable from the past. The goal is neither the traditional African nor the black European but the modern African. This means that a tradition seen rationally, whose values are made explicit and renewed, must assimilate those European elements which modern times demand; and in this process the European elements are so transformed and adapted that a modern, viable *African* culture arises out of the whole. It is a question, therefore, of a genuine Renaissance, which does not remain a merely formal renewal and imitation of the past, but permits something new to emerge. This something new is already at hand; we call it neo-African culture.'

Aftermath of Colonialism

African intellectuals understand that the ending of colonialism will not of itself produce a new Black Heaven. The problems of de-colonisation—of political institutions and economies no less than of the mind—will present challenges as grave as the struggle against colonialism itself. Two broad schools of thought have emerged from discussions of this problem : the one wishes gradually to reform society while preserving the outward forms of what has been achieved; and the other desires 'a Copernican revolution'. We have already seen how in the political struggles those divisions produced the Casablanca Powers and the Monrovia States. But if many of the political motives for these divisions are questionable, the in-tellectual arguments are at least less open to confusion. Aimé Césaire, is the clearest exponent of the 'Copernican' view. If we want to understand the idea that lies behind the modern slogan of 'decolonisation' Césaire repays study.

'. . . Decolonisation is not automatic; and still more, not all forms of decolonisation are of equal value. . . . This is proved by the in-equalities in the development of the liberated countries, some of whom have difficulty in shaking off the aftermath of colonialism, while others, on the contrary, blossom rapidly and fully in the bright sunlight of independence. . . . It is clear that for us there is not, and cannot be, any decolonisation which is bad in itself, and that for the very simple reason that the worst decolonisation will always be a hundredfold superior to the best colonisation. The difference between [them] is not one of degree but of kind. . . . One too often sees perpetuated or reconstituted within the societies con-stituted by nations which have been liberated from the colonial yoke, structures which are in verity colonial or colonialist. Or again, inside imperfectly decolonised nations, there is a danger that typic-ally colonialist phenomena of recurrence will be seen to emerge at any moment, utilised no longer by a colonialist or an imperialist, but by a group of men or a class of men who from that moment, inside the liberated nation, take on the rôle of the Epigonoi of colonialism and use the instruments invented by colonialism. Think of the race struggles in Central or Latin America to take only one example, and you will observe that it is a question there of an inheritance or a survival from the colonial systems which have, nevertheless, achieved independence for the last hundred and fifty years. And if I recall that ... it is only to make ourselves realise one thing : that the combat against colonialism is not over so soon as one thinks and *because imperialism has been conquered in the military sense*. In short, there can be no question for us of displacing colonialism or making servitude an internal affair. What we must do is to destroy it, to extirpate it, in the proper sense of the word, to tear up its roots, and that is why *true decolonisation will be revolutionary or nothing*. This point of view enables us to understand how vain is the temptation felt by certain people to believe in the idea that between the colonial epoch and the time of liberty we must adjust ourselves by phases and transitions....'[138]

Karl Marx in Africa

'Many of us are Marxists,' said Leopold Senghor at the first Congress of Negro Writers and Artists.[139] 'But Marx was not an African. His doctrine was born from the situation of men in Western Europe. And he said himself that his theory of Capital was only valid for Western Europe.'

Marxist ideas have contributed to the thinking of both the English-speaking and the French-speaking *avant garde* of Pan-Africanists. In Britain the sponsors of the sixth Pan-African Congress in 1945—leaders like Padmore, James, Abrahams, Makonnen, Nkrumah and Kenyatta—had all had Marxist training. In the French African struggle many of the RDA leaders—like Sékou Touré and Modeiba Keita—were Marxists. And in the *negritude* movement Aimé Césaire and Leopold Senghor (who is a Catholic at the same time) are but two of the many Marxists who helped to influence attitudes. Although the Marxists were probably in a small minority they were often in a position of dominance in the leadership.

All the Marxist leaders I have referred to have one thing in common : they unequivocally reject International Communism and Moscow's leadership. Some of them had at one time or another been prominent protagonists of the Comintern (Padmore, James, Richard Wright, etc.) or of the latter-day Cominform (notably Césaire). They had all ended up in the camp of those whom 'the gods had failed'. The strength of their anti-communism therefore lies rooted in their own experiences of it. Those who have remained

Marxists repudiate its Russian version.* George Padmore, by the title of his most important political work—*Pan-Africanism or Communism?*—defines the nature of the challenge as he saw it.

M. Sékou Touré, who led the first breakaway of the African working-class from the communist-dominated WFTU, declared : 'The Marxism which served to mobilise the African populations, and in particular the working-class, and to lead that class to success, has been amputated of those of its characteristics which did not correspond to the African realities.'[140]

The nature of African Marxist realities will be briefly considered in the next chapter. For an idea of the vehemence with which African Marxists have repudiated communism, and for the intellectual arguments leading to this repudiation, it is sufficient to read George Padmore and Césaire on this subject. Césaire's letter of resignation to Maurice Thorez, Secretary-General of the French Communist Party, in October 1956 following Khruschev's disclosures at the Twentieth Party Congress about Stalin's misdeeds, ranks high in Pan-African literature and, one would hope, also in the wider political literature of our times.[141]

'I could easily express my feelings towards both the French Communist Party and a Communist International as it has been shaped by the patronage of the Soviet Union; the list of dissensions and grievances would be long,' he begins. 'Lately, we have had a record-breaking crop; and Khruschev's disclosures concerning Stalin are such that everyone, no matter what the extent of his participation in communist activity, has been thrown—or, at least, so I trust—into an abyss of dismay, of pain and of shame.'

After attacking the French Communist Party for their 'pig-headed obstinateness in error, perseverance in lies, the fantastic pretence of never once having been wrong', he writes of 'the bankruptcy of an ideal and pathetic illustration of a whole generation's failure'. Then, mounting his Pan-African horse, he deals with 'considerations which have to do with my condition and quality as a coloured man' : 'Let's say it straight out : that in the light of events (and having appreciated the existence of a shameless anti-semitism whose manifestations have occurred and, it appears, still are occurring in countries that call themselves socialist), I have acquired the conviction that our ways and destinies, and those of communism, such as it is put into practice, are not purely and simply identical; that they cannot be purely and simply identified. One fact, crucial in so far as I am concerned, is this : that we coloured men, in this specific moment of historical evolution, have

* See pages 32, 127–29, 220.

consciously grasped, and grasped in its full breadth, the notion of our peculiar uniqueness, the notion of just who we are and what, and that we are ready, on every plane and in every department, to assume the responsibilities which proceed from this coming into consciousness. The peculiarity of "our place in the world" which isn't to be confused with anybody else's. The peculiarity of our problems, which aren't to be reduced to subordinate forms of any other problem. The peculiarity of our history, laced with terrible misfortunes which belong to no other history. The peculiarity of our culture, which we intend to live and to make live in an ever realler manner.'

No longer, he goes on to say, is he willing to see colonial questions treated as 'a subsidiary part of some more important global matter ... over which deals can be arranged.* He makes it clear that he is alluding to the French Communist Party's vote on Algeria. 'In any case, it is patently established that our colonialism, the struggle of coloured peoples against racism, is much more complex, indeed it is of a totally different nature than the struggle of the French workers against French capitalism, and cannot in any case be considered as a part, as a fragment of that struggle.'

On questions of tactics he has decided that, rather than submit to the 'Prussianising of a few', he prefers 'a form of organisation in which the Marxists would not be drowned, but where they would act as a leaven, would assume the inspirational, the orientating rôle and not the rôle which, objectively, they play as things now stand : that of the dividers of popular forces.'

His letter goes on to make it clear that his wish is to see 'Marxism and communism harnessed into the service of coloured peoples, and not coloured peoples into the service of Marxism and communism. That the doctrine and the movement be tailored to fit men, not men to fit the movement. And of course that goes for others besides communists. If I were a Christian or a Moslem, I'd say the same thing.'

Building on his colour-consciousness he goes on to say : 'There exists a Chinese communism. Though I have no first-hand acquaintance with it, I am strongly prejudiced in favour. And I expect it not to sink into the monstrous errors that have disfigured European communism. But it would also interest me even more to see the African brand of communism blossom forth and flourish. In all likelihood it would offer us variants—useful, valuable, original

* This charge, it is interesting to recall, is identical with that made by George Padmore and C. L. R. James 20 years before they had broken with the International Communists.

variants, and the wisdom in us that is our age-old heritage would, I am certain, shade or complete a good many of the doctrine's points.'

Césaire rejects that there should be communism in any of the French-speaking territories just 'because the French Communist Party conceives its duties towards colonial peoples in terms of a tutorship...' He rejects the offer of solidarity 'with the French proletariat and, *via* communism, with all the world's proletariats. I don't make light of these solidarities.... But I don't want to see them blown up into metaphysics. There are no allies by divine right ... if communism pillages our most vivifying friendships, wastes the bond that weds us to other West Indian islands, the tie that makes us Africa's child, then I say that communism has served us ill in having us swap a living brotherhood for what looks to have the features of the coldest of all chill abstractions.'

He anticipates and rejects the charge of provincialism. 'I have a different idea of a universal. It is of a universal rich with all the particulars there are, the deepening of each particular, the coexistence of them all.' And he concludes : 'Succinctly put, as of now we consider it is our duty to conjugate our efforts with those of all men fired by the love of justice and truth, and in their company to build organisations, apt honestly and effectively to aid the dark peoples in their struggle for a today and for a tomorrow : a fight for justice; a fight for culture; a fight for dignity and for freedom; organisations capable of preparing them in every domain to assume, autonomously, the heavy responsibilities history at this moment makes weigh so heavily upon their shoulders.'

Césaire was the leading member of a group of African Marxists who met separately during the second Congress of Negro Writers and Artists in Rome to consider their attitude to communism in the light of the conditions of under-developed countries, especially in Africa.* While accepting that Marxism can be broadened to accord with African realities they invited African Marxists to develop their doctrine in the light of three conclusions : 1. The cultural references in Marx's thought are nearly all drawn from Western experience. 2. The economic situation of the Western proletariat cannot be strictly identified with that of the under-developed people. 3. A doctrine is all the more universal in so far as it takes account of all experience (historic, economic, etc.), the diversity of the cultural genius of peoples, and the need for its application to be controlled by a really representative authority.

* See Appendix 20 for the full text of this statement.

Black Aliens in Africa

Earlier references have been made to the uneasiness felt by Negro delegations from Africa attending the two Congresses of Negro Writers and Artists. To what extent does their sense of not altogether belonging reflect a wider sense of separation? It is a difficult question to answer because it is so easy to overlook related factors which might lead to the conclusion that it is not only the Negro from America, or from the West Indies, who feels himself out of place at these gatherings. For example, the Ghanaian delegation was highly critical of the way in which the French-speaking intellectuals dominated the proceedings at the Rome Congress, and this had nothing to do with politics. It is not, therefore, a question which only affects the Negro from the New World.

What happens when he goes to Africa? I have already referred to Langston Hughes' experience of being treated as a stranger and a 'white man' in West Africa.* In *Black Power* the late Richard Wright recorded his own difficulties when he visited Ghana for the first time in 1953.[142] Everywhere he found himself treated as a stranger rather than as 'a brother'. I do not accept that the experiences of these two writers were typical, although they undoubtedly reflect an important part of what Negroes might feel—especially when they try to come to terms with the 'ordinary folk', or with the brash young nationalist politicians. But when they established contact with Africans of their own social and intellectual class these differences diminished greatly, as one would expect.

What happens when Negroes from America or the West Indies go to settle is a different question. Here, again, it is difficult to generalise without misleading. One could point to the experience of Gabriel Lisette who came from the French West Indies and became the first Prime Minister of Chad. Subsequently he was deposed; the fact that he was a West Indian was used against him. One could argue that the fact of his having become Prime Minister is a more important test of acceptance than his deposition was of rejection, on the grounds that one cannot be certain how much was due to his being a West Indian, and how much to normal political intrigue.

There must be some significance in the fact that not many Negroes from the New World have come to settle in the independent countries of Africa. Many who came intending to settle have left. A small number stayed on—some because they genuinely like

* See page 17.

it; some because they feel they can't go 'home' again; and some who intend finally to leave. Those who come to join the civil service or to teach generally leave (always allowing for the outstanding exceptions); many with unhappy experiences. Dr. Harold R. Isaacs recently published the results of a survey he undertook among American Negroes in West Africa.[143]

> 'They had come looking for freedom from racism and prejudice, or at least for a racial situation that counted them in instead of out—that provided solace and a sense of identity in a world where everybody was black. They had also looked for a chance to share in the new pride of achievement stemming from the black man's reassertion of himself and his "African personality". In West Africa, in a small way and for a short time, the Negro pilgrim can find some of this. But it does not last long—hardly past the first flush of the sensation of being in a place where the white man is not master. Almost invariably the Negro pilgrim in Africa soon finds himself not free at all, more than ever without solace and a sense of identity, fighting new patterns of prejudice, and suffering the pangs of a new kind of outsiderness. He had thought that he was alien in America, but he discovers that he is much more alien in Africa. Whether he likes it or not, he is American, and in Africa he becomes an American-in-exile.'

If one accepts that this assessment is correct, what conclusions should be drawn from it? Obviously the Negro feels more 'at home' in America than in a strange environment. That there are exceptions one knows; also that many Negroes find it easier to adapt to Liberia than to Ghana; and to West Africa than to East Africa. White Americans often find themselves in similar situations of 'strangeness' in Europe. And Israel's modern folklore is full of wry and amusing examples of the inability of American Jews to adapt themselves to life in the Jewish State. They may be passionate Zionists at home; but Israel is not home for them. This strangeness felt by American Jews in Israel does not however invalidate the reality of the sense of Jewish identity which inspires Zionism any more than the inability of many (probably the great majority of) American Negroes to transplant themselves would invalidate the reality of Pan-African feelings. What it might suggest, however, is that the 'Back to Africa' movement lays a false trail. It may not have been so in the last century when they thought to return to Africa as leaders; but it offers little appeal or practical alternative for Negroes dissatisfied with their present situation in America or the West Indies.

Do the experiences of Negroes in Africa invalidate the idea of 'black solidarity'? Are all blacks really brothers under the skin? How much kinship is there in the skinship of *negritude*? To answer this question satisfactorily it is necessary first to disentangle the sense of *political* solidarity from that of *social* solidarity. Black peoples have demonstrated in a political sense that they feel together and aspire towards common aims; these do not, however, include the desire to return to Africa. Garvey's dream, therefore, is likely to remain an illusion; at least within the present situation.

At this point it is necessary to make another distinction. The experiences of 'strangeness', of being made to 'feel inferior and different' related by American Negroes living in West Africa, applies *equally* to Africans from other parts of the continent living and teaching in West Africa. Almost every experience of unease and strangeness recounted by Mr. Isaacs in his survey has been repeated to me *in almost the same words* by Africans from South Africa living in Ghana and Nigeria. The strangeness of American Negroes is not, therefore, something that is peculiar to themselves. It is not only conditioned by the fact that they have grown up in a society outside of Africa.

CHAPTER VII

MODERN POLITICAL IDEAS

Pan-Africanism has produced a language of its own which conditions the thinking and the politics of the entire continent. It cuts across the English-French language barrier, and across the Sahara. Emotions have been converted into ideas, and ideas into slogans. It matters little today whether a Pan-African speech is being made in Cairo or Capetown, Dar-es-Salaam or Dakar; the political language, with its slogans and appeals, is immediately identifiable. Here is one striking example:

> 'We know that even after our independence has been achieved that *African Personality* which we would build up will depend upon the consolidation of our *unity,* not only in sentiment but in fact. We know that a *balkanised* Africa however loudly it might proclaim to the world its independence and all that, will in fact be an easy prey to the forces of neo-imperialism [*neo-colonialism*]. The weak and divided can never hope to maintain a *dignified independence* however much they may proclaim their desire to be strong and united; for the desire to unite is a very different thing from actual unity. One can foresee the forces of neo-imperialism manipulating these little states in Africa, making them complacently smug in this mere sentimental desire to be one, and at the same time doing everything possible to prevent the realisation of that unity. . . .'[144]

Some of these sloganised concepts have never been clearly defined; they have simply developed. Their meaning emerges from their context. Not infrequently they contradict each other in the sense in which they are used. But such contradictions are not peculiar to Africa. What does *democracy* mean when used in Europe or America? The point is that there is a common understanding to which particular words or concepts are related even when they are being used for different purposes. For example, *nonalignment* is interpreted in widely different ways; but few can doubt its essential meaning.

Non-alignment

How the *positive neutrality* of Delhi and Bandung evolved into the narrowly defined *non-alignment* of Cairo and Belgrade has already been told. What follows is an attempt to reflect the dominant attitudes that have developed around this concept, but without trying to relate precept to practice.[145]

Non-alignment expresses freedom of decision and of choice in deciding each international issue on its merits; in effect an untied and independent policy.

'We say what we believe whether this pleases or displeases.' (President Nasser.)[146]

'We do not tend to support one bloc against the other, but we are bent on finding the best solutions to the problems pressing on us, whether it be colonialism, disarmament, atomic tests or Germany. We shall study all existing views and we shall express ourselves in support of those providing for the most objective settlements.' (President Modeiba Keita.)[147]

'Our standing in the eyes of the world will be greatly enhanced if we consistently express our views on international disputes, without fear or favour, and act in accordance with the moral dictates of our conscience.' (President Osman of Somalia.)[148]

'We consider it wrong for the Nigerian Federal Government to associate itself as a matter of routine with any of the power blocs. . . . This freedom of action will be an essential feature of our policy . . . our policies will be founded on Nigeria's interests and will be consistent with the moral and democratic principles on which our constitution is based.' (Prime Minister Sir Abubaker Tafawa Balewa.)[149]

'The gravamen of any policy endorsed by us should be based upon an independent and not a neutral attitude, especially with reference to issues which affect the destiny of Africa or the people of African descent no matter where they may live.' (Dr. Nnamdi Azikiwe.)[150]

'Non-alignment implies for each nation the right to establish the type of government it desires, to freely choose its régime, its economic and social system, and its way of life—in short, to act in accordance with its own guiding spirit unhampered by any pressure from outside.' (Ben Yousseff Ben Khedda, President of the Algerian Provisional Government.)[151]

Non-alignment is *not* neutrality.

'This policy . . . must not be confused with *équilibrisme*, with a balancing act which takes up no fundamental position and which aligns itself now with one, now with the other, of the two blocs according to circumstances.... We examine international problems in the light of our national interests and of the interests of Africa, and at the same time in the light of our desire for peace and for the peaceful co-existence of all countries, and we decide our policy in the light of these principles alone. If our policy then coincides with that of the Eastern or Western bloc, this is entirely a matter of chance and not the result of calculation. A balancing *équilibriste* policy causes a country to lose its entire personality. It can be blackmailed by both blocs....' (Modeiba Keita.)[152] 'Ghana stands for positive neutralism and non-alignment as against what I might describe as negative neutralism [which] believes that armed conflict between the Great Powers can only bring misery and destruction to those who participate in it. I consider this view to be unrealistic. Those who hold it believe that in the world of today a State can secure its safety if it withdraws itself entirely from the international problems of peace and war and avoids taking a definitive stand on issues which affect the balance of power in the world today.' (Dr. Nkrumah.)[153]

Nor is non-alignment isolationist. It is not fearful of becoming involved in world affairs. On the contrary, it demands to be involved, but not on the Great Powers' terms.

'We should remain in constant touch with the two conflicting military camps, since non-alignment does not mean that we isolate ourselves from problems; it means that we should contribute positively to the consolidation of understanding, and to the opening of channels for the passage of ideas and thoughts across the deep chasms caused by crises.' (Colonel Nasser.)[154]

'We, the small nations, cannot stand aloof from this suicidal race . . . of armament. It is our duty to the world to put the Great Powers wise to the dangers of their activities.' (President Abboud of the Sudan.)[155]

'Our neutralism does not mean isolation or detachment from one part of humanity; on the contrary, it means the search for and acceptance of whatever is true and just in the sum total of human thinking. Our neutralism is dynamic and alive; its sole concern is to save human values and to promote the peace and progress of the human race.' (The King of Morocco.)[156]

Non-alignment rejects the view that Africa must inevitably end up by falling into either the camp of the West or the East.

'. . . The West always talked about the dangers of Communism infiltrating into Africa. "We think this is not a danger." It was not really a question of the newly-independent

African States being Communist or capitalist. "People used to say that I was a Communist. Now we read the same thing about Guinea and Sékou Touré." (Colonel Nasser in an interview.)[157]

'We must stress that our enemies often attempt to have it believed that Africa is being taken in tow either by the West or by the USSR—in any event that it obeys a foreign force or concept. . . . Of course Africa is not unaware of the existence of two blocs which influence world politics. What is of interest to know today is the doctrine of Africa. The East-West conflict often makes one lose sight of the necessity of putting this question to Africa, at least for those who are not aware of whether or not this Continent has its own views and its own doctrine, and consequently whether it represents a coherent system distinct from the other systems.' (Sékou Touré.)[158]

'The people who anxiously watch to see whether we will become "Communist" or "Western democrats" will both be disconcerted. We do not have to be either . . . but we have the lessons of the East and the West before us, and we have our own traditions to contribute to mankind's pool of knowledge.' (Prime Minister Julius Nyerere.)[159]

'I will not become the stooge or satellite or pawn or hireling of anybody.' (Colonel Nasser.)[160]

'As we would not have British masters, so we would not have Russian masters.' (Dr. Nkrumah.)[161]

Non-alignment looks to both blocs for economic and technical aid, but expects it to be untied.

'When certain nations grant aid . . . they are surprised that the receiving countries do not follow their policies in international affairs. . . .' (Modeiba Keita.)[162]

'Soviet bloc aid comes without strings; US aid carries unacceptable conditions amounting to control. Communist aid "helped us to survive" and to "escape domination from the West".' (Colonel Nasser.)[163]

'[We shall develop] . . . with the interest and support of the West or . . . be compelled to turn elsewhere. This is not a warning or a threat, but a straight statement of political reality.' (Dr. Nkrumah.)[164]

'As a result of its economic weakness the non-aligned world has become a stake that is to be won by the granting of economic assistance, a stake in the hands of the great Powers, each of which is attempting to secure political support, strategic strong points, and sources of raw materials and markets. The non-aligned world is aware of its strength and unity and is refusing to become the instrument of alien designs.' (The King of Morocco.)[165]

'Bilateral international assistance . . . has been based on political propaganda, and not on social and economic concepts. . . . The endeavours of the underdeveloped countries to liquidate the old economic forms which gave rise to the present-day disparity in economic development, requires the co-operation of the rich countries . . . in this great international effort. . . . It is needless to state that, under no circumstances, shall we accept assistance from any country which may be tinged with any conditions that will infringe on our sovereignty and independence. . . .' (General Abboud.)[166]

Non-alignment does not constitute a third *bloc*, though it is sometimes spoken of as a third *force*.

'The non-aligned countries have no intention of forming any bloc.' (Colonel Nasser.)[167]

'We are not here to constitute ourselves into a third bloc, yet by this very conference we are constituting ourselves into a moral force and influence between the East and the West in the cause of peace.' (Dr. Nkrumah.)[168]

'The purpose of this conference should not be to organise ourselves into a third bloc.' (President Osman of Somalia.)[169]

Non-alignment allows for the development of friendly feelings towards both blocs; it feels free both to praise and to criticise them.

'I believe that there is a great fund of goodwill for Africa in the United States of America and we in Ghana will certainly do all we can to foster good relations.' (Dr. Nkrumah.)[170]

'The United States . . . should be the first to appreciate the realistic reasons why we as a small country should endeavour to preserve normal relations with the two other great powers of the world today—the Soviet Union and China.' (Dr. Nkrumah.)[171]

'The Governments of the USSR and Ghana declare that they resolutely condemn imperialism and colonialism in all its forms and manifestations, and express their firm confidence that, at present, given the unity of all the progressive forces in the world there exists prerequisites for doing away with the system of colonial oppression and exploitation for good.' (A joint declaration.)[172]

'. . . Colonialism may come to us yet in a different guise, not necessarily from Europe.' (Dr. Nkrumah.)[173]

'Local Communist parties . . . always work to seize power . . . their objectives are dangerous—and that is why the Communist Party is illegal in Egypt. But our people do not have to like Communism to feel friendship and sympathy for Russia.' (Colonel Nasser.)[174]

'I am aware that . . . such a conference for non-aligned

States is an attempt unwelcomed and disapproved by several Powers hostile to peace, foremost among which are the colonial powers wishing to stifle all voices of conscience and extinguish every torch of freedom, if only they could.' (Colonel Nasser.)[175]
'Guinea condemns colonialism and not countries or people. It wants the equality and unity of peoples and of men, without consideration of colour or religion. It remains totally aware that fraternal co-operation, peaceful co-existence and peace between peoples, constitute a clear indication of human progress in work, justice and democracy, and expresses the wish that all the peoples of the world commit themselves firmly to the harmonious development of the destiny of mankind. . . . We are of the generation of Africa which holds out fraternal hands to all peoples to advance towards the greater and real happiness of man. . . .' (Sékou Touré.)[176]
'We have noted—I am telling you the conclusions reached by Africans and Asians and I must report them to you objectively—that the countries of the Eastern bloc, whatever may be their reasons, unreservedly support the peoples struggling for liberation from the colonial yoke. . . . Moreover we have found that help from the Eastern bloc is always immediate help and does not offend the susceptibility or the dignity of the receiving country . . . we have come to the conclusion that the countries of the Western bloc are timidly trying at present to revise their attitude with regard to the *tiers monde*, where they are always outpaced by the countries of the Eastern bloc.' (Modeiba Keita.)[177]
'President Modeiba Keita of Mali said . . . that world crises could be settled if Premier Khruschev showed the same spirit of goodwill as President Kennedy demonstrated this week. . . . Mr. Keita expressed the hope that there would be an "echo" of the President's attitude from Mr. Khruschev's meeting with President Nkrumah and Prime Minister Nehru.'[178]

Non-alignment implies non-participation in military alliances with Great Powers (denying the right to maintain bases). This is laid down in the definition adopted at the Cairo preparatory conference for the Belgrade meeting.*

'This right (to choose one's own system of government) and freedom of choice are incompatible with any participation in a military alliance.' (Ben Yousseff Ben Khedda, President of the Algerian Provisional Government.)[179]

Non-alignment is often presented as being in the best interests of the West itself.

* See page 60.

'The policy of aligning with the West creates a burning issue for Communists. So long as they have a legitimate issue to fight, persecution only adds fuel to the flame. Paradoxical as it may sound, the safest way of aligning with the West is not to align with the West.' (Dunduza K. Chisiza, Parliamentary Secretary of Finance, Nyasaland.)[180]

'. . . I think the best thing to do, for those of us who have achieved independence, and for the West—especially for the West, with its ideology based on freedom and human dignity—is to play down a bit this business of national pride. . . . (President Bourguiba of Tunisia.)[181]

'In foreign affairs my Government intends to practise a policy of neutrality. We believe that an underdeveloped country . . . cannot sensibly do otherwise. But it goes without saying that our links with "Western countries" are much closer than those with "Eastern" countries are ever likely to be.' (President Sylvanus Olympio of Togo.)[182]

'After talking with President Kennedy in March 1961, Nkrumah declared his preference for the United States over the Communist camp, and warned Americans not to equate anti-colonialism with Communism.'[183]

'The Indo-Chinese, the Madagascans and the Guineans repeat unceasingly "we love and we always want to love France, but we cannot in any way merge our love for France with infidelity to our own country. Constraint kills love: liberty expands and enriches it." ' (Jacques Rabemananjara.)[184]

'We have said that independence does not mean a rupture with France, that it does not mean an end to co-operation with France whose culture and language will continue to serve the Guineans. . . . From the moment of our independence, without acrimony, without preconceived ideas, we have held out our hands to France. What we wanted, and what we still want, is that new relationships may be established between the French nation and the young Guinean nation to the greater advantage of both peoples.' (Sékou Touré.)[185]

'President Keita said that at present technicians in Mali were mainly French. If however relations between Mali and France did not return to normal and the French in Mali were threatened by the French Government with the loss of their nationality if they remained in Mali, the Republic of Mali would seek the technical assistance essential to her survival from all countries of the world.[186]

African Personality

No phrase is in more constant use than *African personality*; yet it is seldom defined : Aimé Césaire illustrates the vagueness with which it is often used when he discusses Sékou Touré's answers to the question of how Africa will find the 'ways and means' for its growth and development.

With regard to the economy, for example, Sékou Touré would say it must 'rediscover its *African personality*'. With regard to law, that it must be worked out on the basis of 'the *African personality*'. Of education, that its mission is 'the rehabilitation and blossoming of the *African personality*'. Always the same word, always the same fundamental requirement, Africa; and the same endeavour to dislodge the 'spirit of singularity' in all places at the same time.'[187]

Explaining the significance of the first Conference of Independent African States Dr. Nkrumah said : 'For too long in our history, Africa has spoken through the voice of others. Now, what I have called an *African personality* in international affairs will have a chance of making a proper impact through the voices of Africa's own sons.'[188] Mr. Tom Mboya says : 'The *African personality* would be meaningless unless it were to be identified with the noble things Africa fought for. . . . She has a clean past and a new start, and instead of joining any of the present power blocs or forming just another bloc, she should concentrate on establishing her own personality in the context of dedication to basic individual freedoms and civil liberties.'[189]

The clearest definition is that offered by the writer Alioun Diop : 'The *African personality*, which is the basis and foundation of our humanism, aspires . . . to being freed from the Western grip. *It requires that our people should speak through us.* . . . Our peoples only mean to give expression to what they alone can show forth : how they see themselves, how they identify themselves in the context of the world situation and of the great problems of mankind. . . .'[190]

Neo-Colonialism

'By *neo-colonialism* we mean the practice of granting a sort of independence with the concealed intention of making the liberated country a client-state, and controlling it effectively by means other than political ones. What has happened in the Congo is an example.' (Alex Quaison-Sackey, Ghana's Representative at the UN.)[191]

'*Neo-colonialism* emerged attempting to attain the same aims of exploitation as the old colonialism, using new methods which outwardly appear to be more in line with the spirit of the age. In this domain, military pacts are directed more against internal fronts of nations seeking to free themselves . . . rather than against foreign aggression. In the same way aid and trade were used as a veil to dominate the resources of nations and exhaust them to the benefit of the exploiters. The policy of economic and monopoly blocs was equally directed to this end.' (Colonel Nasser.)[192]

'The Imperialists of today endeavour to achieve their ends not merely by military means, but by economic penetration, cultural assimilation, ideological domination, psychological infiltration, and subversive activities even to the point of inspiring and promoting assassination and civil strife.' (Dr. Nkrumah.)[193]

'. . . The European Common Market . . . is but the economic and financial arm of *neo-colonialism* and the bastion of European economic imperialism in Africa. The Treaty of Rome, which brought into being the European Common Market, can be compared to the treaty that emanated from the Congress of Berlin in the nineteenth century. The former treaty established the undisputed sway of colonialism in Africa; the latter marks the advent of *neo-colonialism* in Africa. In another sense it may be said that the Treaty of Rome, particularly in its effects on Africa, bears unquestionably the marks of French *neo-colonialism*. Indeed, the former French Investment Fund for Economic and Social Development has become the Fund for Financial Assistance and Co-operation, and the European Fund claiming to help newly-independent African States economically and financially are now one and the same thing. The Fund . . . simply reduces that territory to the position of an exclusive market for the economy of the metropolitan country.' (Dr. Nkrumah.)[194]

Although *neo-colonialism* recognises the danger that new forms of subjection may come from sources other than Western,* its commonly accepted meaning is of a threat by the former colonial powers to establish 'backdoor colonialism'. It derives principally from a suspicion of Western intentions based on the history of former colonial relationships. It is quick to point to the fact that out of approximately £185 million granted by France for spending in Africa in 1962, more than £57 million is for French military forces and installations.[195]

'Balkanisation'

The first application of this term to Africa is attributed to President Senghor. It is the favourite running-mate of *neo-colonialism*.

* See page 115.

'The colonialists are ready to "finance" as much independence as one wants; they are ready to flatter African Governments and to wax enthusiastic before the three million free
Guineans, before the thirty million Nigerians, etc. . . . But
their Machiavellian plan still aims at dividing the African in
order to remain master of the Continent.' (Sékou Touré.)[196]

'We are convinced that the States of Africa will never be
independent, in the full sense of the word, if they remain
small States, more or less opposed one to another, each having
its own policy, its own economy, each taking no account of
the policy of the others.' (Modeiba Keita.)[197]

'The *balkanisation* of Africa is a source of weakness to our
Continent. The forces of imperialism and of neo-imperialism
will find their own strength in this basic weakness of our
Continent. Surely, one would have expected that if we have
a chance to undo part of the harm that has already been done
by this *balkanisation* of our Continent, we would not hesitate
in taking that chance.' (Prime Minister Nyerere.)[198]

'As the former colonial territories become independent, new
dangers await us. The European colonial powers, although
they are now being compelled by the force of African nationalism to grant independence, are nonetheless planning to continue to dominate Africa by a new system of foreign domination, namely the *balkanisation* of Africa. They are ready to
grant independence, but under certain conditions, such as the
negotiation of defence agreements and the guarantee of
economic advantages such as would satisfy the demands of
African nationalism. By this means, they expect to be able to
create a large number of small independent States, but which
shall continue to be dependent upon the former colonial
powers perpetually for their economic, technological, social
and cultural development.' (Ako Adjei, Foreign Minister of
Ghana.)[199]

Instances of *balkanisation* frequently cited by sections of African
leaders are the secession of Katanga; the separate independence of
Mauritania, and Togo; and the break-up of the Mali Federation.
The leaders of these three countries, and their supporters, naturally
take a different view.

Dr. Azikiwe, too, has given a different perspective to this
question.

'From the evidence at our disposal it would appear that
whilst European nations may be rightly accused of *balkanising*
Africa in the nineteenth century, yet they have atoned for it
by federating many African territories, which are now being
balkanised by African nationalists on the attainment of the
independence of their countries. The British West Africa,

French West Africa and French Equatorial Africa are examples of *balkanisation* by African nationalists, and the Central African Federation is an example of *balkanisation* in process brought about by the racial segregation and discrimination practices by a small minority of European settlers against the African majority who are the owners of their countries.'[200]

Closely allied with *balkanisation* are the popular current ideas about tribalism and federalism *versus* strong central government, puppet rulers, and African unity.

'The Congo provides a striking example of how federation can be used as a cloak to conceal new colonialism. In fact this type of federalism is not federation at all. It is separation. It does not unite, it *balkanises*. . . . Fundamentally the reason African ethnic groups failed to maintain their independence and succumbed to colonialism was that they were too small and not economically viable. The whole history of colonial penetration of Africa was the history of the colonial powers supporting one ethnic group against the other and exploiting African differences so that, in the end, all came equally under the colonial yoke. . . . The masses who struggled for independence did not do so in order to put a handful of puppets into power. . . . But we have, or should have, an effective answer to *balkanisation*, and the answer is African unity.' (Dr. Nkrumah.)[201]

African Democracy

Rejection of dictatorship and belief in the democratic ideal are attitudes common to virtually all African leaders.

'If I thought Africans could not produce a democracy I would leave politics.' (Leopold Senghor.)[202]

'With the failure of parliamentary democracy in many newly-independent countries, it has become fashionable for a school of political philosophers to assert, sometimes with an air of superiority, and often with that of finality, that democracy cannot be exported. . . . Some . . . even assert that the African or the Asiatic (*sic*) is basically authoritarian and dictatorial. It would seem that these philosophers do not appreciate the difference between the failure of parliamentary democracy on the one hand and the failure of democracy on the other; the Westminster brand of democracy, or what has been referred to as "cricket" democracy, is one method of ensuring democracy as a form of government. If that method fails, another might succeed. . . . The failure of parliamentary democracy in a newly independent country should therefore be regarded

rather as a temporary aberration than as a permanent deviation from the democratic ideal.' (Sir Abubaker Tafawa
Balewa.)[203]

'Every mortal blow that is struck by an independent African
nation at the vitals of democracy is rationalised by [these]
theorists as the African's peculiar method of adapting democratic usages to his barbaric and primitive environment. . . .
The outrageous declaration by an African leader that a one-
party system is in accord with the democratic way of life has
been ably defended by [these] spokesmen of the Western
democracies. . . . But it is an affront to the African race to
suggest that they are incapable of applying these principles.
. . . Communists have laid down dogmatic methods for the
practice of Communism. Any deviation . . . is condemned and
denounced. . . . There are no dogmas for the practice of
democracy; and democrats cannot and must not censure any
nation on the grounds of deviationism. But they must at least
have the courage and honesty to insist that a flagrant departure
from the ideal of democracy is not an acceptable variant of the
most beneficent and ennobling form of government which
mankind . . . has evolved.' (Chief Awolowo, Leader of Nigeria's
Opposition.)[204]

'I must say that . . . I have my own doubts about the
suitability for Africa of the Anglo-Saxon form of democracy.'
(Julius Nyerere.)[205]

'There are two ways of governing a country. In the first
way, the State may substitute itself for all initiative, all men,
all consciences. At that moment it deprives the people of their
liberty of initiative, places them under conditions and in consequence passes itself off as omniscient by trying to solve general
problems and problems of details simultaneously. Such a State
can only be anti-democratic and oppressive. We have adopted
the second way and chosen to be a democratic State.' (Sékou
Touré.)[206]

Democracy by Discussion

'Democracy is essentially government by *discussion*. . . .'
(Sir Abubaker Tafawa Balewa.)[207]

'To the ancient Greeks "democracy" meant simply government by discussion. . . . But not all the people assembled for
these discussions . . . those who took part in them were the
"equals". . . . The two factors of democracy which I want to
bring out here are "*discussion*" and "*equality*". Both are
essential to it, and both contain a third element "freedom".'
(Julius Nyerere.)[208]

'Democracy, the freedom of all the supporters to exert
themselves in the conception of the problems, in the *discussion*

of the problems, and in the choice of solutions to be carried out. On the other hand, the leadership of the Party for its part, has complete freedom in the achievement of the tasks decided upon, and in the judgment of the forms of action appropriate to the objective conditions of this achievement.' (Sékou Touré.)[209]

For and against the One-Party State

'An organised opposition is *not* an essential element. . . . An organised opposition may arise, or it may not; but whether it does or not depends entirely upon the choice of the people themselves and makes little difference to free discussion and equality in freedom.' (Julius Nyerere.)[210]

'I can understand that some countries may find a second party superfluous if nearly everyone is agreed on the essentials. In this case, what is important is that minority opinion should be able to express itself, independently or within the party, without intimidation. I would agree with my friend Julius Nyerere . . . that the test of a democratic régime in Africa might not necessarily be the actual presence of a second party, or several parties, so much as whether or not the régime tolerated individualists. This is a crucial point, for societies are not built or improved by conformists.' (Sylvanus Olympio.)[211]

'Opposition parties must develop not because the text books say so but rather as a normal and natural process of the individual freedom of speech and freedom to criticise government, and the right of a people to return a government of their choice by use of the ballot box. . . . In practice when a country has just won its independence . . . [there will be room only] for a very weak and small opposition . . . at least in the initial period. Unless a split occurs in the ranks of the new nationalist Government, this situation may continue for ten or even more years. This does not mean the abandonment of democracy, but it is a situation which calls for great vigilance on the part of the people in respect of their individual freedoms.' (Tom Mboya.)[212]

'Leaders of opposition parties, who may have fought for independence just as valiantly as anybody else, find themselves the recipients of practically nothing. Herein lies the rub. It is only natural for these people to feel they have been given a raw deal . . . they are almost certain to despise and denounce their opponents. . . . Their opponents will regard this as mischievous detraction. . . . And so the stage is set for full-scale mudslinging which sometimes culminates in the governing party clamping down on their opponents with the force of law. . . . The problem we are facing here is how to make it

possible for leaders of opposition parties to share in the gratitude and admiration which the masses lavish on their rivals in
the early years of independence. For this there seems to be no
better idea than that during the first ten years or so there
should be "national" Governments. . . .' (Dunduza K.
Chisiza.)[213]

'The greatest danger to the survival of the Opposition
arises where the Government has an overwhelming majority.
The party which "brings in" independence . . . almost in-
variably gets overwhelming support at the start of independence . . . the Government party is often tempted to rule
without regard to the rights or views of the Opposition. Some
countries even go to the length of being hostile to the Opposition and their supporters. This . . . is undemocratic.' (Chief
H. O. Davies, QC.)[214]

'Both the Government and the Opposition must be strong
to survive. But they must not crush the Opposition. One must
be pragmatic like the English. When the Opposition is within
the law, allow it; but when it is against the law, don't stand
for it.' (Leopold Senghor.)[215]

'Democracy and a one-party system of government are, in
my opinion, mutually exclusive. Under a one-party system the
party in power arrogates to itself the right to be the only
ruling party for all time. . . .' (Chief Awolowo.)[216]

'Unless an Opposition, as a "Shadow Cabinet" which is
capable of replacing the Government exists, democracy becomes a sham. . . . Failure to tolerate the existence of an
Opposition party would be disastrous to the existence of
democracy.' (Dr. N. Azikiwe.)[217]

Democratic Centralism

'Although we have only one political party . . . free
democratic practice is respected at our meetings. All opinions
are expressed and that which gains the most votes is considered to be the right one and consequently the one whose
policy is applied. . . .' (Modeiba Keita.)[218]

Modeiba Keita's description is that of *democratic centralism* to
which he, Sékou Touré and Dr. Nkrumah subscribe. Its basis is
that the Party and the State are the same; both rest on the people's
will, and they must be democratically consulted in the *formulation*
of policy.

'*Democratic centralism* carries the following principles :
(*a*) All responsible men in the Party are directly and democratically chosen by the supporters who enjoy total liberty of
conscience and of expression within the Party. (*b*) An affair

of the State of Guinea is the affair of all the citizens of Guinea. The programme of the Party is democratically discussed. As long as no decision has been made, each is free to say what he thinks or what he wishes. But when, after extensive discussion in congress or in assembly, a decision has been arrived at by a unanimous vote or by a majority, the supporters and the leaders are bound to apply it correctly. (c) The responsibility for leadership is not shared. Only the responsibility for a decision is shared. Thus, no distortion of discipline should be permitted.' (Sékou Touré.)[219]

'In our Party all are equal regardless of their race or tribe. All are free to express their views. But once a majority decision is taken, we expect such a decision to be loyally executed, even by those who have opposed that decision. This we consider and proclaim to be the truest form of *democratic centralism*— decisions freely arrived at and loyally executed. This applies from the lowest to the highest level. None is privileged and no one shall escape disciplinary action.' (Dr. Nkrumah.)[220]

African Law and Justice

'The question is to transform, to renovate, to reconvert the *matter* as well as the *spirit* of Justice ... It is not to African peoples that one needs to speak about Justice because there is not one African, not one coloured man who, since his coming of age, has not longed for real justice ... because in the course of history ... coloured people, through incomprehension, self-ishness, wickedness, have been bullied, humiliated, discredited, disqualified. . . . The qualitative change in our judicial practices and political behaviour of our magistrates are the two elements of a single problem : Justice—rapid, demo-cratic and humane.' (Sékou Touré.)[221]

'The Government believe that the courts of law should be absolutely independent of the Executive, and should be a bulwark for the defence of the rights of the individual ... Un-fortunately it is impossible to include fundamental rights ... in the Independent Order in Council, but it is the Govern-ment's intention to include these fundamental rights in the constitution once Independence has been granted.' (Dr. Nkrumah.)[222]

The Law of Lagos* 'to safeguard and advance the will of the people and the political rights of the individual' was enacted at a conference on the Rule of Law organised by the International Commission of Jurists in the Nigerian capital in January 1961. It was attended by one hundred and ninety-four judges, members of

* See Appendix 18.

the legal and academic profession from twenty-three African countries. One of the questions the Conference discussed was Preventive Detention. Almost unanimously they condemned its practice, while at the same time recognising the difficulties faced by newly-independent countries.

'The most crucial issue in the discussions was the concern felt by all the participants for the observance of the fundamental human rights and the limits within which these should be fostered with due regard for the security of the State. Most participants deplored all attempts by Governments to muzzle criticisms of their actions by well-disposed persons anxious for the supremacy of the Rule of Law, and everyone felt that there should be real freedom of expression and of the Press, but that the need for State security should not be overlooked.' (Dr. T. O. Elias, Attorney-General and Minister of Justice, Nigeria.)[223]

'Some of the participants questioned whether specifically African needs do not call for the recognition of a specifically African legality. This may be recognised without falling into contradiction, for there is a universal principle of legality according to which all political, economic and juridical institutions should be conceived for man and not vice versa, while there are at the same time principles of legality peculiar to Africa ... In Africa the liberation of man ... cannot be obtained except through observance of the essential requirements of independence, unity, democracy and economic development. Similarly, principles of law applied in Africa must achieve a synthesis between more recent and customary law.' (Gabriel d'Arboussier, Minister of Justice, Senegal.)[224]

In his proposals for establishing 'a concert of Africa', Dr. Azikiwe has put forward the idea that it should promulgate 'an African Convention of Human Rights as an earnest of their belief in the rule of law, democracy as a way of life, respect for individual freedom, and respect for human dignity. This convention of human rights should declare categorically the faith of the Members of the concert of Africa in freedom under the law.'*

Summing-Up

No African leader believes that the Anglo-Saxon or Westminster model of parliamentary government can be transplanted to Africa. All *say* they believe in democracy, although this need not necessarily be parliamentary democracy (Abubaker, Nyerere, Olympio, Nkrumah, Sékou Touré, Modeiba Keita, Mboya). Some, however,

* See Appendix 25.

insist on the model of parliamentary democracy, because they believe in the essential safeguard of an organised Opposition (Awolowo, Azikiwe). The right of an organised Opposition to exist is also recognised by those who do not necessarily subscribe to 'parliamentary democracy'. (Abubaker, Nyerere, Mboya, Olympio, Senghor, Chisiza, Bourguiba). But not everybody in this latter category accepts that an organised Opposition is essential to the working of democracy, at least not in the early stages of independence. (Mboya, Nyerere, Olympio). There is a widespread belief that because of the nature of the circumstances in which many African States come to their independence, a period of *national government* might be the right answer (Chisiza, Mboya). A special category of leaders either believe in, or subscribe to *democratic centralism*.

How have these diverse views worked out in practice in the independent African States? Of the twenty-eight States (excluding South Africa), seven have established Coalition or National Governments while permitting the existence of political parties and of elections (Cameroun, Chad, Congo (Brazzaville), Congo (Leopoldville), Dahomey, Gabon and Somalia).

Eight maintain one-party States in which no other political parties either exist or are allowed to exist (Central African Republic, Guinea, Mali, Ivory Coast, Mauritania, Niger, UAR, Upper Volta).

Six have Governments in which a single party controls all, or virtually all, the seats; but allow for opposition parties to organise themselves and to participate in elections (Ghana, Liberia, Senegal, Tanganyika, Togo, Tunisia).

One has military rule (the Sudan); one has Imperial rule (Ethiopia); one has semi-Imperial rule (Libya); and one has a mixture of Imperial rule and party political freedom (Morocco).

Only two maintain a system of parliamentary democracy (Nigeria and Sierra Leone).

African Socialism and Marxism

In the language of the left-wing of African nationalism, socialism and Marxism are seldom differentiated as between 'Marxist socialism' and 'democratic socialism'. The emphasis is always heavily on 'African socialism'.

> 'The Marxism which served to mobilise the African populations, and in particular the working class, and to lead that class to success, has been amputated of those of its characteristics

which did not correspond to the African realities.' (Sékou Touré.)[225]

'Socialism is based, by definition, not only on race, but also on geography and history—political and economic. It is these values, especially the cultural values of sentiment, which constitute the contribution which the new Negroes can make to the rendezvous of giving and receiving : to the convergent current of socialism, in a word to the "New Directions of Socialism"... We have developed co-operation, not *collectivist,* but *communal.* For co-operation—of family, village, tribe—has always been honoured in Black Africa; once again, not in collectivist form, not as an aggregate of individuals, but in communal form, as mutual agreement.' (Leopold Senghor.)[226]

'These aims [of the CPP] embrace the creation of a welfare state based upon African socialist principles, adapted to suit Ghanaian conditions, in which all citizens, regardless of class, tribe, colour or creed, shall have equal opportunity... our party also seeks to promote popular democracy based upon universal suffrage—on"one man one vote".' (Dr. Nkrumah.)[227]

Arab socialism repeats the same theme.

'The Arab socialist feels free to be inspired by all that has been created by human thought. He feels free to construct and to add to his heritage. While the communist strictly obeys the principles which are the basis of his indoctrination, the Arab socialist is a faithful adherent to the history of the problems and realities of his people and his country.' (Mohammed Hassanine Heikal.)[228]

'The [Egyptian] Revolution laid down for itself six principles, declared in the name of the people to achieve Arab socialism. These principles were inspired by the past—its errors and its sins—and by the present with its positive strides, and by both the foreseeable and the far-off future. These were : eradication of imperialism and its agents; eradication of feudalism; eradication of monopoly and the control of capital over the Executive; setting up a strong national army; establishing social justice; setting up a sound democratic life.' (Aly Sabry, UAR Minister for Presidential Affairs.)[229]

'African socialism', is in its essence *deviationist.** It permits 'borrowing' of ideas, but rejects the importation of international communist ideology. Although Sékou Touré, Dr. Nkrumah and others talk about the 'working class', 'the peasants', etc., they quarrel *a priori* with the class-war. Sékou Touré's draft of the CGTA manifesto† 'rejects the class struggle because of African social groups' identity of living conditions and lack of differentia-

* See *Karl Marx in Africa,* page 104.   † See page 82.

tion into antagonistic classes, and because of the economic and political alienation to which the peoples of tropical Africa are at present subjected.'[230] 'We have rejected from scientific socialism, atheism and violence, as being fundamentally contrary to our nature . . .' (Leopold Senghor.)[231] In his *Autobiography* Dr. Nkrumah describes himself as a 'Christian Marxist'.

CHAPTER VIII

CONCLUSION

If we look at Pan-Africanism today, just four years after its transplantation to Africa's soil, we see unmistakable signs of severe strains developing between its component parts. But we see something else as well. Despite all the setbacks, quarrels and divisions the desire for unity has grown stronger, not weaker, in these last four years. More, not fewer, leaders, movements and governments have embraced the cause of unity. Their argument is not over the need for unity, but about the best way of achieving it. Admittedly such arguments often produce a divisive rather than a unifying result, because in the end the argument becomes more important than the objective. But this has not yet happened in Africa. That the urge towards closer unity is still stronger than the divisive forces is not altogether surprising. Modern Pan-Africanism is reacting realistically to Africa's fundamental problem: its disunity. Tribalisms, a plethora of unviable states, vying nationalisms, rival ideas, and divergent loyalties are part of Africa's disorder. Everywhere the need is for unity: unity within the new states still struggling to become real nation-states; unity between states; unity in economic programmes to allow for a swift, co-ordinated effort to lift Africa out of its poverty; unity in the fight to get rid of the remnants of colonialism, and to ward off neo-colonialism; and unity to establish Africa's voice in international affairs.

If Africa is to avoid either the neo-colonialist inheritance that came to Latin America or the divisions of Asia, it will need a Pan-African movement capable of creating a framework of unity. If this movement divides against itself—as there are signs of its doing —Africa will become, like all the others, a divided continent.

Are there special reasons—historical, economic or political—that would lead one to believe that Africa might succeed where the others have failed? Pan-Africanists claim they have a common history of colonialism and a determination to make up, through revolutionary crash-programmes, for the crucial century lost in the race towards modern technical, economic and educational development. Is this enough? Pan-African unity is strongest when it is fighting against colonialism. But this is no guarantee that its leaders can unite among themselves when the task is to work together, and not simply to fight against a 'common enemy'.

There are those who believe that Pan-Africanism is finished; that it has fulfilled what was a limited political rôle during the period of colonial oppression; and that it has nothing constructive to offer to an independent Africa. But Africa is not yet independent. There are still colonies—Portuguese, Spanish and a few British. There is still the great problem of Algeria, and the still greater problem of South Africa. Even after colonialism, suspicions about neo-colonialism will remain. Economically and politically the continent has everything to gain from Pan-African planning; more even than Europe, and much more than Asia. Africa alone has produced a highly-developed 'pan-continental' movement. This is surely not without some significance. At the very least it demonstrates a belief in the value of a wider unity. Africa's modern leaders are being brought up in the tradition of Pan-Africanism. Is it something they will surrender quickly or easily? Can they succeed?

The chauvinisms, jealousies, suspicions, love of power, devotion to the sanctity of sovereignty, and all the weaknesses and foibles of politicians, political movements and governments known to every part of the world operate equally strongly in Africa. Pan-Africanists claim that Africa starts with a 'clean-sheet'; this is an anti-historical view. They claim they are a moral force of a kind no longer dominant in the West or in the East. Everybody likes to believe they are more moral than anybody else. The truth is that few are.

Nowhere in this book have I made any claims about Pan-Africanism. I have tried to describe it as objectively as I can. I have no views of my own about whether it will succeed or fail in the end. I am more concerned at this stage to understand it, to be 'with it' (in the modern phrase), than to pass judgments on it. That it is a dynamic movement nobody can deny. That it is evolving new ideas and methods with great rapidity is plain. But who can say with any degree of confidence where it will lead?

APPENDICES

I

THE PAN-AFRICAN CONGRESS
Paris, *1919*

RESOLUTION

(a) That the Allied and Associated Powers establish a code of law for the international protection of the natives of Africa, similar to the proposed international code for labour.

(b) That the League of Nations establish a permanent Bureau charged with the special duty of overseeing the application of these laws to the political, social and economic welfare of the natives.

(c) The Negroes of the world demand that hereafter the natives of Africa and the peoples of African descent be governed according to the following principles:

(i) *The Land.* The land and its natural resources shall be held in trust for the natives and at all times they shall have effective ownership of as much land as they can profitably develop.

(ii) *Capital.* The investment of capital and granting of concessions shall be so regulated as to prevent the exploitation of the natives and the exhaustion of the natural wealth of the country. Concessions shall always be limited in time and subject to State control. The growing social needs of the natives must be regarded and the profits taxed for social and material benefit of the natives.

(iii) *Labour.* Slavery and corporal punishment shall be abolished and forced labour except in punishment of crime, and the general conditions of labour shall be prescribed and regulated by the State.

(iv) *Education.* It shall be the right of every native child to learn to read and write his own language, and the language of the trustee nation, at public expense, and to be given technical instruction in some branch of industry. The State shall also educate as large a number of natives as possible in higher technical and cultural training and maintain a corps of native teachers.

(v) *The State.* The natives of Africa must have the right to participate in the Government as fast as their development permits, in conformity with the principle that the Government exists for the natives, and not the natives for the Government. They shall at once be allowed to participate in local and tribal government, according to ancient usage, and this participation shall gradually extend, as education and experience proceed, to the higher offices of states; to the end that, in time, Africa is ruled by consent of the Africans . . . whenever it is proven that African natives are not receiving just treatment at the hands of any State or that any State deliberately excludes its civilised citizens or subjects of Negro descent from its body politic and culture, it shall be the duty of the League of Nations to bring the matter to the notice of the civilised world.

2

THE PAN-AFRICAN CONGRESS
Manchester, 1945

The following are some of the principal resolutions passed:

I

To secure equal opportunities for all colonial and coloured people in Great Britain, this Congress demands that discrimination on account of race, creed or colour be made a criminal offence by law.

That all employments and occupations shall be opened to all qualified Africans, and that to bar such applicants because of race, colour or creed shall be deemed an offence against the law.

In connection with the political situation, the Congress observed:

(a) That since the advent of British, French, Belgian and other Europeans in West Africa, there has been regression instead of progress as a result of systematic exploitation by these alien imperialist Powers. The claims of "partnership", "Trusteeship", "guardianship", and the "mandate system", do not serve the political wishes of the people of West Africa.

(b) That the democratic nature of the indigenous institutions of the peoples of West Africa has been crushed by obnoxious and oppressive laws and regulations, and replaced by autocratic systems of government which are inimical to the wishes of the people of West Africa.

(c) That the introduction of pretentious constitutional reforms in West African territories are nothing but spurious attempts on the part of alien imperialist Powers to continue the political enslavement of the peoples.

(d) That the introduction of Indirect Rule is not only an instrument of oppression but also an encroachment on the right of the West African natural rulers.

(e) That the artificial divisions and territorial boundaries created by the imperialist Powers are deliberate steps to obstruct the political unity of the West African peoples.

II

Economic. As regards the West African economic set-up, the Resolution asserted:

(a) That there has been a systematic exploitation of the economic resources of the West African territories by imperialist Powers to the detriment of the inhabitants.

(b) That the industrialisation of West Africa by the indigenes has been discouraged and obstructed by the imperialist rulers, with the result that the standard of living has fallen below subsistence level.

(c) That the land, the rightful property of West Africans, is gradually passing into the hands of foreign Governments and other agencies through various devices and ordinances.

(d) That the workers and farmers of West Africa have not been allowed independent trade unions and co-operative movements without official interference.

(e) That the mining industries are in the hands of foreign monopolies of finance capital, with the result that wherever a mining industry has developed there has been a tendency to deprive the people of their land holdings (e.g. mineral rights in Nigeria and Sierra Leone now the property of the British Government).

(f) That the British Government in West Africa is virtually controlled by a merchants' united front, whose main objective is the exploitation of the people, thus rendering the indigenous population economically helpless.

(g) That when a country is compelled to rely on one crop (e.g. cocoa) for a single monopolistic market, and is obliged to cultivate only for export while at the same time its farmers and workers find themselves in the grip of finance capital, then it is evident that the Government of that country is incompetent to assume responsibility for it.

Commenting on the social needs of the area, the Resolution said:

(a) That the democratic organisations and institutions of the West African peoples have been interfered with, that alien rule has not improved education, health or the nutrition of the West African peoples, but on the contrary tolerates mass illiteracy, ill-health, malnutrition, prostitution, and many other social evils.

(b) That organised Christianity in West Africa is identified with the political and economic exploitation of the West African peoples by alien Powers.

III

1. The principles of the Four Freedoms and the Atlantic Charter be put into practice at once.

2. The abolition of land laws which allow Europeans to take land from the Africans. Immediate cessation of any further settlement by Europeans in Kenya or in any other territory in East Africa. All available land to be distributed to the landless Africans.

3. The right of Africans to develop the economic resources of their country without hindrance.

4. The immediate abolition of all racial and other discriminatory laws at once (the Kipande system in particular) and the system of equal citizenship to be introduced forthwith.

5. Freedom of speech, Press, association and assembly.

6. Revision of the system of taxation and of the civil and criminal codes.

7. Compulsory free and uniform education for all children up to the age of sixteen, with free meals, free books and school equipment.

8. Granting of the franchise, i.e. the right of every man and woman over the age of twenty-one to elect and be elected to the Legislative Council, Provincial Council and all other Divisional and Municipal Councils.

9. A State medical, health and welfare service to be made available to all.

10. Abolition of forced labour, and the introduction of the principle of equal pay for equal work.

IV

DECLARATION TO THE COLONIAL POWERS

The delegates believe in peace. How could it be otherwise, when for centuries the African peoples have been the victims of violence and slavery? Yet if the Western world is still determined to rule mankind by force, then Africans, as a last resort, may have to appeal to force in the effort to achieve freedom, even if force destroys them and the world.

We are determined to be free. We want education. We want the right to earn a decent living; the right to express our thoughts and emotions, to adopt and create forms of beauty. We demand for Black Africa autonomy and independence, so far and no further than it is possible in this One World for groups and peoples to rule themselves subject to inevitable world unity and federation.

We are not ashamed to have been an age-long patient people. We continue willingly to sacrifice and strive. But we are unwilling to starve any longer while doing the world's drudgery, in order to support by our poverty and ignorance a false aristocracy and a discarded imperialism.

We condemn the monopoly of capital and the rule of private wealth and industry for private profit alone. We welcome economic democracy as the only real democracy.

Therefore, we shall complain, appeal and arraign. We will make the world listen to the facts of our condition. We will fight in every way we can for freedom, democracy and social betterment.

V

DECLARATION TO THE COLONIAL PEOPLES

We affirm the right of all colonial peoples to control their own destiny. All colonies must be free from foreign imperialist control, whether political or economic.

The peoples of the colonies must have the right to elect their own Governments, without restrictions from foreign Powers. We say to the peoples of the colonies that they must fight for these ends by all means at their disposal.

The object of imperialist Powers is to exploit. By granting the right to colonial peoples to govern themselves that object is defeated. Therefore, the struggle for political power by colonial and subject peoples is the first step towards, and the necessary prerequisite to, complete social, economic and political emancipation. The Fifth Pan-African Congress therefore calls on the workers and farmers of the Colonies to organise effectively. Colonial workers must be in the front of the battle against imperialism. Your weapons—the strike and the boycott—are invincible.

We also call upon the intellectuals and professional classes of the colonies to awaken to their responsibilities. By fighting for trade union rights, the right to form co-operatives, freedom of the Press, assembly, demonstration and strike, freedom to print and read the literature which is necessary for the education of the masses, you will be using the only means by which your liberties will be won and maintained. Today there is only one road to effective action—the organisation of the masses. And in that organisation the educated colonials must join. Colonial and subject peoples of the world, Unite!

3

EXTRACTS FROM
THE BANDUNG DECLARATION
1955

1. Respect for fundamental human rights and for the purposes and principles of the Charter of the United Nations.

2. Respect for the sovereignty and territorial integrity of all nations.

3. Recognition of the equality of all races and of the equality of all nations large and small.

4. Abstention from intervention or interference in the internal affairs of another country.

5. Respect for the right of each nation to defend itself singly or collectively, in conformity with the Charter of the United Nations.

6. (*a*) Abstention from the use of arrangements of collective defence to serve the particular interests of any of the big Powers.

(*b*) Abstention by any country from exerting pressures on other countries.

7. Refraining from acts or threats of aggression or the use of force against the territorial integrity or political independence of any country.

8. Settlement of all international disputes by peaceful means, such as negotiations, conciliations, arbitration or judicial settlement as well as other peaceful means of the parties' own choice, in conformity with the Charter of the United Nations.

9. Promotion of mutual interest and co-operation.

10. Respect for justice and international obligations.

The Asian-African Conference declares its conviction that friendly co-operation in accordance with these principles would effectively contribute to the maintenance and promotion of international peace and security, while co-operation in the economic, social and cultural fields would help bring about the common prosperity and well-being of all.

4

THE FIRST CONFERENCE OF
INDEPENDENT AFRICAN STATES
Accra, April 15–22, 1958

DECLARATION

We, the African States assembled here in Accra, in this our first Conference, conscious of our responsibilities to humanity and especially to the peoples of Africa, and desiring to assert our African personality on the side of peace, hereby proclaim and solemnly reaffirm our unswerving loyalty to the Charter of the United Nations, the Universal Declaration of Human Rights and the Declaration of the Asian-African Conference held at Bandung.

We further assert and proclaim the unity among ourselves and our solidarity with the dependent peoples of Africa as well as our friendship with all nations. We resolve to preserve the unity of purpose and action in international affairs which we have forged among ourselves in this historic Conference; to safeguard our hard-won independence, sovereignty and territorial integrity; and to preserve among ourselves the fundamental unity of outlook on foreign policy so that a distinctive African Personality will play its part in co-operation with other peace-loving nations to further the cause of peace.

We pledge ourselves to apply all our endeavours to avoid being committed to any action which might entangle our countries to the detriment of our interests and freedom; to recognise the right of the African peoples to independence and self-determination and to take appropriate steps to hasten the realisation of this right; to affirm the right of the Algerian people to independence and self-determination and to exert all possible effort to hasten the realisation of their independence; to uproot forever the evil of racial discrimination in all its forms wherever it may be found; to persuade the Great Powers to discontinue the production and testing of nuclear and thermo-nuclear weapons; and to reduce conventional weapons.

Furthermore, mindful of the urgent need to raise the living standards of our peoples by developing to the fullest possible advantage the great and varied resources of our lands, We hereby pledge ourselves to co-ordinate our economic planning through a joint economic effort and study the economic potentialities, the technical possibilities and related problems existing in our respective States; to promote co-ordinated industrial planning either through our own individual efforts and/or through co-operation with Specialised Agencies of the United Nations; to take measures to increase trade among our countries by improving communications between our respective countries; and to encourage the investment of foreign capital and skills provided they do not compromise the independence, sovereignty and territorial integrity of our States.

Desirous of mobilising the human resources of our respective countries in furtherance of our social and cultural aspirations, We will endeavour to promote and facilitate the exchange of teachers, professors, students, exhibitions, educational, cultural and scientific material which will improve cultural relations between the African States and inculcate greater knowledge amongst us through such efforts as joint youth festivals, sporting events, etc.; We will encourage and strengthen studies of African culture, history and geography in the institutions of learning in the African States; and We will take all measures in our respective countries to ensure that such studies are correctly orientated.

We have charged our Permanent Representatives at the United Nations to be the permanent machinery for co-ordinating all matters of common concern to our States; for examining and making recommendations on concrete practical steps for implementing our decisions; and for preparing the grounds for future Conferences.

Faithful to the obligations and responsibilities which history has thrown upon us as the vanguard of the complete emancipation of Africa, we do hereby affirm our dedication to the causes which we have proclaimed.

RESOLUTIONS

1. Exchange of Views on Foreign Policy

The Conference of Independent African States,

Having made the widest exchange of views on all aspects of foreign policy,

Having achieved a unanimity on fundamental aims and principles,

Desiring to pursue a common foreign policy with a view to safeguarding the hard-won independence, sovereignty and territorial integrity of the Participating States,

Deploring the division of the greater part of the world into two antagonistic blocs,

1. Affirms the following fundamental principles:

   A. Unswerving loyalty to and support of the Charter of the United Nations and respect for decisions of the United Nations;

   B. Adherence to the principles enunciated at the Bandung Conference, namely:

   (i) Respect for the fundamental human rights and for the purposes and principles of the Charter of the United Nations.

   (ii) Respect for the sovereignty and territorial integrity of all nations.

   (iii) Recognition of the equality of all races and of the equality of all nations, large and small.

   (iv) Abstention from intervention or interference in the internal affairs of another country.

   (v) Respect for the right of each nation to defend itself singly or collectively in conformity with the Charter of the United Nations.

   (vi) Abstention from the use of arrangements of collective defence to serve the particular interests of any of the big Powers.

Abstention by any country from exerting pressure on other countries.

(vii) Refraining from acts or threats of aggression or the use of force against the territorial integrity or political independence of any country.

(viii) Settlement of all international disputes by peaceful means such as negotiation, conciliation, arbitration or judicial settlement, as well as other peaceful means of the parties' own choice in conformity with the Charter of the United Nations.

(ix) Promotion of mutual interest and co-operation.

(x) Respect for justice and international obligations.

2. Affirms its conviction that all Participating Governments shall avoid being committed to any action which might entangle them to the detriment of their interest and freedom;

3. Believes that as long as the fundamental unity of outlook on foreign policy is preserved, the Independent African States will be able to assert a distinctive African Personality which will speak with a concerted voice in the cause of Peace in co-operation with other peace-loving nations at the United Nations and other international forums.

2. The Future of the Dependent Territories in Africa

The Conference of Independent African States,

Recognising that the existence of colonialism in any shape or form is a threat to the security and independence of the African States and to world peace,

Considering that the problems and the future of dependent territories in Africa are not the exclusive concern of the Colonial Powers but the responsibility of all members of the United Nations and in particular of the Independent African States,

Condemning categorically all colonial systems still enforced in our Continent and which impose arbitrary rule and repression on the people of Africa,

Convinced that a definite date should be set for the attainment of independence by each of the Colonial Territories in accordance with the will of the people of the territories and the provisions of the Charter of the United Nations,

1. Calls upon the Administering Powers to respect the Charter of the United Nations in this regard, and to take rapid steps to implement the provisions of the Charter and the political aspirations of the people, namely self-determination and independence, according to the will of the people;

2. Calls upon the Administering Powers to refrain from repression and arbitrary rule in these territories and to respect all human rights as provided for in the Charter of the United Nations and the Universal Declaration of Human Rights;

3. Calls upon the Administering Powers to bring to an end immediately every form of discrimination in these territories;

4. Recommends that all Participating Governments should give all possible assistance to the dependent peoples in their struggle to achieve self-determination and independence;

5. Recommends that the Independent African States assembled here should offer facilities for training and educating peoples of the dependent territories;

6. Decides that the 15th April of every year be celebrated as Africa Freedom Day.

3. The Question of Algeria

The Conference of Independent African States,

Deeply concerned by the continuance of war in Algeria and the denial by France to the Algerian people of the right of independence and self-determination despite various United Nations resolutions and appeals urging a peaceful settlement, notably the offer of good offices made by the Moroccan and Tunisian Heads of State,

Considering that the present situation in Algeria constitutes a threat to international peace and the security of Africa in particular,

1. Recognises the right of the Algerian people to independence and self-determination;

2. Deplores the grave extent of hostilities and bloodshed resulting from the continuance of the war in Algeria;

3. Urges France
    (a) to recognise the right of the people of Algeria to independence and self-determination;
    (b) to put an end to the hostilities and to withdraw all her troops from Algeria;
    (c) to enter into immediate peaceful negotiation with the Algerian Liberation Front with a view to reaching a final and just settlement;

4. Appeals to all peace-loving nations to exercise pressure on France to adopt a policy which is in conformity with the principles of the Charter of the United Nations;

5. Appeals to the friends and allies of France to refrain from helping France, whether directly or indirectly, in her military operations in Algeria;

6. Affirms its determination to make every possible effort to help the Algerian people towards the attainment of independence;

7. Recommends that the representatives of the Independent African States at the United Nations be instructed by their various Governments to consult each other constantly and acquaint members of the United Nations with true states of affairs in Algeria and solicit their support for a just and peaceful settlement and to recommend to the Independent African States measures which may from time to time become necessary to be taken and in particular find ways and means whereby the Independent African States may enlighten world opinion on the Algerian situation including the appointment of a mission as soon as possible to tour the capitals of the world to enlist world support of Governments.

4. Racialism

The Conference of Independent African States,

Considering that the practice of racial discrimination and segregation is evil and inhuman,

Deeply convinced that racialism is a negation of the basic principles of human rights and dignity to the extent where it is becoming an element of such explosiveness which is spreading its poisonous influence more and more widely in some parts of Africa that it may well engulf our Continent in violence and bloodshed,

Noting with abhorrence the recent statement made by the head of the South African Government on his re-election to the effect that he will pursue a more relentless policy of discrimination and persecution of the coloured people in South Africa,

1. Condemns the practice of racial discrimination and segregation in all its aspects all over the world, especially in the Union of South Africa, in the Central African Federation, Kenya and in other parts of Africa;

2. Appeals to the religious bodies and spiritual leaders of the world to support all efforts directed towards the eradication of racialism and segregation;

3. Calls upon all members of the United Nations and all peoples of the world to associate themselves with the Resolutions passed by the United Nations and the Bandung Conference condemning this inhuman practice;

4. Calls upon all members of the United Nations to intensify their efforts to combat and eradicate this degrading form of injustice;

5. Recommends that all Participating Governments should take vigorous measures to eradicate where they arise vestiges of racial discrimination in in their respective countries.

5. Steps to be taken to Safeguard the Independence, Sovereignty and the Territorial Integrity of the Independent African States

The Conference of Independent African States,

Determined to safeguard the hard-won independence, sovereignty and territorial integrity of each of its members,

Believing that the getting together and consulting among Independent African States, as in the present Conference of Accra, is essential for the effectiveness of their contribution to world peace,

1. Declares the determination of all Participating Governments
    (a) to respect the independence, sovereignty and territorial integrity of one another,
    (b) to co-operate with one another to safeguard their independence, sovereignty and territorial integrity,
    (c) to co-operate in their economic, technical and scientific developments and in raising the standard of living of their respective peoples,
    (d) to resort to direct negotiations to settle differences among themselves and if necessary to conciliation or mediation by other African Independent States;

2. Condemns all forms of outside interference directed against the independence, sovereignty and territorial integrity of the Independent African States.

6. Togoland under French Administration

The Conference of Independent African States,

Having examined the Memorandum on the situation in Togoland under French Administration submitted by the Juvento Party, and the statement made by the Representative of this Party during the hearing granted to him in the Conference,

Bearing in mind the objectives of the International Trusteeship System and the objectives proclaimed by the Bandung Conference,

Having regard to the extremely important responsibilities laid upon the Legislative Assembly to be elected on 27th April, 1958, as to the future of the territory by paragraphs 7 and 8 of the operative part of the United Nations Resolution of 29th November, 1957,

1. Expresses grave concern regarding the present electoral laws and system of the Territory;

2. Strongly urges that the Administering Authority will co-operate fully with the United Nations Commissioner in order to ensure fair and democratic elections in the Territory.

7. Cameroons Under French Administration

The Conference of Independent African States,

Having examined the Memorandum on the situation in the Cameroons under French Administration submitted by the Union of the Populations of Cameroons, and the statement made by the Representative of this Party during the hearing granted to him in the Conference,

Bearing in mind the objectives of the International Trusteeship System and the objectives proclaimed by the Bandung Conference,

1. Condemns the use of military force against the unarmed people in the Trust Territory of the Cameroons under French Administration as contrary to the spirit of the United Nations;

2. Calls upon the Administering Powers to comply with the Charter of the United Nations and satisfy the legitimate aspirations of the people concerned by opening direct negotiations with their representatives;

3. Appeals to the United Nations to intensify its efforts in helping the people of the Cameroons to achieve their legitimate political aspirations.

8. Examination of Ways and Means of Promoting Economic Co-operation between the African States, based on the Exchange of Technical, Scientific and Educational Information, with Special Regard to Industrial Planning and Agricultural Development

The Conference of Independent African States,

Having discussed the economic and social conditions in their respective countries,

Considering that these countries have great and various economic resources, mineral, agriculture and animal,

Considering that there are now possibilities for commercial exchange between Independent African States and that these possibilities should be greatly encouraged,

Considering that steps should be taken to bring about economic emancipation in these countries,

Considering that hitherto non-African forces have arbitrarily divided the African Continent into economic regions, and that the Conference does not recognise this division,

Considering further that Africa could be developed as an economic unit,

Noting that the incorporation of dependent African territories in the economic systems of colonial Powers is not in the best interests of these peoples,

Recommends to the Participating African States:

1. The establishment within each Independent African State of an Economic Research Committee to survey the economic conditions and to study the economic and technical problems within the State;

2. The establishment of a Joint Economic Research Commission

(a) to co-ordinate information and exchange of views on economic and technical matters of the various Independent African States;

(b) to find measures whereby trade among African countries could be developed and encouraged;

(c) to make proper and detailed investigation as to the possibilities of co-ordinating the economic planning in each State towards the achievement of an all-African economic co-operation;

(d) to find ways and means for common industrial planning within the African States and the possibilities of making available mineral resources and other African products among the African States;

(e) to lay down proposals by which Independent African States can receive foreign capital and employ foreign experts, and to encourage co-operation with other countries in such manner as not to affect their independence, sovereignty and unity;

3. To take steps in order to collect and exchange knowledge and technological information among themselves;

4. To establish joint African enterprises;

5. To hold economic conferences and African exhibitions;

6. To strengthen their co-operation with the Specialised Agencies of the United Nations and especially with the newly proposed Economic Commission for Africa;

7. To make joint efforts as far as practicable to construct means of communications between African States;

8. To investigate the possibility of eventual establishing of an African common market;

9. To provide facilities for exchange of labour and labour information and to encourage co-operation among national trade union organisations;

10. To strengthen the co-operation with the International Labour Organisation;

11. To take joint action for the prevention of diseases among human beings, in agriculture and in animal husbandry, and to act against the ravages of locusts;

12. To ensure the establishment of equitable social and economic policies which will provide national prosperity and social security for all citizens.

9. On the Cultural level, the formulation of concrete Proposals for the Exchange of Visiting Missions between the various Countries, both Government and non-Government, which may lead to first-hand Knowledge of one Country to another, and to a mutual appreciation of their respective Cultures

The Conference of Independent African States,

Having made the widest exchange of views on all aspects of the cultures of all Participating Countries,

Desiring to promote the widest dissemination of the cultures of all Participating Countries,

A. Upholds the principles of the Charter of the United Nations and reaffirms the principles approved by the Bandung Conference of April, 1955, concerning Cultural co-operation, and accordingly;

1. States that colonialism is prejudicial to national culture and as such hinders any possible cultural co-operation;

2. Calls for the development of Cultural Co-operation among African States in the larger context of world co-operation and in the spirit of the United Nations Educational, Scientific and Cultural Organisation;

B. Recommends to all Participating Members;

1. To promote and facilitate the exchange of teachers and professors;

2. To encourage the establishment of cultural centres in each other's country on the approval of the country in which such a centre may be established and in conformity with its laws, regulations and practices;

3. To encourage and facilitate the exchange of their students, each providing a certain number of scholarships for students from other African countries;

4. To facilitate the exchange of exhibitions, educational, scientific and cultural material including books, periodicals, bulletins, audio visual aids and other cultural and educational material;

5. To ensure that syllabi of history and geography applied in the schools and educational institutions of each include such material as may help to give each student an accurate information of the way of life and culture in the other African countries;

6. To spare no efforts to revise history and geography, text books and syllabi used in their schools with the view to removing any incorrect information due to colonial or other foreign influences;

7. To co-ordinate their school systems at all levels and to recognise the certificates, diplomas and degrees awarded by their educational institutions and universities of equivalent status;

8. To encourage reciprocal visits by their different organisations of youths, teachers, Press, labour, women, artists, sports, etc., granting them all possible facilities;

9. To strive to include principal African languages in the curriculum of the secondary school and colleges with the view to facilitating the cultural co-operation envisaged;

10. To hold inter-African periodic and *ad hoc* conferences for their educators, scientists, men of letters, journalists, etc., with the view to discussing common problems and to extend all possible facilities for such purposes;

11. To conclude mutual cultural agreements among them for the promotion of cultural co-operation.

12. To encourage in their universities and institutes of higher learning research on African culture and civilisation creating fellowships for this purpose;

13. To encourage the establishment of African publishing centres and to make concerted efforts to publish an African journal edited and contributed to by Africans introducing Africa's culture, civilisa-

tion and development to the world and to the various African countries;

14. To set up an annual prize for works which promote closer solidarity among the African States, the ideas of liberty, friendship and peace and which disseminate knowledge about African civilisation and culture;

15. To encourage the translation of books dealing with African culture and civilisation into their principal languages, e.g. creating fellowships for this purpose;

16. To establish an annual inter-African sports meeting and an annual youth festival;

17. To set up, each in its respective country, a local organisation whose functions will be the promotion and development of cultural co-operation among African countries.

10. Consideration of the Problem of International Peace and Conformity with the Charter of the United Nations and the Re-affirmation of the Principles of the Bandung Conference

The Conference of Independent African States,

Alarmed at the prospect of nuclear and thermo-nuclear energy being used by the Great Powers for military purposes,

Desiring to strengthen their contribution to world peace and security,

Realising that world peace is a prerequisite for the progress and prosperity of all peoples,

Taking into account the fact that no African nation is at present represented in the international bodies concerned with the problems of disarmament,

1. Calls upon the Great Powers to discontinue the production of nuclear and thermo-nuclear weapons and to suspend all such tests not only in the interest of world peace but as a symbol of their avowed devotion to the rights of man;

2. Views with grave alarm and strongly condemns all atomic tests in any part of the world and in particular the intention to carry out such tests in the Sahara;

3. Appeals to the Great Powers to use atomic, nuclear and thermo-nuclear energy exclusively for peaceful purposes;

4. Affirms the view that the reduction of conventional armaments is essential in the interest of international peace and security and appeals to the Great Powers to make every possible effort to reach a settlement of this important matter;

5. Condemns the policy of using the sale of arms as a means of exerting pressure on Governments and interfering in the internal affairs of other countries;

6. Urges the United Nations to ensure that the African nations are represented equitably on all international bodies concerned with the problems of disarmament;

7. Considers that meeting and consultation on international affairs should not be limited to the big Powers;

8. Expresses its deep concern over the non-compliance with United Nations resolutions, calls upon the Member States to respect such resolutions, and urges a just solution of the outstanding international problems;

9. Expresses its deep concern over the question of Palestine which is a disturbing factor of World Peace and Security, and urges a just solution of the Palestine question;

10. Expresses its deep concern over the South-West African and similar questions which are disturbing factors of World Peace and Security, and urges a just solution to them.

11. The Setting up of a Permanent Machinery after the Conference

The Conference of Independent African States,

Firmly convinced that a machinery for consultation and co-operation is essential,

1. Decides to constitute the Permanent Representatives of the Participating Governments at the United Nations as the informal permanent machinery,

(a) for co-ordinating all matters of common concern to the African States,

(b) for examining and making recommendations on concrete practical steps which may be taken to implement the decisions of this and similar future conferences, and

(c) for making preparatory arrangements for future conferences of Independent African States;

2. Agrees that meetings of Foreign Ministers, other Ministers or experts be convened from time to time as and when necessary to study and deal with particular problems of common concern to the African States;

3. Agrees that the Conference of the Independent African States should be held at least once every two years;

4. Agrees that the next Conference shall be held within the next two years and accepts the kind invitation of the Government of Ethiopia to hold the next Conference in Addis Ababa.

5

THE SECOND CONFERENCE OF INDEPENDENT AFRICAN STATES
Addis Ababa, June 15–24, 1960

1. The Strengthening of International Peace and Security in Conformity with the Charter of the United Nations and the Bandung and Accra Resolutions

The Conference of Independent African States meeting at Addis Ababa,

Reaffirming unswerving loyalty to the Charter of the United Nations, the Universal Declaration of Human Rights and the Declarations of the Bandung and Accra Conferences,

Animated by a sincere desire that Africa, in solidarity with the rest of the world, should play its role in strengthening world peace and security,

Convinced that colonialism is one of the factors which provoke friction between peoples and endanger international peace and security,

Welcoming the progress made at the negotiations conducted in Geneva among the interested States towards the discontinuation of nuclear and thermo-nuclear tests,

Believing that progress in disarmament is an essential condition for reducing international tension and promoting peace,

Viewing with alarm the renewed tension in the world due to the failure of the Summit Conference which was to be held in Paris in May, 1960, among France, the United Kingdom, the United States of America and the Union of Soviet Socialist Republics,

1. Appeals to all States, especially to the Great Powers, to exert their efforts to reduce the international tension;
2. Expresses the hope that:
   (*a*) The efforts made at the United Nations regarding disarmament will lead to positive results,
   (*b*) The discussions held in Geneva between the States concerned on the discontinuance of nuclear and thermo-nuclear tests by effective international control will be concluded successfully;
3. Expresses concern for the non-implementation of the United Nations General Assembly resolutions, the Bandung Declaration and Accra resolutions pertaining to the solution of the problem of Palestine, which is a disturbing factor to world peace and security in the north-east of the African Continent.

2. First Resolution on Algeria

The Conference of Independent African States meeting in Addis Ababa,

Deeply concerned by the continuation of hostilities in Algeria which constitute a great threat to peace and security in Africa and in the world at large,

Confirming Resolutions adopted on Algeria at the Accra and Monrovia Conferences of Independent African States,

Believing:

(a) That the right to self-determination and independence of the Algerian people is a basis upon which a lasting solution can be achieved,

(b) That the conditions for the implementation of the right of self-determination of the Algerian people must be negotiated by the two parties concerned, namely, France and the Provisional Government of the Algerian Republic,

Noting that the two parties have accepted the right of self-determination as a basis for a just and democratic solution of the Algerian problem,

Welcoming the offer made by General de Gaulle on June 14, 1960, for immediate discussions with the Representatives of the Provisional Government of the Algerian Republic, with a view to a settlement of the Algerian problem,

Noting the willingness of the Provisional Government of the Algerian Republic to enter into negotiations with the Government of France on the basis of self-determination for the Algerian people,

Expressing satisfaction at the efforts of those, in France, who have always supported a peaceful and negotiated settlement in Algeria,

Invites France and the Provisional Government of the Algerian Republic to negotiate and reach an agreement on conditions for a fair and sincere implementation of the right of self-determination of the Algerian people, including conditions for a cease-fire.

3. Second Resolution on Algeria

The Conference of Independent African States meeting in Addis Ababa,

Deeply concerned by the continuation of hostilities in Algeria which constitutes a great threat to Peace and Security in Africa and in the world at large,

Confirming Resolutions adopted on Algeria at the Accra and Monrovia Conferences of Independent African States,

Recommends to all Governments of the Independent African States:

(a) continuation of material and diplomatic support for the Algerian cause,

(b) continuation of active and united support for the Algerian cause at the United Nations,

(c) consultation and exchange of views between the Governments on the Algerian question, whenever a situation warranting such action arises,

(d) joint representation by the Independent African States to the Government of France to help in achieving a peaceful and a negotiated settlement based upon the self-determination of the Algerian people,

(e) that missions composed of representatives of the Independent

African States be despatched to the capitals of the world, with a view to soliciting support for the Algerian cause,

(f) that a joint representation should be made by the Independent African States to the NATO Powers, with a view to urging France to desist from using in Algeria arms supplied by that Organisation for defensive purposes,

(g) the withdrawal of all African troops being used by France in Algeria.

4. Resolution on the Question of South-West Africa

The Conference of Independent African States, meeting in Addis Ababa,

(a) Having considered the question of the Territory of South-West Africa,

(b) Recalling United Nations Resolution 1361 (XIV) of November 17, 1959, which drew "the attention of Member States to the conclusions of the special report of the Committee on South-West Africa, covering the legal action open to Member States to refer any dispute with the Union of South Africa concerning the interpretation or the application of the Mandate for South-West Africa to the International Court of Justice for adjudication, in accordance with Article 37 of the Statute of the Court,

1. Concludes that the international obligations of the Union of South Africa concerning the Territory of South-West Africa should be submitted to the International Court of Justice for adjudication;

2. Notes that the Governments of Ethiopia and of Liberia have signified their intention to institute such a proceeding;

3. Decides that a Steering Committee of four African States, including the delegations of Ethiopia and of Liberia, should be established to determine the procedures and tactics incident to the conduct of the juridical proceedings in this matter.

5. Resolution on the Future Status of the Informal Permanent Machinery of the Independent African States

The Conference of Independent African States meeting in Addis Ababa,

Having discussed the future status of the Informal Permanent Machinery of the Independent African States;

Recalling Resolution 13 of the first Conference of Independent African States, meeting in Accra in 1958, which decided to constitute the Permanent Representatives of the participating Governments at the United Nations as the Informal Permanent Machinery;

Expressing great satisfaction at the work done by the Informal Permanent Machinery for co-ordinating the policies of the Independent African States at the United Nations and for making preparatory arrangements for the Conferences;

Noting with the greatest appreciation that the activities of the Informal Permanent Machinery have contributed to the progressive creation of a distinctive African Personality in international affairs;

Decides to request the Informal Permanent Machinery to continue as a transitional organisation pending the establishment of a Permanent

Organisation with a seat in Africa to fulfil its functions in accordance with Resolution 13 of the Accra Conference.

6. The Banning of Nuclear and Thermo-Nuclear Tests in Africa

The Conference of Independent African States meeting at Addis Ababa,

Deeply concerned by the decision of France to continue testing her nuclear and thermo-nuclear devices in the Sahara;

Deploring the defiance of France of the previous appeals and protests of the African States and her disregard of the recommendation of the United Nations contained in General Assembly Resolution 1379 (XIV) of November 20, 1959;

Regretting that France's decision to conduct her tests had come at a time when the other nuclear Powers had agreed to stop all tests, with a view to reaching a final agreement to ban nuclear and thermo-nuclear devices;

1. Strongly condemns the policy of France to continue to use the Sahara as a testing ground for atomic devices;

2. Appeals to the United Nations to urge France to comply with General Assembly Resolution 1379 (XIV) which requested France to refrain from such tests;

3. Recommends that the Independent African States continue to take appropriate measures with a view to preventing atomic tests in the Sahara or any other part of Africa.

7. Promotion of African Unity

The Conference of Independent African States meeting in Addis Ababa,

Having discussed the question of the Promotion of African Unity;

Considering that co-operation and unity among African States are essential for the maintenance of the independence and sovereignty of Africa;

Recalling Resolution V of the Accra Conference, which expressed that the getting together and consulting among Independent African States is essential for the effectiveness of their contribution to world peace;

Noting that Chapter VIII of the United Nations Charter encourages the creation of Regional Organisations;

1. Requests the President of the Conference of Independent African States to address a communication to the Heads of these States to initiate consultations through diplomatic channels with a view to promoting African unity;

2. Decides to inscribe this item on the agenda of the next regular session of the Conference of Independent African States.

8. Resolution on the Appraisal of the Implementation of the Resolutions of the Accra and Monrovia Conferences*

The Conference of Independent African States meeting in Addis Ababa,

Having studied the report of the Informal Permanent Machinery of the African Representatives to the United Nations;

* These conferences refer to the first Conference at Accra in 1958 and to the Conference of Foreign Ministers in Monrovia. See Appendix 9

Expresses its satisfaction with the tangible results obtained in implementing the resolutions of the Accra and Monrovia Conferences;

Congratulates the Informal Permanent Machinery on the way in which it has carried out the tasks assigned to it by virtue of Resolution No. 11 of the Conference of Independent African States held in Accra.

9. Eradication of Colonial Rule from Africa

The Conference of the Independent African States meeting in Addis Ababa,

Recalling the declaration of Bandung and the resolutions of Accra and Monrovia proclaiming that colonialism in all its manifestations constitutes an evil which should speedily be brought to an end;

Reaffirming that the subjugation of peoples to alien domination and exploitation constitutes a denial of fundamental rights which is contrary to the Charter of the United Nations and the Universal Declaration of Human Rights, and is an impediment to the promotion of World Peace and Co-operation;

Considering that Africa is the only Continent where a large proportion of the inhabitants still live under colonial domination with all its privations and indignities;

Considering further that the present awakening of the people of Africa and the independence movements can no longer be contained, without the risk of seriously compromising relations between the diverse nations;

Believing that the restoration of natural rights and human dignity to the Africans, in those parts of Africa, at present under foreign subjugation, as well as the peaceful enjoyment of the hard-won freedom by the peoples of the Independent African States, could only be achieved through the complete eradication of colonial rule from our Continent;

Recalling the courageous stand taken by the freedom fighters in Africa, and saluting the memory of those who sacrificed their lives in defending the liberty of their respective countries;

Conscious of the responsibility of the Independent African States towards those peoples fighting for independence and also of the active solidarity which should be shown towards all African freedom fighters;

Taking into consideration the petitions presented by the representatives of the nationalist movements in the non-independent countries of Africa (Angola, Kenya, Uganda, Northern and Southern Rhodesia, Ruanda-Urundi, the Union of South Africa and South-West Africa);

1. Urges the Colonial Powers to fix dates in conformity with the will of the people for the immediate attainment of Independence by all non-independent countries and to communicate those dates to the people concerned;

2. Resolves that the Independent African States continue to exert concerted action to achieve through all possible peaceful means the complete eradication of colonial rule from Africa;

3. Condemns the practice of colonial Powers of enlisting Africans, against their own will, in foreign armed forces to suppress the liberation movements in Africa;

4. Appeals to the conscience of all Africans to resist enlistment in such foreign armed forces;

5. Appeals further to leaders, political parties and other organisations

of non-independent countries, at this historical phase of their struggle, to unite in a national front to achieve speedy liberation of their countries;

6. Decides to establish a special fund to aid Freedom Fighters in Africa (Africa Freedom Fund);

7. Decides that such a fund be administered by an organ to be established by the Conference in accordance with rules and regulations to be adopted by the Conference;

8. Agrees that the Independent African State contribute to the Africa Freedom Fund on the basis of equitable shares to be agreed upon by the Conference;

9. Recommends to extend assistance and to accord facilities to genuine African political refugees;

10. Decides to offer, if so desired, its good offices to assist in settling differences among leaders and political parties of non-independent countries through its permanent machinery;

11. Appeals to the colonial Powers to refrain from suppressing national liberation movements, to release immediately all political prisoners, detainees and persons under restrictive orders.

10. Eradication of Colonial Rule from Africa: Means to Prevent New Forms of Colonialism in Africa

The Conference of the Independent African States meeting in Addis Ababa,

Welcoming the recent attainment of independence by several countries of Africa;

Reaffirming its faith in the total liberation and emancipation of Africa in the shortest possible time;

Considering the difficulties with which the emerging nations of Africa may be confronted in the political, economic and social fields;

Noting that new forms of colonialism could be introduced into these territories, under the guise of economic, financial and technical assistance;

Considering that some of the non-independent countries may, out of necessity and under pressure, enter into agreements and pacts with foreign Powers which would restrict in advance their total independence and hinder their future freedom of action;

1. Calls upon all colonial Powers to refrain from any action which might compromise the sovereignty and independence of the emerging States;

2. Declares that assistance to the emerging States should be without political conditions;

3. Urges the leaders of the emerging States to consider seriously this question before committing themselves to action which might prejudice the future of their countries;

4. Recommends that independent African States should consider the possibility of introducing a system whereby economic and technical aid can be provided by them collectively;

5. Urges the leaders of non-independent countries to resist any attempt at Balkanisation which is detrimental to the ultimate goal of African unity;

6. Recommends that the Independent African States be wary of colonial penetration through economic means and that they institute effective

control over the working machineries of foreign companies operating in their territories.

11. Resolution on Nyasaland, Southern Rhodesia and Northern Rhodesia

The Conference of Independent African States meeting in Addis Ababa,

Convinced that it is the intention of the settlers to create another South Africa in Central Africa;

Recognising that it is its duty to support the people of Africa in the struggle for independence from foreign rule;

Convinced that the British Government, by its undue delay in carrying out its duty to prepare the Protectorate of Northern Rhodesia and Nyasaland for self-government, and by its forcible imposition of the settlers to control the Government of the Central African Federation;

Demands:

1. that the British Government take immediate steps to dissolve the Federation of Central Africa;

2. that effect be given to all such measures as may be necessary to confer self-government on Northern Rhodesia and Nyasaland, so that they may be free to choose, when, and with which country to federate, according to the wishes of their own people;

3. that the Constitution of Southern Rhodesia be democratised by introducing the principle of "one man, one vote," since the Conference does not consider a Senate with nominated Africans as a sufficient safeguard for the people;

4. that the protective clauses in the present constitutional legislation be maintained until such time as the democratic constitution has been promulgated;

5. that all Political detainees in Northern Rhodesia, Nyasaland and Southern Rhodesia be released and that the ban on the Copperbelt Division of the United National Independent Party of Northern Rhodesia be lifted.

12. Policy of Apartheid and Racial Discrimination in Africa

The Conference of Independent African States meeting in Addis Ababa,

Having learned with indignation of the death of many African political leaders in the prisons of the Union of South Africa, thus adding to the already long list of victims of the shameful policy of racial discrimination;

Recalling resolution No. 1375 (XIV), adopted by the United Nations General Assembly, condemning the policy of apartheid and racial discrimination practised by the Government of the Union of South Africa;

Recalling further the Security Council's Resolution of April 1, 1960, recognising the existence of a situation in South Africa which, if continued, might endanger international peace and security;

Reaffirming the declaration of Bandung and the resolutions adopted at Accra and Monrovia regarding this shameful policy;

Noting that, despite world opinion and the resolutions adopted by the United Nations, the Government of the Union of South Africa still persists in its evil policy of apartheid and racial discrimination;

1. Desires to pay homage to all victims of the shameful policy of apartheid and racial discrimination;

2. Decides to assist the victims of racial discrimination and furnish them with all the means necessary to attain their political objectives of liberty and democracy;

3. Calls upon Member States to sever diplomatic relations or refrain from establishing diplomatic relations, as the case may be, to close African ports to all vessels flying the South African flag, to enact legislation prohibiting their ships from entering South African ports, to boycott all South African goods, to refuse landing and passage facilities to all aircraft belonging to the Government and companies registered under the laws of the Union of South Africa and to prohibit all South African aircraft from flying over the air-space of the Independent African States;

4. Invites the Arab States to approach all petroleum companies with a view to preventing Arab oil from being sold to the Union of South Africa and recommends that the African States refuse any concession to any company which continues to sell petroleum to the Union of South Africa;

5. Invites the Independent African States which are members of the British Commonwealth to take all possible steps to secure the exclusion of the Union of South Africa from the British Commonwealth;

6. Recommends that appropriate measures be taken by the United Nations in accordance with Article 41 of the Charter;

7. Appeals to world public opinion to persevere in the effort to put an end to the terrible situation caused by apartheid and racial discrimination;

8. Decides to instruct the Informal Permanent Machinery to take all steps necessary to secure that effect shall be given to the above recommendations and to furnish full information on cases of racial discrimination in the Union of South Africa, so that the outside world may be correctly informed about such practices.

13. Resolution for the Creation of an Organisation for African Economic Co-operation

The Conference of Independent African States meeting in Addis Ababa,

Having examined the economic problems confronting Africa;

Considering that the effects of the collective measures taken by European Powers are inimical to the interests and the prosperity of African countries;

Considering economic co-operation between African Independent States is indispensable to their stability and the survival of their independence;

Understanding how important it is to organise technical assistance among the African States;

Considering that it is necessary to establish a collective approach by the Independent African States to the Economic Commission for Africa and to the specialist institutions of the United Nations;

Recognising the important role of the Economic Commission for Africa in the sphere of economic and social development and conscious of the increasing need of such a contribution for the development of economic co-operation in Africa;

Taking into account the lack of a competent organisation able to organise, co-ordinate, establish and maintain African economic unity;

Conscious moreover that the creation of an organisation for African economic co-operation will contribute immensely to the economic stability of the Independent African States and of those which are on the point of becoming independent;

Recommends:

1. The creation of an organisation which shall be named African Council of Economic Co-operation;

2. An immediate meeting of experts of the Independent African States to formulate the functions, the jurisdiction and other details concerning this Council, and provided their report is approved by the Member States, to propose a date for the first meeting of this Council;

3. An invitation to the member countries to give effect to all the resolutions of an economic character adopted by the Conferences of the Independent African States.

14. Education, Culture and Science

The Conference of Independent African States,

Recalling Resolution No. 9, Point 3, on cultural questions adopted by the first Conference of Independent African States at Accra;

Desirous of putting into practice the decisions of the said resolution;

Convinced that their implementation is indispensable to the maintenance and development of African culture and to the development of educational, cultural and scientific co-operation between the African States;

Recommends:

1. The creation of an organisation to be known as the "Council for Educational, Cultural and Scientific Co-operation in Africa";

2. The immediate convocation of a meeting of specialists in matters of education, culture and science from the African States to formulate the functions, jurisdiction and other details of the organisation above-mentioned, and if the report of these experts is approved by the Member States, they should propose a suitable date for the meeting of this organisation;

Invites the Member States and the Council for Educational, Cultural and Scientific Co-operation in Africa to apply all the resolutions relative to educational, cultural and scientific questions adopted by the Conferences of Independent African States.

15. The Promotion of Economic Co-operation among African States

The Conference of Independent African States meeting in Addis Ababa,

1. Believing that the development of economic and social conditions in Africa is conducive to the improvement of the standard of living of the African peoples and a guarantee of the stability and independence of the African States;

2. Considering that closer economic relations between the African States constitutes one of the means to realise the above objective; and further,

3. Considering that it has now become urgent to stimulate trade relations between the African States in this respect;

4. Recalling Sub-section 4 of the Resolution on Economic and Social

matters of item No. 2 of the First Conference of the Independent African States held at Accra; and further,

A.

5. Recalling Resolution No. 11 of the Second Session of the Economic Commission for Africa, held in Tangiers; and in order to meet the specific needs of the African Countries;

Recommends:

1. That a joint African Development Bank be established;
2. That a joint African Commercial Bank be established;
3. That the Council for African Economic Co-operation shall immediately upon its establishment call a committee of experts from among Member States:

(a) To submit to it draft articles of Agreement;
(b) To propose capital quotas to be allotted to each Member State;
(c) To study payment difficulties among Member States, and propose concrete measures for the removal of these difficulties;
(d) To undertake all measures necessary to expedite the creation of such Banks;

Authorises the committee of experts to seek (through the Economic Commission for Africa) the assistance of the appropriate international bodies in carrying out this project.

B.

Considering that an ever-increasing movement of persons, commodities and ideas is conducive to unity; and further,

Considering that the structure of customs tariffs of Member States is paramount for expanding such movement among African States;

Recalling Sub-section 2 (b) of the Resolution on Economic and Social matters of item No. 2 of the First Conference of Independent African States held at Accra; and further,

Recalling Resolution No. 8 of the Second Session of the Economic Commission for Africa held in Tangiers;

Recommends:

1. That the Council for African Economic Co-operation shall immediately upon its establishment call a committee of experts from among Member States:

(a) To review the structure of customs tariffs of the Independent African States;
(b) To propose to Member States specific improvements in their customs tariffs;
(c) As a first step, to propose preferential treatments, to be applied among themselves; and

2. That the committee of experts shall submit a report to the Council for Economic Co-operation;

3. Authorises the experts' committee to seek through the Economic Commission for Africa, the assistance of the appropriate international bodies.

C.

Considering that the improvement of the media of communication is a pre-condition to the promotion of economic, social and cultural relations among Member States;

Recalling Sub-sections 4 and 7 of the Resolution on Economic and

Social matters of item No. 2 of the First Conference of the Independent African States held at Accra;

Recommends:

1. That the Council for African Economic Co-operation shall immediately upon its establishment call a Conference of the Civil Aviation Authorities of Member States:

(a) To standardise licensing procedures for transport, equipment, flying personnel, overhaul, maintenance and inspection of transport vehicles and related units and equipment;

(b) To standardise charges and allied services.

2. That a meeting of the African National Air Carrier Operators be called as often as need be:

(a) To establish a closer co-operation between national African Air Lines;

(b) To study the feasibility of the creation of an Air Union of Africa and to submit to Member States a plan for the implementation thereof.

3. That similar efforts be made in other fields of communications, including telecommunications.

16. Congo

Telegram to H.E. The Minister of Foreign Affairs, Brussels

The Second Conference of Independent African States is deeply concerned at certain news reports referring to large scale movments of troops from neighbouring countries at the frontiers of the Belgian Congo. The Conference wishes to remind your Government that such troop movements can constitute a threat to the territorial integrity of the Congo for whose defence your Government are still fully responsible. The Conference would like to be informed of the veracity of this news and to receive an assurance from the Belgian Government that all necessary steps have been taken to counter this threat.

6

DECLARATION OF THE GHANA–GUINEA UNION
May 1, 1959

Basic Principles of the Union of Independent African States

1. Membership of the Union shall be open to all independent African States or Federations adhering to the principles on which the Union is based.

2. Each State or Federation which is a member of the Union shall preserve its own individuality and structure. The member States or Federations will decide in common what portion of sovereignty shall be surrendered to the Union in the full interest of the African community.

3. The Union shall have a flag, an anthem and a motto. Each member State or Federation will also have its flag, anthem and motto distinct from the flag, anthem and motto of the Union.

4. The Union flag shall be red, gold and green with as many five-pointed black stars as there are member States of the Union.

5. The motto of the Union of Independent African States shall be Independence and Unity.

6. (*a*) The general policy of the Union shall be to build up a free and prosperous African community in the interest of its peoples and world peace. (*b*) This policy shall be based essentially on the maintenance of diplomatic, economic and cultural relations on the basis of equality and reciprocity with all the States of the world which adopt a position not contrary to African interests and compatible with African dignity and personality. (*c*) Its main objective will be to help our African brothers subjected to domination with a view to ending their state of dependence, widening and consolidating with them the Union of Independent African States.

7. The States or Federations shall have their own foreign representation, nevertheless every member of the Union can entrust any other member State with its representation in certain countries.

8. (*a*) The acts of States or Federations which are members of the Union shall be determined in relation to the essential objectives which are Independence, Unity, the African personality, as well as the interest of the peoples. (*b*) They shall not act in obedience to any one group or bloc but will take account of external forces working for or against them.

9. Apart from their own citizenship, the nationals of the States or Federations which are members of the Union will have a Union citizenship. No visa will be required for travel from one State to another within the African Union.

10. Heads of States which are members of the Union will determine common policy on matters of defence, each State or Federation will have its own army.

11. (*a*) An Economic Council of the Union composed of an equal number of members designated by each member State will have the task of determining the general economic policy and studying all economic and financial problems of interest to the Union as a whole or in part. (*b*) A common bank of issue known as the Union Bank will be set up. Its task will be to issue and back the respective currencies of the different States or Federations which are members of the Union.

12. Finally to bring Africans closer together, the Union will take the necessary measures to co-ordinate historical research, the teaching of languages and cultural activities designed to promote the harmonious development of African civilisations.

7

THE SANNIQUELLIE DECLARATION
July 19, 1959

Joint Declaration by the Governments of Liberia, Ghana and Guinea Issued at Sanniquellie, Liberia

Resolved to assist, foster and speed up the total liberation of African non-independent territories whose peoples are struggling for national independence and self-determination, racial equality and human dignity,

Conscious of the fact that freedom, equality, justice and dignity are noble objectives of all peoples and are essential to the achievement of the legitimate aims and aspirations of the African peoples,

Determined to bring about unity, co-operation, harmony, coherence and mutual understanding among ourselves,

Bearing in mind the historical differences among the peoples of Africa in various fields, but convinced that joint action is necessary to attain our common purpose,

The President of the Republic of Liberia, the President of the Republic of Guinea and the Prime Minister of Ghana, after a frank exchange of views, have agreed on the necessity for immediate action and, in the light of this, they have reviewed the two communiqués issued by Ghana and Guinea, on the one hand, and the Official Gazette Extraordinary issued by Liberia, on the other hand, and have proposed the holding of a Special Conference in 1960 of all independent States of Africa as well as non-independent States which have fixed dates on which they will achieve independence to discuss and work out a Charter which will achieve their ultimate goal of unity between independent African States.

They have agreed further on a Declaration of Principles which will be presented to the special Conference of Independent African States as well as those dependent States invited to participate as the basis for the discussions of the Special Conference.

These principles are:

1. The name of the organisation shall be The Community of Independent African States.

2. Africans, like all other peoples, have the inherent right to independence and self-determination and to decide the form of Government under which they wish to live.

3. Each State and Federation, which is a member of the Community, shall maintain its own national identity and constitutional structure. The Community is being formed with a view to achieving unity among independent African States. It is not designed to prejudice the present or future international policies, relations and obligations of the States involved.

4. Each member of the Community accepts the principle that it shall not interfere in the internal affairs of any other member.

5. (a) The acts of States or Federations, which are members of the Community, shall be determined in relation to the essential objectives which are Freedom, Independence, Unity, the African Personality, as well as the interest of the African peoples.

(b) Each member State or Federation shall, in its acts or policies, do nothing contrary to the spirit and objective of the Community.

6. (a) The general policy of the Community shall be to build up a free and prosperous African Community for the benefit of its peoples and the peoples of the world and in the interest of international peace and security.

(b) This policy shall be based essentially on the maintenance of diplomatic, economic and cultural relations, on the basis of equality and reciprocity with all the States of the world which adopt a position compatible with African interests and African dignity.

(c) Its main objective will be to hold other African territories subjected to domination, with a view to accelerating the end of their non-independent status.

7. The Community shall set up an Economic Council, a Cultural Council and a Scientific and Research Council.

8. Membership in the Community shall be open to all independent African States and Federations, and any non-independent country of Africa shall have the right to join the Community upon its attainment of independence.

9. The Community shall have a Flag and an Anthem to be agreed upon at a later date.

10. The motto of the Community shall be "Independence and Unity".

8

STATEMENT BY THE PRESIDENT OF GHANA, OSAGYEFO DR. KWAME NKRUMAH, ON THE SANNIQUELLIE DECLARATION*

The first step along the road towards African union was taken on 23 November, 1958, when Ghana and the Republic of Guinea united. We realised that our union might involve many difficult issues, but we were determined to unite in order to form a nucleus for a union of African States. In July, 1959, I met the Presidents of Liberia and Guinea for a three-day conference at Sanniquellie. We discussed matters of common concern, and the whole question of African emancipation and unity. At the end of our talks we issued a Declaration of Principles which, I believe, may one day be regarded as of great historical significance.

The concept of a union of African States may seem visionary to some, but at least everyone would agree that great political forces have been released and are at work in Africa. With goodwill, sympathy and understanding, it should be possible to guide these forces into constructive and positive channels. We all have everything to lose from a failure to achieve a peaceful liberation of Africa.

* Kwame Nkrumah, *I Speak of Freedom*, Heinemann, London, 1961.

9

THE MONROVIA CONFERENCE OF
FOREIGN MINISTERS OF
INDEPENDENT AFRICAN STATES*
August 4–8, 1959

1. Resolution on the War in Algeria

The Conference of Independent African States meeting in a Special Session in Monrovia from the 4th to the 8th of August, 1959, with a Delegation from the Provisional Government of the Algerian Republic participating,

Deeply concerned with the continuation and spread of hostilities in Algeria and the deterioration in the situation which stems from it, constituting a grave threat to international peace and security,

Bearing in mind the resolution passed on Algeria at the Accra Conference in April, 1958, as well as the Joint Communiqué issued at Sanniquellie on July 19, 1959.

Considering that it is through negotiation between the two parties concerned that a just, peaceful and democratic solution can be found in conformity with the Charter of the United Nations,

Taking note of the willingness of the Provisional Government of the Algerian Republic to enter into negotiation with the Government of France,

1. Urges France:

(*a*) to recognise the right of the Algerian people to self-determination and independence;

(*b*) to put an end to the hostilities and to withdraw all her troops from Algeria;

(*c*) to enter into negotiation with the Provisional Government of the Algerian Republic.

2. Appeals to the members of the North Atlantic Treaty Organisation (NATO) with a view to urging France to desist from using in Algeria arms supplied by that organisation for defensive purposes.

3. Requests all the friends and allies of France, and all peace-loving nations and peoples to use their influence with the Government of France with a view to bringing to an end the bloodshed in Algeria and enabling the Algerian people to achieve their legitimate aspirations towards independence and liberty.

* States represented were Liberia, Morocco, Ghana, Guinea, Tunisia, U.A.R., Sudan, Ethiopia, Libya and the Provisional Government of Algeria.

4. Denounces, as an act of fratricide, the use of African troops in the French Army fighting in Algeria.

5. Hopes that all peoples and Governments, the world over, will support and recognise the Provisional Government of the Algerian Republic.

6. Recommends to the Governments of the Independent African States:

(*a*) the active preparation for the debate on the Algerian Question at the Fourteenth Session of the General Assembly of the United Nations;

(*b*) continuation of diplomatic action in favour of the Algerian cause;

(*c*) the widest possible dissemination of information in support of the cause of Algeria by every available means;

(*d*) to render material aid to Algeria, leaving it to each Government to decide the character and extent of such help;

(*e*) the proclamation of the 1st of November as Algeria Day, as an expression of solidarity with the struggle of the Algerian people;

(*f*) consultation and exchange of views whenever a situation warranting such action arises in Algeria, either at the governmental level or at the level of the Informal Permanent Machinery of the Independent African States at the United Nations.

2. Resolution on Nuclear Tests in the Sahara

The Conference of Independent African States meeting in a Special Session in Monrovia, Liberia, from the 4th to the 8th of August, 1959,

Noting with concern the decision of the French Government to carry out nuclear tests in the Sahara,

Recalling the resolution of the Accra Conference of Independent African States which viewed with grave alarm and strongly condemned all atomic tests in any part of the world and in particular the intention to carry out such tests in the Sahara,

Referring also to the Joint Communiqué issued at Sanniquellie on July 19, 1959,

Considering the grave dangers these nuclear tests will hold for the people of Africa in general and in particular those living in the Sahara and the adjacent territories.

1. Denounces vigorously and with profound indignation the decision of any government to carry out nuclear tests in the Sahara or in any other part of Africa.

2. Appeals to the conscience of the world to condemn this threat to the lives and security of the African people.

3. Recommends to the governments and peoples of Africa to protest in the most energetic and formal manner to the French Government to desist from carrying out the proposed tests in the Sahara.

4. Authorises the Informal Permanent Machinery of the Independent African States at the United Nations to examine and take such steps as may be appropriate with a view to enlisting the support of the United Nations and any other organisations to remove this grave threat that hangs over the Sahara in particular and over the peoples of Africa in general.

3. Resolution on the Cameroons now under French Administration

The Conference of Independent African States,

1. Welcomes the independence of the Cameroons which will become effective on the 1st January, 1960.

2. Considers that free elections under United Nations supervision before independence is the most effective and democratic means of solving the present crisis, which is in strict conformity with the objectives of the International Trusteeship System.

3. Deplores the present situation in that Territory and calls upon the Government, and the Opposition in and out of the Territory, to come together in the interest of their Country and to find a just solution to their differences so that the Independent Cameroons will be able to take its rightful place among the Independent African States and the Nations of the world.

4. Offers its good offices to search for appropriate means for bringing about this objective.

5. Failing that, appeals to the conscience of the world and the members of the United Nations to support all efforts to bring the matter before the next session of the General Assembly of the United Nations.

4. Resolution on Racial Discrimination

The Conference of Independent African States,

Deeply convinced that the practice of racial discrimination and segregation is evil and inhuman and diametrically opposed to the provisions of the Universal Declaration of Human Rights,

Considering that racialism is a threat to international peace and security wherever it is practised,

Noting with concern the relentless manner in which the Government of South Africa is putting into practice its apartheid policy,

1. Condemns the practice of racial discrimination and segregation in all of its aspects all over the world, especially in the Union of South Africa, in the Central African Federation, in Kenya and in other parts of Africa.

2. Calls upon all members of the United Nations and all peoples of the world to associate themselves with the resolutions passed by the United Nations and the Bandung and Accra Conferences condemning this inhuman practice.

3. Recommends that the different Governments take such measures as to contribute effectively to persuade the Union of South Africa to implement the resolutions of the United Nations on racial questions.

5. Resolution on Non-Independent Territories

The Conference of Independent African States,

After hearing petitioners from Uganda, Angola, Southern Rhodesia,

Reaffirms Resolution II of the Independent African States held in Accra in April 1958 concerning the future of dependent territories in Africa,

Recognises the right of non-independent territories in Africa to self-determination and independence,

1. Calls upon the Administering Powers to respect the Charter of the United Nations in this regard, to take rapid steps to implement the

provisions of the Charter and to take due account of the political aspirations of the people, and their right to self-determination and independence.

2. Appeals to the conscience of the world and the members of the United Nations to assist these territories in realising their legitimate aspirations and to attain their independence in conformity with the Charter of the United Nations.

6. Resolution on the Question of South-West Africa

The Conference of Independent African States,

Deeply concerned by the situation in the territory of South-West Africa,

1. Urges the Government of the Union of South Africa to implement the Resolutions of the United Nations concerning the territory of South-West Africa.

2. Maintains that this territory is in fact a Trust Territory of the United Nations, and as such the United Nations cannot relinquish its legal and moral responsibilities to the indigenous inhabitants who are entitled to the same treatment given to other Trust Territories.

3. Appeals to the United Nations to fix a date for the independence of the territory of South-West Africa.

7. Resolution on the Question of Nyasaland

The Conference of Independent African States,

Having examined the grave situation now prevailing in Nyasaland, the memorandum submitted by the Nyasaland African Congress and the statement made by the representative of this Congress during the hearing granted to him in the Conference,

Having further been made aware of the findings of the Devlin Report,

Bearing in mind the objectives of Chapter XI of the Charter of the United Nations on the Declaration regarding non-self-governing territories and the objectives proclaimed by the Accra Conference of Independent African States,

1. Calls upon the United Kingdom Government to lift the State of Emergency in Nyasaland, to release all those unlawfully detained and to lift the ban on the Nyasaland African Congress.

2. Calls upon the Government of the United Kingdom to respect the Charter of the United Nations in this regard and to take rapid steps to implement the provisions of the Charter and to take due account of the political aspirations of the people, namely self-determination and independence.

8. Resolution Expression of Thanks to the Liberian Government

The Independent African States,

Having accepted the gracious invitation of the Government of Liberia to convene in Monrovia from 4th to 8th August, 1959,

Considering the historical significance of their Conference,

Acknowledge with deep appreciation this amicable gesture of the Liberian Government,

Express their total satisfaction for the arrangements made by the Government of Liberia, and the warm hospitality extended to members of the delegations of the participating Governments by the President, the Government and the people of Liberia,

Take this opportunity to declare their profound gratitude to the President, Government and people of Liberia.

9. Resolution

The Conference of Independent African States,

Having been deeply impressed by the efficiency of the work of the Officials of this Conference,

Takes this opportunity to place on record its appreciation and thanks to the Members of the Secretariat and other Officials responsible for the preparatory and technical administration of the Conference.

I O

EXTRACTS FROM THE STATEMENT BY THE GHANA MINISTER OF FOREIGN AFFAIRS, THE HON. AKO ADJEI, AT THE SECOND CONFERENCE OF INDEPENDENT AFRICAN STATES
Addis Ababa, June, 1960

It is clear from this declaration of principles (the Sanniquellie Declaration) that the Union of African States, which the three leaders discussed and agreed upon, is intended to be a political Union. Such a political Union, in their view, will provide the framework within which any plans for economic, social and cultural co-operation can, in fact, operate to the best advantage of all.

To us in Ghana, the concept of African Unity is an article of faith. It is a cardinal objective in our national policy. We sincerely believe that the Independent African States can, and may some day, form a real political Union—the Union of African States.

As a result of our faith in African Unity, our electorate, in exercise of their sovereign rights, recently voted in a plebiscite on the new republican constitution of Ghana. The constitution specifically states that Ghana is prepared, at any time, to surrender her sovereignty, in whole or in part, in the interest of a Union of African States.

Therefore, to us in Ghana, the idea or concept of African Unity is no longer a matter for public political debate. We have passed beyond the talking stage.

The idea of African Unity is now part of our fundamental law—the new republican constitution, which will be inaugurated on the first day of July this year.

The Union of African States is the ultimate goal. It does not matter whether you start with an Association of African States or whether with economic or cultural co-operation. Certainly, we must start from somewhere, but certainly the Union can be achieved in the end.

In our view, it is the complete political Union of African States that can save Africa from the maelstrom into which it may easily fall.

In the view of the Ghana Delegation, a Union of African States is inevitable, and we shall devote our efforts towards achieving that goal.

Against this background, and in the light of statements made by Dr. Kwame Nkrumah, Prime Minister of Ghana, and by other leaders in Africa on the question of African Unity, the Ghana Delegation proposes that this Conference should recommend the establishment of a Committee of Experts with specific terms of reference to work out the details of the

Union of African States. The Committee may consist of Ministers, diplomats, economists and so on; and some of the subjects to be worked out may include the formation of a Customs Union, the Removal of Trade Barriers, and the establishment of an African Development Fund. Ghana is prepared to co-operate fully in such a venture.

In final summation, I wish to emphasise, Mr. President, that the problems confronting our peoples in Africa today are so important and so vital to our very existence, that we cannot afford to dissipate our energies in fruitless argument and academic polemical debate.

The present situation in Africa demands of us a complete change in our traditional attitudes, and a drastic reorganisation of our thinking habits.

We must think and plan for the future. We must think in larger terms, and act on a wider plane of ideas. It is only by projecting our thinking beyond our own narrow national boundaries that we shall succeed in establishing, with our neighbours, that fellowship or community of ideas which is so essential for peace and prosperity in Africa and in the wider world.

In the times that lie ahead of us, the States of Africa can depend upon the Government and people of Ghana for full co-operation, in all fields of human endeavour, calculated to ensure a lasting peace, prosperity, happiness, independence and unity of the African peoples.

EXTRACTS FROM THE STATEMENT OF THE
LEADER OF THE NIGERIAN DELEGATION,
THE HON. Y. M. SULE, AT THE SECOND
CONFERENCE OF INDEPENDENT AFRICAN
STATES
Addis Ababa, June, 1960

The world today is in such a state that whatever may be our differences
of opinion here in Africa we must close our rank and file and move
together as one people irrespective of nationality, creed or religion. We
will either hang together and firmly too, like a bunch of grapes, or fall one
by one. While claims and counter claims by the Power Blocs have become
the order of the day and world peace is always being threatened, it is not
unlikely that there may also be another move by certain countries to knock
our heads together so that this excellent idea of Africa uniting to be one
may never come to be true. Such countries feel that it would be detrimental to their own interests economically and politically if Africa
unites. They may also have the feeling that so long as the African States
form a united front and refuse to allow any propaganda or hypocrisy to
disunite them, Africa will be the answer continent and all the world will
turn to Africa. But whether anybody likes it or not Africa, by the grace of
God, has been destined to play a major role, if not the leading role, in the
affairs of the world. The question of African leadership is, therefore,
merely a question of time. But if we are to be worthy of this responsibility
we must constantly remember that once we begin to wash our dirty linen
in public and so long as we do not sink and bury our differences and if we
indulge in mud slinging against one another, enemies of African unity—
and we must remember we have them—will quickly take advantage and
ruin the excellent work we have so far been able to achieve. Enemies of
African unity are equally as interested—and as eager—to disband us as
we, the Africans, are to unite ourselves.

Pan-Africanism is the only solution to our problems in Africa, no matter
what kind of problems they are. No one in Africa doubts the need to
promote Pan-Africanism. One cannot over-emphasise the need of our
being in friendly relationship with our neighbours in African territories.
But we must not be sentimental; we must be realistic. It is for this reason
that we would like to point out that at this moment the idea of forming a
Union of African States is premature. On the other hand we do not
dispute the sincerity and indeed the good intentions of those people that
advocate it. But we feel that such a move is too radical—perhaps too
ambitious—to be of any lasting benefit. Gradual development of ideas and

thoughts is more lasting. It must be remembered also that nations are like ordinary individual human beings and must therefore be treated as such. Hence, it is essential to remember that whatever ideas we may have about Pan-Africanism will not materialise or at least will not materialise as quickly as we would like them to if we start building from the top downwards. We must first prepare the minds of the different African countries —we must start from the known to the unknown.

At the moment we in Nigeria cannot afford to form union by government with any African States by surrendering our sovereignty. We need to wait until the African States are independent and have formed governments of their own. We believe that many of the African States would very much prefer to rule themselves by themselves, and that they would like to taste the atmosphere of freedom after having been under foreign domination for some time. Furthermore, it may happen that some of them—we hope, however, that this may NOT happen—may adopt unbearable policies. We need to wait and see the types of governments they make and the policy they pursue. Some African territories may surrender their sovereignty to some foreign government—we hope they will choose unity with other African States. However, we do not know what circumstances may dictate.

President Tubman's idea of the association of state is therefore more acceptable for it is yet premature to form a Union of States under one sovereignty. We must first break all artificial barriers; build international roads, promote mutual exchanges—exchange of information, scientific and otherwise, etc., lifting any ban on the movement of free trade and people between the various African countries. All these must be done in order to pave the way for this Union of African States. But while it is true to say that the formation of a Union of African States is premature, yet one can hardly ignore the necessity for the emerging African States, more especially West African States, to be united under one sovereignty. Something of a loose federation at first having got the way clear may be a good beginning. Sooner or later the unity will come by necessity or circumstantially. Africans are Africans. They are African by colour, they are African by soil, by culture, by ways of thinking and, indeed, Africans are inseparable. The unity of Africans comes as a natural course and there can exist no barrier against it. It is by unity that Africa will be able to project her identity before the eyes of the world. It is by unity that African States will be able to command respect among other nations of the world and it is by unity that we shall be able to satisfactorily achieve peace and prosperity.

Any move made to promote co-operation, understanding and mutual help among African countries is indeed welcome. I must warn, however, that while the whole idea is good and acceptable to us all, individual ambition and greed for power may spoil everything; it will spoil the good work we have done and ruin the good work we are capable of doing in the future. Personal ambition therefore will not help us for it will create in the minds of people a feeling of suspicion and lack of confidence. If therefore we are really sincere—and I am sure we all are—in our declared policy that it is the unity of Africa and the interests of her people that we value most and place first and foremost in our minds then we must set aside partial affection, personal prejudices and personal ambition. Our aim and ambition should be directed towards achieving a United States of

Africa no matter who leads. All that we must have is honest, impartial and incorruptible leadership coupled with the fear of God.

At this juncture I wish to seize this opportunity to congratulate those African leaders who have made such excellent contributions to the Pan-African movement. For them we have undying love and respect. For they are the pioneers that have set the ball rolling. But, and this is a big but, if anybody makes the mistake of feeling that he is a Messiah who has got a mission to lead Africa the whole purpose of Pan-Africanism will, I fear, be defeated. We all can recall what Hitler thought and did in Nazi Germany and what that meant to the whole world. Hitler thought he had a mission to rule the whole world and in pursuance of his mission he tried to destroy other world Powers and plunged the whole of Europe—and indeed the whole world—into war.

Therefore, we must be careful not to set ourselves against ourselves. Personal ambition may set certain countries bitterly against one another. We must treat ourselves like brothers and sisters, and we must not go out and make some of our brothers and sisters objects of ridicule in the eyes of the world for our selfish interests. If we feel that any one of the African countries is not pursuing the right policy let us by all means try to convince that country in a brotherly way to abandon that policy and take to the right one. Why should we, for example, go all out to campaign against a fellow African country in an international organisation simply because we disagree or believe it is a satellite of a foreign country? I feel the best we can do to that country is to make her realise her own folly or mistake, if so it is, in a way and manner that will be understood and appreciated by her. In short we must not be too bitter against one another no matter what our differences. This and only this is the way to achieve our objective and get to our goal.

I 2

DECLARATION BY GHANA–GUINEA–MALI
Conakry, December 24, 1960

We, the President of the Republic of Ghana, the President of the Republic of Guinea, and the President of the Republic of Mali, meeting at Conakry on the 24th December, 1960, having reviewed all important African and international problems have decided with a view to harmonising and co-ordinating the policies of our three States:

1. To establish a union of our three States.
2. To promote a common economic and monetary policy.

In this regard, two special committees have been set up to examine practical methods for achieving objectives.

We have also decided that each year the three Heads of State will meet quarterly in Accra, Bamako and Conakry.

Concerning the situation in the Congo, we unanimously regretted the inability of the United Nations to enforce the resolutions of the Security Council in regard to the maintenance of the political independence of the Congo, its territorial integrity and the normal functioning of its democratic institutions.

The Head of State of the Republic of Mali took note of the recent statement made by Ghana and Guinea on the Congo situation and has associated himself with it.

The Head of State of the Republic of Ghana has taken note of the decision of the Governments of Guinea and Mali to withdraw their troops from the Congo and has decided to issue a statement concerning the Ghana troops now serving in the Congo.

The three Heads of State deplored the attitude taken by certain African Heads of State whose recent stand is likely to jeopardise the unity of Africa and strengthen neo-colonialism. They condemn all forms of African regroupment based on languages of the colonial Powers. They therefore appeal to these Heads of State to follow a higher and more healthy conception of African unity.

13

THE BRAZZAVILLE DECLARATION
December 19, 1960

Communiqué

Les Etats Africains et Malgache soussignés se sont réunis à Brazzaville du 15 au 19 décembre 1960, dans le but de réaliser de nouveaux progrès dans la voie de leur coopération interafricaine, fondée sur le voisinage, la culture et la communauté des intérêts. Ce faisant, ils entendent travailler efficacement au maintien de la Paix en Afrique et dans le monde.

En face de la grave situation, qui est, aujourd'hui celle de l'Afrique, ils sont pleinement conscients des responsabilités oui sont les leurs. Aussi, ont-ils choisi comme méthode, non pas de se donner l'apparence de résoudre les problèmes, mais d'essayer de les résoudre concrètement, non pas de prendre parti, mais de consilier les parties, non pas de proposer n'importe quel compromis, mais d'inviter les parties au dialogue, d'où seul peut sortir une solution qui constitue un progrès positif pour la Paix et la coopération internationale.

La Mauritanie

Les Etats soussignés adressent leurs fraternelles félicitations à la Mauritanie qui, le 28 novembre 1960, a accédé à la souveraineté internationale.

La Mauritanie a déjà été reconnue par de nombreux Etats comme Etat souverain et indépendant. C'est le devoir de l'Organisation des Nations Unies de l'admettre en son sein.

Les Etats soussignés regrettent que l'U.R.S.S., par son veto, ait empêché cette admission. Ils s'étonnent qu'un grand pays, qui a déposé, à la XVe session de l'O.N.U., une résolution sur l'Indépendance immédiate des Pays colonisés par voie de négociations, s'oppose à l'admission d'une ancienne colonie, qui vient précisément d'obtenir son indépendance par voie de négociations.

Ils invitent tous les Etats Africains soucieux de défendre, avec la dignité, la liberté de l'Afrique et d'éviter la guerre froide sur le Continent, à redoubler d'efforts pour l'admission de la Mauritanie.

Dans sa lutte héroïque et pacifique d'hier pour son indépendance, la Mauritanie, a reçu le soutien de ses amis. Aujourd'hui, dans sa lutte pour son admission à l'O.N.U., la Mauritanie peut compter sur la solidarité agissant de nos Etats affectés, mais non découragés, par la grande injustice dont elle vient d'être victime du fait du veto russe.

Problème algérien

Les Etats soussignés, tout en rendant hommage au général de Gaulle, initiateur de la décolonisation en France, qui a accordé l'indépendance à treize pays africains et malgache, ne peuvent taire leur angoisse devant la persistance de la guerre d'Algérie, qui continue avec son cortège de morts, de ruines et de haines raciales.

Les Etats soussignés, attachés au principe de décolonisation pour lequel ils ont tant lutté, mais conscients du danger, mortel pour l'Afrique, de la prolongation de la guerre en Algérie, ont pris la seule attitude qui permette, par des négociations, l'application honnête et démocratique du principe de l'autodétermination, proclamé solennellement par le général de Gaulle.

Ils n'ont pas voulu s'associer à une solution de facilité, peu pratique, négative même, qui consiste en un recours illusoire à l'O.N.U. pour l'organisation et le contrôle d'un référendum dans un pays ne se trouvant pas sous la tutelle de l'O.N.U.

Les Etats soussignés ont foi en l'O.N.U. Mais ils constatent que, jusqu'à ce jour, la Charte de cette Organisation internationale n'a jamais prévu de mesures coercitives contre ceux qui refusent d'appliquer des résolutions votées par la majorité ou même l'unanimité de ses membres.

Bien que n'appartenant pas tous à la Communauté, ils n'ont jamais caché leur amitié pour la France. Mais ce n'est pas cette amitié qui a dicté et qui dicte encore leur comportement d'aujourd'hui.

C'est dans la crainte de voir dégénérer le drame algérien en un conflit mondial dont l'Afrique ferait en définitive les frais, qu'ils sont résolus à demander, avec insistance, à la France de se dépasser pour mettre fin, en 1961, à la guerre d'Algérie et, après des négociations franches, d'appliquer honnêtement le principe de l'autodétermination, étant entendue que des garanties politiques seraient données réciproquement aux parties.

La France montrera ainsi qu'en libérant les quinze Etats qui sortent du régime colonial et en permettant aux Algériens de choisir librement leur destin, elle reste fidèle à ses propres principes et à sa tradition.

Problème congolais

Les Etats Africains et Malgache soussignés, saluent l'effort que l'Organisation des Nations Unies a entrepris pour sauver le Congo-Leopoldville du chaos et de l'anarchie. Ils adressent leurs félicitations à Monsieur Hammarskjoeld, Secrétaire général de l'Organisation, qui, respectant l'esprit de la Charte, s'est efforcé d'empêcher l'existence de la guerre froide à cette partie du Continent.

Malheureusement, les blocs rivaux ont tenté et tentent encore de recoloniser le Congo-Leopoldville, soit directement, soit indirectement par l'intermédiaire de certains Etats asiatiques et africains. Les Etats Africains et Malgache soussignés dénoncent, devant la conscience mondiale, cette nouvelle forme du colonialisme.

L'indépendance réelle du Congo-Leopoldville veut sans doute, que l'O.N.U. continue de lui apporter son assistance technique, mais elle exige surtout qu'aucun autre Etat n'intervienne, par l'intermédiaire de ses soldats ou de ses diplomates, dans les affaires intérieures du Congo-Leopoldville.

La solution politique du problème congolais ne peut être trouvée que dans une Conférence de la Table Ronde qui, grouperait les représentants de tous les Partis sans exception.

Hors de ce principe démocratique, tout le reste est racisme et guerre froide.

Pour

Le Cameroun	Ahidjo
La République Centrafricaine	Dacko
Le Congo Brazzavile	Fulbert Youlu
La Côte d'Ivoire	Houphouet Boigny
Le Dahomey	Maga
Le Gabon	Léon M'Ba
La Haute Volta	Yameogo
Madagascar	Tsiranana
La Mauritanie	Moktar Ould Daddah
Le Niger	Hamani Diori
Le Sénégal..	Senghor
Le Tchad	Tombalbaye

RESOLUTION SUR LA CONFERENCE ECONOMIQUE

Les Etats ci-après soussignés représentés par les Chefs d'Etats et de Gouvernements signataires;

Considérant la nécessité d'affermir leur indépendance politique par la promotion économique et sociale de leurs populations;

Considérant que la réalisation de ces objectifs exige une action régionale concertée respectant leur personalité politique, menée à leur initiative et sous leur responsabilité;

Désireux d'apporter une contribution à l'accroissement de la solidarité interafricaine par le renforcement des liens économiques qui les unisse, dans le respect des engagements internationaux auxquels ils ont souscrit,

DECIDENT :

La création d'un Comité d'Etudes composé au maximum de trois représentants par Etat.

Ce Comité d'Etudes se réunira le 30 janvier 1961 à Dakar et aura pour mission d'étudier et de proposer, en vue d'établir un Projet d'organisation africaine et malgache de Coopération économique, des solutions adéquates aux problèmes suivants:

1. Problème de monnaie et de crédit dans l'optique d'une politique de développement des économies africaine et malgache.

2. Problèmes du soutien des productions des Etats membres et de l'organisation des marchés des produits agricoles et industriels, grâce à la création de fonds de stabilisation des prix—au renforcement et à l'élargissement des unions régionales douanières à l'harmonisation de la fiscalité, et, d'une façon générale, grâce à la recherche d'une meilleure coordination dans le domaine des échanges commerciaux.

3. Problèmes de l'harmonisation des différents plans nationaux et de leur financement et, concommittent, l'étude d'un code africain et malgache d'investissements comportant l'octroi de garanties aux

investissements privés, la création d'un Fonds Africain et Malgache de Solidarité pour le développment économi que et social, et, enfin celle d'une Banque Africaine et Malgache d'Investissements.

Le Comité étudiera, en outre, les problèmes poses par l'adhésion éventuelle ou déjà acquise des Etats membres de la Conférence, aux diverses organisations de la Communauté économique Européenne, ainsi qu'à diverses organisations internationales de caractère économique et fiancier, dans le souci de la sauvegarde de leurs économies naissantes. Il se saisira enfin, de tous les problèmes particuliers que pose, d'ores et déjà l'industrialisation de leur pays.

(Translation)

THE COMMUNIQUÉ

The undersigned African States and Madagascar met at Brazzaville from 15 to 19 December with the aim of realising new progress on the road to their inter-African co-operation, founded on neighbourhood, culture and community of interests, and to work effectively towards the maintenance of peace in Africa and in the world.

In face of the grave situation which is today that of Africa, they are fully conscious of their responsibilities. However, the method that they have chosen is not to take sides—but to reconcile the sides, not to propose any particular compromise but to invite both sides to a dialogue from which can only emerge a solution which constitutes a positive progress for international peace and co-operation.

Mauritania

The undersigned States address their fraternal felicitations to Mauritania, which acceded to international sovereignty on the 28th November, 1960.

Mauritania has already been recognised by numerous States as an independent and sovereign State. It is the duty of UNO to admit her to her ranks.

The undersigned States regret that the U.S.S.R. has vetoed this admission. They are astonished that a Great Power, which put forward a resolution at the 15th session of UNO asking for the immediate independence, through negotiations, of all colonial territories, opposes the admission of a former colony, which gained independence precisely by these means.

They invite all African States anxious for the liberty and dignity of Africa, and anxious to avoid the cold war on our continent, to redouble their efforts for the admission of Mauritania.

Yesterday, in her heroic and pacific struggle for independence, Mauritania received the support of her friends. Today, in her struggle for her admission to UNO, Mauritania can count on the active solidarity of our States, who are affected, but not discouraged, by the great injustice done to her through the Russian veto.

The Algerian Problem

The undersigned States, whilst rendering homage to General de Gaulle who began French decolonialisation, granted independence to thirteen African States including Madagascar, cannot conceal their anguish in face of the persistence of the Algerian war which continues with its cortège of death, destruction and racial hate.

The undersigned States, attached to the principle of decolonialisation for which they have struggled so much; but aware of the danger for Africa which lies in prolonging the Algerian war, have taken the only attitude which by negotiation allows the honest and democratic application of the principle of self-determination solemnly proclaimed by General de Gaulle.

They do not want to associate themselves with the hardly practicable and negative solution, consisting in an illusory resort to UNO, for the organisation and control of a referendum in a country which does not come under the guardianship of UNO.

The undersigned States have faith in UNO but they believe that until today, the Charter of this international organisation has never anticipated forceful measures against those who refuse to apply the resolution voted by the majority or even unanimity of the members.

Although not belonging to the Community, they have not hidden their friendship for France. But it is not this friendship which dictates their behaviour today.

It is in the fear of watching the Algerian drama degenerate into a world conflict, in which Africa will bear the cost, that they have resolved to ask France firmly to conclude the war in Algeria in 1961, and after frank negotiations to apply honestly the principle of self-determination; it being understood that political guarantees would be granted reciprocally to both sides.

Thus France will show that by liberating the fifteen States which grew out of the colonial régime and in permitting the Algerians freely to choose their destiny, she stays faithful to her own principles and to her traditions.

The Congolese Problem

The undersigned States and Madagascar salute the effort undertaken by UNO to save the Congo (Leopoldville) from chaos and anarchy. They render thanks to Mr. Hammarskjoeld, Secretary-General of UNO, who, respecting the spirit of the Charter, has striven to stop the cold war extending to this part of the Continent. Unfortunately the rival blocs have tried and are still trying to recolonise the Congo (Leopoldville) either directly or indirectly through the intermediary of certain Asiatic and African States.

The undersigned States and Madagascar denounce before the conscience of the world this new form of colonisation. The real independence of the Congo (Leopoldville) needs, without doubt, UNO continuing to bring its technical assistance but UNO is not required to substitute for the Congolese authorities. Above all, what is required in the Congo (Leopoldville) is that no other State intervenes in her domestic affairs through the intermediary of soldiers or diplomats.

The practical solution of the Congolese problem can only be found at a Round Table Conference, which would group together the representatives of every party without exception.

Outside of this democratic principle, all the rest is a resort to the cold war.

For:	*Signed:*
CAMEROUN	Ahidjo
CENTRAL AFRICAN REPUBLIC	Dacko
CONGO (Brazzaville)	Fulbert Youlu
IVORY COAST	Houphouet Boigny
DAHOMEY	Maga
GABON	Léon M'Ba
UPPER VOLTA	Yameogo
MADAGASCAR	Tsiranana
MAURITANIA	Moktar Ould Daddah
NIGER	Hamani Diori
SENEGAL	Senghor
CHAD	Tombalbaye

RESOLUTION OF THE ECONOMIC CONFERENCE

The above-signed States represented by their Chiefs of State,

Considering the necessity to affirm their political independence through the economic and social advance of their populations;

Considering that to realise these objectives demands concerted regional action; respecting their political personality, led by their initiative and under their responsibilities;

Wishing to bring forward a contribution for the enlargement of inter-African solidarity through reinforcing economic ties which already unite them, meanwhile respecting any other international commitments to which they have subscribed,

Decide:

The creation of a Commission composed of a maximum of three representatives for each State.

This Commission will meet on January 30th at Dakar and its object will be to study and to propose, with a view to establishing a plan of African and Madagascan economic co-operation, adequate solutions to the following problems:

1. Problems relating to money and credit seen in the perspective of a policy of developing Madagascan and African economies.

2. Problems relating to the support of the production of Member States, and the organisation of the sale of their agricultural and industrial products through the creation of price-stabilisation funds; the reinforcement and enlargement of regional customs unions; the harmonisation of fiscal policies; and generally through the pursuit of better co-ordination in the domain of commercial exchange.

3. Problems of harmonising and financing the different national plans. The Commission will have to study the establishment of an African and Madagascan code of investment, including the granting of guarantees to private investment, and to work out the basis of an African and Madagascan solidarity in economic and social development. Lastly it will have to study the creation of an African and Madagascan investment bank.

The Commission will study, moreover, problems posed by the adhesion, to come or already achieved, of Member States of the Conference to various organisations of the European Economic Community as well as to various international organisations of a financial and economic character, in the hope of safeguarding their emergent national economies. Finally it will be concerned with all individual problems arising, now and in the future, from the industrialisation of their countries.

14

CHARTER FOR "THE UNION OF AFRICAN STATES"
*Accra, July 1, 1961**

The President of the Republic of Ghana, the President of the Republic of Guinea, and the President of the Republic of Mali, meeting in Accra on the 27th, 28th and 29th April, 1961,

Having regard to

(*a*) The Joint Communiqué issued in Accra on the 23rd of November, 1958, which brought into being the Ghana–Guinea Union,

(*b*) The Joint Communiqué issued in Conakry on the 1st of May, 1959, laying down the practical basis for the achievement of such a Union, and setting out the basic principles for a wider African Community owing no allegiance to any foreign Power,

(*c*) The Joint Communiqué of the Heads of State of the Republic of Ghana and the Republic of Mali, issued in Bamako in November, 1960, regarding the achievement of African Unity,

(*d*) The Joint Communiqué by the Head of State of the Republic of Guinea and the Republic of Mali issued at Siguiri on the 5th of December, 1960, recommending a Union of the two States, and deciding that the friendly relations and the ties of co-operation binding them to the Republic of Ghana should be intensified,

(*e*) The Joint Communiqué that emerged from a meeting between Presidents Kwame Nkrumah, Sékou Touré and Modibo Keita, at Conakry on the 24th December, 1960, reaffirming their joint determination to create a Union between Guinea, Mali and Ghana, giving a mandate to a Special Committee to formulate concrete proposals for implementing such a Union;

Having regard to

The conclusions reached by this Special Committee meeting in Accra from the 13th to the 18th January, 1960, and subject to approval by their respective Parliaments decide that:

Section 1
GENERAL PROVISIONS

Article 1. There shall be established between the Republics of Ghana, Guinea and Mali a Union to be known as "The Union of African States (UAS)".

Article 2. The Union of African States (UAS) shall be regarded as the

* Publication date in Ghana, Guinea and Mali.

nucleus of the United States of Africa. It is open to every State or Federation of African States which accepts its aims and objectives. It reaffirms the complete adherence of its members to the African Charter and the Casablanca Resolutions.

Article 3. The aims of the Union of African States (UAS) are as follows:

to strengthen and develop ties of friendship and fraternal co-operation between the Member States politically, diplomatically, economically and culturally;

to pool their resources in order to consolidate their indpendence and safeguard their territorial integrity;

to work jointly to achieve the complete liquidation of imperialism, colonialism and neo-colonialism in Africa and the building up of African Unity;

to harmonise the domestic and foreign policy of its Members, so that their activities may prove more effective and contribute more worthily to safeguarding the peace of the world.

Article 4. The Union's activities shall be exercised mainly in the following fields:

(*a*) *Domestic Policy.* The working out of a common orientation for the States.

(*b*) *Foreign Policy.* The strict observance of a concerted diplomacy, calculated to achieve closer co-operation.

(*c*) *Defence.* The organisation of a system of Joint Defence, which will make it possible to mobilise all the means of defence at the disposal of the State, in favour of any State of the Union which may become a victim of aggression.

(*d*) *Economy.* Defining a common set of directives relating to Economic Planning, aiming at the complete decolonisation of the set-ups inherited from the colonial system, and organising the development of the wealth of their countries in the interest of their peoples.

(*e*) Culture. The rehabilitation and development of African culture, and frequent and diversified cultural exchange.

Section 2

POLITICAL

Article 5. The Supreme Executive Organ of the Union of African States shall be the Conference of Heads of State of the Union.

1. *The Union Conference.* This shall meet once a quarter in Accra, Bamako and Conakry respectively. It shall be presided over by the Head of State in the host country, who shall fix the date of the Conference.

The Draft Agenda shall be drawn up by him, on the basis of items forwarded by Heads of State.

The Union Conference shall pass resolutions, which shall become effective immediately.

2. *Preparatory Committee.* The Union Conference shall always be preceded by a meeting of a Committee entrusted with the task of preparing the ground for it. This Preparatory Committee may be convened at any time by the Head of State of the host country. He shall determine the number of delegates per State having regard to the items on the Draft Agenda.

The Preparatory Committee shall make recommendations for the consideration of the Union Conference.

3. *Co-ordinating Committees of the Mass Organisations of the Union.* There shall be established among political organisations, Trade Union Organisations, Women's Movements and Youth Movements of the Union States, a Co-ordinating Committee for organisational purposes, to impart to the said bodies a common ideological orientation which is absolutely necessary for the development of the Union.

These Committees shall be established within three months after the publication of the present Document.

Each of the Co-ordinating Committees here envisaged, at its first Constituent Meeting shall draw up standing rules and shall determine the practical methods to be employed for the attainment of the objectives jointly agreed upon.

4. *National Days.* Before any Union Day is decided upon, the National Days of the Union States shall be marked by celebrations in all the States, in the form of ceremonies and public meetings.

Such occasions may be declared Public Holidays in whole or in part, according to the needs of the countries concerned.

Section 3

DIPLOMACY

Article 6. The principle of harmonisation of the foreign policy of the Union States shall be based upon a concerted diplomacy.

To achieve such harmonisation, the following steps should be taken:

(*a*) at each Union Conference an analysis shall be made by the Heads of State, of the international political situation, and the Union shall decide upon directives to be sent to all the diplomatic Missions of the Member States.

(*b*) Ambassadors, Chargés d'Affaires, Consuls and other Heads of Missions of the three States, serving abroad shall co-ordinate their activities by way of frequent consultation.

(*c*) Every latitude shall be given to each State to be represented by the Embassy of another Member State of the Union. Where there is no representation of any of the three States of the Union, the Member State desirous of entrusting its affairs to the Diplomatic Mission of another State which is not a member of the Union, shall consult the Union Conference before proceeding.

(*d*) At international gatherings, Conferences or Meetings, the delegations of the Union States must as in duty bound consult one another, and arrive at a common stand which no one shall be allowed to ignore, and all are expected to support.

Section 4

JOINT DEFENCE

Article 7. In order to safeguard their sovereignty, the Member States shall oppose any installation of foreign military bases on their soil.

They shall jointly ensure the defence of their territorial integrity. Any aggression against one of the States shall be considered as an act of aggression against other States of the Union.

A common system of defence shall be organised in order to make it possible to secure the permanent defence of the Union States.

Section 5
ECONOMY

ECONOMIC COMMITTEE OF THE UNION

Article 8. The Economic Committee of the Union shall have the task of co-ordinating and harmonising the Economic and Financial Policy of the Union States in accordance with directives jointly agreed upon.

Article 9. The Economic Committee shall consist of a delegation of five members per State chosen from among the officials responsible for economy and finance in each State.

Article 10. It shall hold two sessions every year, in the months of March and September. Each State shall serve as the Headquarters of the Economic Committee of the Union for one year, and shall preside over its meetings during that year.

The Economic Committee of the Union shall draw up its standing rules at its first session. The Sessions of the Economic Committee of the Union may not exceed a fortnight.

During its sessions it shall make recommendations to be submitted to the Heads of State.

Section 6
CULTURE

Article 11. The Union States shall relentlessly pursue the rehabilitation of African Culture and the development of African civilisation.

Teaching in two languages, exchange of staff, rediffusion programmes, the establishment of joint Research Institutes shall be intensified in the Union States.

Section 7
MISCELLANEOUS

Article 12. The Institutions shall become effective from the date when this Charter is proclaimed simultaneously in the Union States.

Article 13. Modifications may be made to the present provisions at a meeting of Heads of State, in the event of the admission of a new State or at the request of a Head of State, with the view to giving greater cohesion to the Union.

Modifications shall be passed unanimously by the Conference of Heads of State.

Article 14. Every African State whose Government accepts the aims and objectives of this Charter, shall be eligible for consideration for membership of the Union of African States, from the date following a clear statement by the Head of the State. This statement shall be transmitted to the Heads of Member States of the Union.

Signed:
MODIBO KEITA
President of the Republic of Mali
SÉKOU TOURÉ
President of the Republic of Guinea
KWAME NKRUMAH
President of the Republic of Ghana

15

THE CASABLANCA CONFERENCE*
January 3–7, 1961

1. THE AFRICAN CHARTER OF CASABLANCA

We, the Heads of the African States, meeting in Casablanca from January 3 to January 7, 1961, conscious of our responsibilities towards the African Continent, proclaim our determination to promote the triumph of liberty all over Africa and to achieve its unity,

Affirm our will to preserve and consolidate our identity of views and unity of action in international affairs, to safeguard our hard won independence, the sovereignty and territorial integrity of our States, to reinforce peace in the world by adopting a policy of non alignment,

Proclaim our determination to liberate the African territories still under foreign domination, by giving them aid and assistance, to liquidate colonialism and neo-colonialism in all their forms, to discourage the maintenance of foreign troops and the establishment of bases which endanger the liberation of Africa and to strive equally to rid the African Continent of political and economic interventions and pressures,

Proclaim the necessity for the Independent African States to direct their political, economic and social policies to the exploitation of the national wealth for the benefit of their peoples and to ensuring an equitable distribution of that wealth among all nationals,

Affirm our will to intensify our efforts for the creation of an effective form of co-operation among the African States in the economic, social and cultural domains,

Aiming at the consolidation of liberty in Africa and building up its unity and security, decide:

1. The creation of an African Consultative Assembly, as soon as conditions permit, composed of the representatives of every African State, having a permanent seat and holding periodical sessions,

2. The creation of the following four committees:

(a) *The African Political Committee*, comprising Heads of State, or their duly accredited representatives, will meet periodically with a view to co-ordinating and unifying the general policy of the various African States;

(b) *The African Economic Committee*, comprising the Ministers of Economic Affairs of the Independent African States, will meet periodically with a view to taking decisions with regard to African Economic Co-operation. One of the most urgent tasks of this

---

* For participants see page 51.

Committee will be to establish postal and telecommunication links among the various African Capitals;

(c) *The African Cultural Committee*, comprising the Ministers of Education of the Independent African States, will meet periodically with a view to preserving and developing African culture and civilisation and intensifying African cultural co-operation and assistance;

(d) *A Joint African High Command*, comprising the Chiefs of Staff of the Independent African States, will meet periodically with a view to ensuring the common defence of Africa in case of aggression against any part of this Continent, and with a view to safeguarding the independence of African States,

3. The creation of a liaison office for establishing effective co-operation among the different organisations mentioned above and particularly for the holding within three months of a meeting of experts charged with defining the practical procedure concerning the functioning of the organisations in question.

We, the Heads of African States, convened in Casablanca from the 3rd January to the 7th January, 1961, reaffirm our faith in the Conferences of the Independent African States, held in Accra in 1958 and in Addis Ababa in 1960, and appeal to all Independent African States to associate themselves with our common action for the consolidation of liberty in Africa and the building up of its unity and security.

We solemnly reaffirm our unshakeable adherence to the United Nations Charter and to the Declaration of the Afro-Asian Conference held in Bandung, with the aim of promoting co-operation among all the peoples of the world and of consolidating international peace.

2. RESOLUTIONS

Resolution on Palestine

The Conference at Casablanca,

Having examined the important problem of Palestine, and deeply concerned about the situation created in Palestine by depriving the Arabs of Palestine of their legitimate rights:

1. Warns against the menace which this situation presents to the peace and security of the Middle East and the international tension which results therefrom.

2. Insists on the necessity to have a just solution to this problem in conformity with the United Nations resolutions and the Asian African resolution of Bandung to restore to the Arabs of Palestine all their legitimate rights.

3. Notes with indignation that Israel has always taken the side of the imperialists each time an important position had to be taken concerning vital problems about Africa, notably Algeria, the Congo and the nuclear tests in Africa, and the Conference, therefore, denounces Israel as an instrument in the service of imperialism and neo-colonialism not only in the Middle East but also in Africa and Asia.

4. Calls upon all the States of Africa and Asia to oppose this new policy which imperialism is carrying out to create bases for itself.

Resolution on Mauritania

The Conference,

Considering the colonialist intrigues aimed at dividing the territories of the African States in order to weaken them;

Considering that France, in order to strengthen her domination over the Sahara, exploits its wealth and secures for herself an outlet on the Atlantic, has severed from Morocco the southern portion of her territory, in Mauritania;

Considering that the setting up of a puppet State, the said Mauritania, against the will of the people concerned, and in disregard of the solemn undertakings given by France, is a violation of international treaties and agreements;

Considering that the setting up of Mauritania as a puppet State is merely a means for France to encircle the African countries, secure for herself bases to which she can retreat, and increase the number of her satellites;

Considering that, in general, the increase in the number of artificial States in Africa is a permanent threat to the security of the African Continent, and, at the same time, a strengthening of the forces of imperialism;

Considering that the objective aimed at by France in Mauritania is the economic exploitation and strategic use of this area, particularly against the African countries, as well as the maintenance of artificial barriers in Africa;

Considering that the defence of the unity and territorial integrity of all African States is, at the same time, the defence of the freedom of Africa;

Solemnly denounces and condemns all forms of economic, political and military exploitation in Africa;

Declares its determination to oppose, by all possible means, every attempt to partition and create satellite States in certain parts of the African Continent;

Approves any action taken by Morocco on Mauritania for the restitution of her legitimate rights.

Resolution on Ruanda-Urundi

With regard to the Trust Territory of Ruanda-Urundi, the Conference denounces Belgium's attempts to divide this country by creating two pseudo-independent States established by a policy of organised repression against the nationalist elements of this country.

The Conference supports unreservedly the cause of the people of Ruanda-Urundi in their struggle for real independence and urges the implementation of the resolutions passed by the General Assembly of the United Nations at its Fifteenth Session concerning the future of Ruanda-Urundi and the constitutional régime of Ruanda-Urundi, namely:

A general and unconditional amnesty for all those involved in the incidents which occurred in November, 1959;

The lifting of the state of emergency and the restoration of democratic liberties and fundamental human rights;

The immediate return of all political refugees;

A national reconciliation;

The safeguard of the national unity and the protection of the territorial integrity of this country.

The Conference denounces the use of the territory of Ruanda-Urundi as a base for aggression against African peoples and the Congo in particular.

The Conference demands the immediate evacuation of all Belgian forces stationed in this territory and the restoration of an atmosphere of peace and security.

Resolution on Apartheid and Racial Discrimination

The Casablanca Conference,

Recalling the resolutions of the United Nations Organisation which denounced the Apartheid policy and the racial discrimination practised by the Government of the Union of South Africa, and

Recalling in particular the resolution of the Security Council of the 1st of April, 1960, which considers the policy of racial discrimination pursued by the Government of the Union of South Africa as a threat to world peace and security,

1. Denounces the Government of the Union of South Africa for its contempt of the decisions taken by the United Nations Organisation and by the African and Asian Conferences and condemns its obstinacy in pursuing a policy which affects human dignity and constitutes a flagrant violation of human rights;

2. Denounces the imperialist Powers who continue to lend moral, political and military support to the racialist Government of the Union of South Africa;

3. Reaffirms and undertakes to implement the decisions taken at the Bandung, Accra, Monrovia and Addis Ababa conferences on this subject and urges all African States to implement these decisions;

4. Calls upon the United Nations Organisation to invoke the sanctions provided for in Articles 40 and 41 of the United Nations Charter should the Government of the Union of South Africa not put an end to its policy of racial discrimination.

Resolution on Nuclear Tests

The Conference,

Vigorously opposes the carrying out of nuclear tests by France on the African continent, in spite of the outraged conscience of the world, the disapproval of African countries, and the recommendations of the United Nations;

Strongly denounces this act of provocation directed against the African peoples, with a view to intimidating them and hindering their march towards the attainment of freedom and unity, and is a permanent danger for the African peoples and a constant threat to world peace;

Denounces and condemns the collusion between France and Israel in regard to nuclear tests, a collusion which threatens peace in the world and particularly in Africa;

Appeals to all peoples and in particular to the peoples of Africa who are most directly threatened, to do everything in their power to prevent these tests from taking place, and oppose the use of African territories for purposes of political domination;

Having noted with satisfaction the refusal by the people of France to allow these tests to take place on their own soil;

Invites all African countries to reconsider their relations with France, faced as they are with France's obstinate insistence on carrying out atomic explosions in Africa.

Resolution on Algeria

The Conference,

Considering that the fifteenth session of the United Nations has recognised the right of the Algerian people to Independence and Self-Determination on the basis of the unity and territorial integrity of Algeria, as well as the responsibility of the United Nations in the implementation of the right in Algeria;

Considering that all political, diplomatic and material aid given to the Algerian people represents a contribution to the liberation of Africa;

Considering that every assistance given to France in her war in Algeria constitutes an act of hostility directed against Africa as a whole;

Considering that the Provisional Government of the Algerian Republic is the only authority qualified to represent and speak on behalf of Algeria;

Considering that the war pursued by France in Algeria constitutes an increasing threat to peace and security in Africa and the world;

Considering that the events and demonstrations which are taking place and developing in Algeria constitute the unequivocal affirmation of the will of the Algerian people to realise their Independence, and of their unanimity in support of the Provisional Government of the Algerian Republic;

Declares its determination to support by all means the Algerian people and the Provisional Government of the Algerian Republic in their struggle for the Independence of Algeria;

Calls upon all the countries which support the Algerian people in their struggle for national liberation to re-enforce their political, diplomatic and material aid to the Provisional Government of the Algerian Republic;

Denounces the assistance given by NATO to France in her war of colonial reconquest in Algeria;

Invites all countries to take steps forthwith to prevent their territories from being used directly or indirectly for operations against the Algerian people;

Calls for the immediate withdrawal of all African troops serving under French command in Algeria;

Approves the enlistment of African and other volunteers in the Army of National Liberation;

Invites all the Governments which have not done so to recognise the Provisional Government of the Algerian Republic;

Declares that the continuation of the war in Algeria is of such nature that it impels the participating countries to reconsider their relations with France;

Opposes the partition of Algeria and rejects any unilateral solution and any constitution either imposed or granted.

DECLARATION

The Conference denounces and condemns all consultations and reference unilaterally organised by France in Algeria, and the results thereof can in no way commit the Algerian people.

3. COMMUNIQUÉ
concerning the situation in the Congo

The Conference at Casablanca convened by His Majesty King Mohammed V of the Kingdom of Morocco, and constituted by the following Heads of States, namely His Majesty King Mohammed V of the Kingdom of Morocco, His Excellency Gamal Abdel Nasser, President of the United Arab Republic, His Excellency Kwame Nkrumah, President of the Republic of Ghana, His Excellency Sékou Touré, President of the Republic of Guinea, His Excellency Modibo Keita, President of the Republic of Mali, His Excellency Ferhat Abbas, Prime Minister of the Provisional Government of Algeria representing the Provisional Government of Algeria, His Excellency Abdelkader El Allam, Minister of Foreign Affairs representing His Majesty King Idriss I of the Kingdom of Libya and His Excellency Alwin B. Perera, Ambassador Extraordinary and Plenipotentiary representing the Prime Minister of Ceylon, having considered the situation in the Congo:

1. Declares the intention and determination of the respective Governments represented to withdraw their troops and other military personnel placed under the United Nations Operational Command in the Congo.

2. Reaffirms their recognition of the elected Parliament and legally constituted Government of the Republic of the Congo which came into being on 30th of June, 1960.

3. Convinced that the only justification for the presence of the United Nations troops in the Congo is:

    i. To answer the appeals of the legitimate Government of the Republic of the Congo at whose request the United Nations decided to create its Operational Command;

    ii. To implement the decisions of the Security Council in respect of the situation in the Congo;

    iii. To safeguard the unity and independence of the Republic of the Congo and preserve its territorial integrity;

Urges the United Nations to act immediately to:

    (a) Disarm and disband the lawless bands of Mobutu;

    (b) Release from prison and detention all members of the Parliament and legitimate Government of the Republic of the Congo;

    (c) Reconvene the Parliament of the Republic of the Congo;

    (d) Eliminate from the Congo all Belgian and other foreign military and para-military personnel not belonging to the United Nations Operational Command whether operating as such or in disguise;

    (e) Release to the legitimate Government of the Congo all civil and military airports, radio-stations and other establishments, now unlawfully withheld from that Government;

    (f) Prevent the Belgians from using the United Nations Trust Territory of Ruanda-Urundi as a base to commit aggression—direct or indirect—to launch armed attacks against the Congolese Republic.

4. Decides that if the purposes and principles which justified the presence of the United Nations Operational Command in the Republic of the Congo are not realised and respected then the States here represented reserve the right to take appropriate action.

16

THE PROTOCOL OF
THE AFRICAN CHARTER
May 5, 1961

1. THE PROTOCOL

In compliance with their determination to implement the African Charter issued at the Casablanca conference, which was held between 3rd and 7th January, 1961, and in accordance with the provisions of the said Charter; the Governments of the African States which signed the Charter agree to this protocol:

Article 1. Co-operation among the member States of the Charter shall be conducted through the following bodies: (a) an African Political Committee; (b) an African Economic Committee; (c) an African Cultural Committee; (d) an African Joint High Command; and (e) a Liaison Office. These bodies which carry out the provisions of the Charter shall have a permanent character.

Article 2. The African Political Committee: The African Political Committee shall be the highest body for the co-ordination and unification of the general policy of the member States, and shall be composed of the Heads of States, or their accredited representatives. At its first meeting, the Committee shall lay down the provisions of its by-laws.

Article 3. Meetings of the African Political Committee: The African Political Committee shall hold an ordinary meeting *once* a year and may hold a number of extraordinary meetings at the request of one member State, upon the approval of the majority of the member States.

Article 4. The African Economic Committee: The African Economic Committee shall consist of the Ministers of Finance of the member States or their representatives. The Committee shall hold periodic meetings and shall submit a report on the problems it is tackling and an annual report on its activities to the African Political Committee. At its first meeting, the Committee shall decide its by-laws.

Article 5. The African Cultural Committee: The African Cultural Committee shall consist of the Ministers of Education of the member States or their representatives. The Committee shall hold periodic meetings, and shall submit a report on the problems it is tackling and an annual report on its activities to the African Political Committee. At its first meeting, the Committee shall decide its by-laws.

Article 6. The African Joint High Command: The African Joint High Command shall consist of the Chiefs of Staffs of the member States or their representatives. The Committee shall hold periodic meetings and shall report to the African Political Committee immediately after every meeting.

Article 7. Recommendations of the African Joint High Command: Recommendations of the African Joint High Command shall become valid as soon as they are approved by the African Political Committee.

Article 8. The Liaison Office: The headquarters of the Liaison Office shall be at Bamako, the capital of the Republic of Mali. It may be transferred to any other place by a decision of the African Political Committee. It shall be headed by a secretary to be appointed by the African Political Committee for a renewable term of three years. He will be assisted by a number of assistant secretaries appointed by the African Political Committee. The secretary of the Liaison Office is the highest administrative official of this body.

Article 9. Officials of the Liaison Office: The secretary of the Liaison Office shall appoint the officials required for the smooth functioning of the various committees and shall submit to the African Political Committee drafts of the by-laws governing the conditions of their appointments.

Article 10. Co-ordination of the Committees' Work: The secretary of the Liaison Office shall submit to the African Political Committee an annual report on the measures which ensure the best possible co-ordination of work among the various bodies provided for in the Casablanca African Charter.

Article 11. The Committees' Secretariat: The secretary or his representative shall carry out the secretarial work during the meetings of the aforementioned bodies.

Article 12. The Budget: The secretary shall prepare the draft budget and shall submit it to the African Political Committee before the beginning of the financial year. The African Political Committee shall then determine the shares to be paid by each of the member States.

Article 13. The Status of the Secretariat Officials: The secretary and the officials of the Liaison Office shall be considered international officials and shall receive no instructions from any member State during the exercise of their duties and tasks. All their actions must be in line with their position as international officials. The member States shall pledge to refrain from any action which would affect the officials while they are carrying out their responsibilities.

Article 14. Privileges and Immunities: the secretary of the Liaison Office, his assistants, his technical officials, the special envoys, and the representatives of the member States shall enjoy the privileges and immunities customarily granted to members of the diplomatic corps during the performance of their duties in the member States.

Article 15. The Liaison Office Building: The building of the Liaison Office shall enjoy all the privileges and immunities agreed upon. The secretary shall conclude an agreement for this purpose with the host State. The committees shall enjoy the same privileges and immunities when they meet outside the Liaison Office.

Article 16. Applications for Membership: Any African State accepting the provisions of the African Charter and this protocol may apply for membership to the president of the African Political Committee and shall become a member upon the approval of the African Political Committee.

Article 17. General Provisions: (a) The member States declare that the obligations and commitments they incur by virtue of their international undertakings shall not contradict their obligations and commitments under the Casablanca African Charter and this protocol and, in particular, the policy of non-alignment provided for in the aforementioned Charter. (b) The member States undertake to inform the secretary of any agreements and treaties they become party to. (c) The Casablanca African Charter and this protocol shall be registered with the UN Secretariat-General in accordance with Para. 1 of Art. No. 102 of the UN Charter.

Article 18. Amendments: At the request of one of the member States and the approval of two-thirds of the member States, this protocol may be amended with a view to strengthening the relations among these States. The proposed amendments shall be submitted to the secretary of the Liaison Office two months before the meeting of the African Political Committee.

Article 19. Signing and Validity of the Protocol: This protocol shall become effective as soon as it is approved by at least two of the member States.

Done at Cairo, UAR, this day Friday 5th May 1961, in three original copies, in Arabic, English, and French, which have equal validity.

MUHAMMAD YAZID, for the Provisional Government of the Algerian Republic; AKO ADJEI, for the Republic of Ghana; LOUIS-LANSANA BEAVOGUI, for the Republic of Guinea; BAREMA COCOUM, for the Republic of Mali; IDRISS MUHAMMADI, for the Kingdom of Morocco; MAHMUD FAWZI, for the United Arab Republic.

2. Statements on the Signing of the Protocol

The Ministers of Foreign Affairs of the Casablanca Summit States concluded on May 5 their Cairo meeting after approving the text of the protocol for an African Charter.

A statement issued at the end of the meeting also said there was complete identity of views on African and international problems which had been discussed during the meeting.

Spokesman for the Ministers said at the end of the meeting:

"The Ministers of Foreign Affairs of the States of the African Charter of Casablanca convened in Cairo from the 13th April to the 5th of May, 1961, to examine the recommendations of the Committee of experts which met in Accra in implementation of the decisions of the African Charter of Casablanca.

The Ministers of Foreign Affairs defined and approved the text of the protocol for the implementation of the African Charter of Casablanca. They took the necessary decisions and measures for the rapid establishment of the organs foreseen by the African Charter of Casablanca.

The Ministers of Foreign Affairs examined African and international problems which have preoccupied Africa and the world. There was complete identity of views on all these problems. They were informed of the latest developments of the situation in the Congo and decided to further strengthen their efforts for safeguarding the independence, the integrity and the national unity of the Congo and renew their support of the legitimate Government of the Congo headed by Mr. Antoine Gizenga.

Algeria

They examined the latest developments of the situation in Algeria and renewed their affirmation of unconditional support to the struggling Algerian people. They expressed their absolute agreement to the policy adopted by the Provisional Government of the Algerian Republic with a view to reaching a negotiated solution, based on the right of the Algerian people to self determination and the territorial integrity of Algeria.

They reiterated their support for the legitimate rights of the Arab people of Palestine and their desire to implement the resolutions on Palestine adopted at Casablanca.

The Ministers of Foreign Affairs studied the recent developments of the national liberation fight going on in different parts of Africa, particularly Angola. They reaffirmed their support to the Angolian people and paid tribute to their heroic struggle.

They discussed the measures to be taken for the implementation of the Casablanca resolutions, particularly those on racial discrimination. There was complete identity of view on the problems of disarmament and the banning of nuclear tests.

The Ministers of Foreign Affairs studied the situation in Laos and affirmed the necessity of preserving the independence and territorial integrity of that State as well as its neutrality.

They condemned foreign intervention in Cuba and expressed their admiration for the Cuban people struggling for the safeguarding of their independence and for the defence of their territory."

The UAR Presidential adviser for political affairs, Mahmud Riyad, held a Press conference on the 9th May, at the headquarters of the Central Government in Heliopolis. He declared that the Foreign Ministers of the African Charter Powers agreed on the following points during their meetings in Cairo as from 30th April to 5th May:

1. The first meeting of the African Economic Committee shall be held at Conakry on 15th July, 1961.

2. The first meeting of the African Cultural Committee shall be held at Casablanca on 31st July, 1961.

3. The first meeting of the African High Command shall be held on 15th July, 1961.

4. The first meeting of the Political Committee shall be held before 15th September, 1961, as the Foreign Ministers recommend, provided that the place of the meeting shall be decided upon through consultations among the member States.

5. Bamako, the capital of the Republic of Mali, shall be the headquarters of the Liaison Office and the temporary secretary shall be Moroccan until such time as the Political Committee meets and appoints a permanent secretary.

His Excellency added that it was agreed to allocate 50,000 pounds for the provisional budget of the liaison office. All member States with the exception of Algeria will pay equal shares, each thus paying 10,000.

Mahmud Riyad was asked if this protocol would be submitted to Heads of States for their approval. He said that the approval of this protocol would be carried out in accordance with the constitutional conditions of each member State. By virtue of their constitutional conditions, some States have already approved the protocol, while in the case of the other States, it will have to pass through the various stages provided for in their systems. The Foreign Ministers, he added, have signed the protocol on the authority of their Heads of State.

Mahmud Riyad said that Article 17 of the protocol provides that the Charter shall be registered with the UN Secretariat-General. It is the duty of the secretary, upon his appointment, to carry out this registration. It was also agreed that the instruments of ratification shall be deposited with the Moroccan Government until the formation of the permanent secretariat.

17

THE MONROVIA CONFERENCE*
May 8–12, 1961

Resolution on the Means of Promoting Better Understanding and Co-operation Towards Achieving Unity in Africa and Malagasy

The Conference of Heads of States and Governments of Africa and Malagasy meeting at Monrovia on 8th to 12th May, 1961:

Recognising the historic importance of the Conference Monrovia, because of the number of participating States;
Noting with deep regret the absence of some of our sister States;
Confident in their intense desire for African solidarity and expressing the hope that they may find it convenient to attend subsequent meetings;
Anxious to promote henceforth a full and brotherly co-operation between Independent African and Malagasy States;
Considering the need for pooling resources and co-ordinating efforts in order to overcome the barriers of growth which confront all African and Malagasy countries on their way to development;

A. Solemnly affirms and adopts the following principles which shall govern the relationship between the African and Malagasy States:

1. Absolute equality of African and Malagasy States whatever may be the size of their territories, the density of their populations, or the value of their possessions;

2. Non-interference in the internal affairs of States;

3. Respect for the sovereignty of each State and its inalienable right to existence and development of its personality;

4. Unqualified condemnation of outside subversive action by neighbouring States;

5. Promotion of co-operation throughout Africa, based upon tolerance, solidarity and good-neighbour relations, periodical exchange of views, and non-acceptance of any leadership;

6. The unity that is aimed to be achieved at the moment is not the political integration of sovereign African States, but unity of aspirations and of action considered from the point of view of African social solidarity and political identity;

B. Urges that all African and Malagasy States shall refrain from encouraging, directly or indirectly, dissident groups or individuals of other States in subversive activities by permitting their own States to be used as bases from which such dissidents may operate, or by financing dissidents in other countries or otherwise;

* For a list of those attending see page 201.

C. Accepts, in principle, that an inter-African and Malagasy Advisory Organisation shall be created, the essential purpose of which shall be to put into effect the above-mentioned principles and to establish this Organisation at the next conference.

D. Decides,

(1) That a technical commission of experts designated by the respective States shall be created and that these experts shall meet in Dakar, Senegal, within three months after the close of this Conference for the purpose of working out detailed plans for economic, educational, cultural, scientific and technical co-operation, as well as for communications and transportation among African and Malagasy States;

(2) That the existing research and technical institutions shall constitute effective machinery for the collection of data and the dissemination of the results of research among African and Malagasy States, and that all States shall so direct;

(3) That all African and Malagasy States shall recognise the desire to promote the revival of African culture and traditions in the interest of preserving the real African heritage;

(4) That all African and Malagasy States shall make a special effort to include in addition to their respective national and official languages the teaching of the French and English languages.

E. Decides, finally, that the next Conference of Heads of African and Malagasy States shall be held in Lagos, Nigeria.

Resolution on Threats to Peace and Stability in Africa and the World

The Conference, profoundly disturbed by the serious threats which hang over peace and stability in Africa and the world,

Considering that the principle of non-interference in the domestic affairs of African States applies only to States already independent and sovereign;

Affirms its unanimous determination to give material and moral assistance to all dependent territories of colonial Powers with a view to accelerating their accession to independence.

The Conference, as concerns the ALGERIAN QUESTION, welcomes the improvement of the situation in Algeria and the decision of the two parties to open negotiations on 20 May, 1961; and

Appeals to the Government of France and the Provisional Government of the Algerian Republic to conclude at the earliest moment an agreement putting an end to the war and accord to Algeria its independence and territorial integrity.

The Conference, as concerns the CONGO,

Reaffirms its faith in the United Nations as the only organisation which, in spite of past weaknesses and mistakes in its work, is best adapted to achieve a real solution of the Congo problem;

Calls on all African States to desist from such activities as the hasty recognition of breakaway régimes in the Republic of the Congo, and generally from taking sides with rival groups in any form or manner;

Condemns assassinations as a means to attain political power;

Condemns the action of certain non-African States which encourage subversion in other African States.

The Conference, as concerns ANGOLA,

Calls on all African and Malagasy States to pledge their wholehearted material and moral support to the Africans in Angola in their struggle for autonomy;

Appeals to the universal conscience against the atrocities and the bloody repression of the Angolian population.

The Conference, as regards the UNION of SOUTH AFRICA,

Condemns unreservedly the theory and practice of apartheid by the Government of the Union of South Africa;

Calls on all African and Malagasy States to apply immediately political and economic sanctions, collectively and individually, against the Government of the Union of South Africa, not only to demonstrate our resentment of the ruthless degradation of the non-whites there, but also ultimately to compel the Government of the Union of South Africa to abandon the iniquitous practice of apartheid;

Calls on all African and Malagasy States to take all necessary steps to give all material and moral support to the Africans and Asians of South Africa in their struggle to regain the stature of man;

Affirms that all the participating African States strongly support the reiterated decision of the Trusteeship Council of the United Nations that the Government of the Union of South Africa must acknowledge the authority of the Council as guardian of the mandate over the Territory of South-West Africa.

The Conference, as concerns DISARMAMENT,

Appeals to all the nuclear Powers to stop the manufacture and stockpiling of nuclear weapons and all further nuclear explosions anywhere in the world;

Decides that the Chairman should make a written appeal in the name of the Conference to the Commission on Nuclear Disarmament, now in session in Geneva, to use their best endeavours to secure the objective stated in the preceding paragraph;

Notes the assurances given by the French Government that they will cease all further nuclear explosions in Africa.

The Conference, as concerns the UNITED NATIONS,

Urges the members of the United Nations to assure a more equitable geographical distribution of the seats of the Security and the Economic and Social Councils and also to work for the expansion of the Councils,

Decides to send a cablegram to members of the Security Council asking them to take a decision in favour of the admission of Mauritania in the United Nations Organisation in conformity with the last Resolution of the General Assembly;

Condemns all attempts to weaken or undermine the authority of the United Nations;

Records the intention of all African and Malagasy States to present a united front in the future to all world problems with which Africa might be faced at the United Nations.

Resolution on Settlement of Conflicts which may Arise Between African States

This Conference of Chiefs of African and Malagasy States and Governments, meeting at Monrovia from 8th to 12th May, 1961,

Recommends:

1. That the settlement of disputes shall be by peaceful means;
2. That a commission shall be created which shall be attached to the Organisation of Co-operation of the African and Malagasy States;
3. That this Conference unanimously resolves that a written appeal be made through the executive authority of the present Conference to their Excellencies the Emperor of Ethiopia and the President of Somalia to make renewed efforts towards a sincere and early solution of all their existing frontier and any other disputes.

Attendance

Who was there:

President William V. S. Tubman of Liberia, presiding; President Felix Houphouet-Boigny of Ivory Coast; President Ahmadou Ahidjo of Cameroun; President Leopold Senghor of Senegal; President Philibert Tsiranana of the Malagasy Republic; President Sylvanus Olympio of Togo; President Hubert Maga of Dahomey; President Francois Tombalbaye of Chad; President Hamani Diori of Niger; President Maurice Yameogo of Upper Volta; President Fulbert Youlou of Congo (Brazzaville); Prime Minister Sir Abubakar Tafawa Balewa of Nigeria; Prime Minister Sir Milton Margai of Sierra Leone; Prime Minister Abdi Rashid Shermarke of Somalia; and Prime Minister Moktar Ould Daddah of Mauritania. In addition, high-level delegations represented Tunisia (whose President Habib Bourghiba could not attend because he was completing State visits to the U.S., U.K. and Canada); the Central African Republic and Gabon (whose Presidents were ill); Ethiopia; and Libya.

Notable Absentees:

The Presidents of Ghana, Guinea and Mali declined to come on the grounds that preparations had been inadequate. Morocco and the United Arab Republic, the fourth and fifth Casablanca Powers, also were unrepresented. Sudan's President Ibrahim Abboud withdrew his acceptance a few days before the conference, on the grounds that he must support Morocco's objection to the insertion of a controversial issue into the meeting—i.e. the presence of Mauritania, whose independence Morocco disputes. The Congo (Leopoldville) was not invited because of the desire to avoid a controversy with the Casablanca nations over credentials.

18

AFRICAN CONFERENCE ON THE RULE OF LAW
Lagos, Nigeria, January, 1961

THE LAW OF LAGOS

The African Conference on the Rule of Law, consisting of 194 judges, practising lawyers and teachers of law from twenty-three African nations as well as nine countries of other continents,

Assembled in Lagos, Nigeria, in January 1961 under the aegis of the International Commission of Jurists,

Having discussed freely and frankly the Rule of Law with particular reference to Africa, and

Having reached conclusions regarding Human Rights in relation to Government security, Human Rights in relation to aspects of criminal and administrative law, and the responsibility of the Judiciary and of the Bar for the protection of the rights of the individual in society,

Now solemnly

Recognises that the Rule of Law is a dynamic concept which should be employed to safeguard and advance the will of the people and the political rights of the individual and to establish social, economic, educational and cultural conditions under which the individual may achieve his dignity and realise his legitimate aspirations in all countries, whether dependent or independent,

Reaffirms the Act of Athens and the Declaration of Delhi with special reference to Africa and

Declares

1. That the principles embodied in the *Conclusions* of this Conference which are annexed hereto should apply to any society, whether free or otherwise, but that the Rule of Law cannot be fully realised unless legislative bodies have been established in accordance with the will of the people who have adopted their Constitution freely;

2. That in order to maintain adequately the Rule of Law all Governments should adhere to the principle of democratic representation in their Legislatures;

3. That fundamental human rights, especially the right to personal liberty, should be written and entrenched in the Constitutions of all countries and that such personal liberty should not in peacetime be restricted without trial in a Court of Law;

4. That in order to give full effect to the Universal Declaration of

Human Rights of 1948, this Conference invites the African Governments to study the possibility of adopting an African Convention of Human Rights in such a manner that the *Conclusions* of this Conference will be safeguarded by the creation of a court of appropriate jurisdiction and that recourse thereto be made available for all persons under the jurisdiction of the signatory States;

5. That in order to promote the principles and the practical application of the Rule of Law, the judges, practising lawyers and teachers of law in African countries should take steps to establish branches of the International Commission of Jurists.

This Resolution shall be known as the Law of Lagos.

Done at Lagos this 7th day of January, 1961.

CONCLUSIONS
COMMITTEE I
Human Rights and Government Security—the Legislative, Executive and Judiciary

I

1. The exigencies of modern society necessitate the practice of the Legislature delegating to the Executive the power to make rules having the force of legislation.

2. The power of the Executive to make rules or regulations having legislative effect should derive from the express mandate of the Legislature; these rules and regulations should be subject to approval by that body. The object and scope of such executive power should be clearly defined.

3. The Judiciary should be given the jurisdiction to determine in every case upon application whether the circumstances have arisen or the conditions have been fulfilled under which such power is to be or has been exercised.

4. Every constitution should provide that, except during a period of emergency, legislation should as far as possible be delegated only in respect of matters of economic and social character and that the exercise of such powers should not infringe upon fundamental human rights.

5. The proclamation of a state of emergency is a matter of most serious concern as it directly affects and may infringe upon human rights. It is the sense of the Conference that the dangers of survival of the nation such as arise from a sudden military challenge may call for urgent and drastic measures by the Executive which by the nature of things are susceptible only to *a posteriori* legislative ratification and judicial review. In any other case, however, it is the Parliament duly convened for the purpose that should declare whether or not the state of emergency exists. Wherever it is impossible or inexpedient to summon Parliament for this purpose, for example during Parliamentary recess, the Executive should be competent to declare a state of emergency, but in such a case Parliament should meet as soon as possible thereafter.

6. The Conference is of the opinion that real danger exists when, to quote the words of the General Rapporteur, "The citizenry, whether by legislative or executive action, or abuse of the judicial process, are made to live as if in a perpetual state of emergency."

7. The Conference feels that in all cases of the exercise of emergency powers, any person who is aggrieved by the violation of his rights should

have access to the courts for determination whether the power has been lawfully exercised.

II

The Conference, having considered the relative rights and obligations of legislative, executive and judicial institutions and their functions as affecting human rights and government security with particular reference to the observance of the Rule of Law in both independent and dependent countries in Africa and elsewhere; and having taken cognizance of allegations that discriminatory legislation based on race, colour or creed exists to the detriment of fundamental human rights of large sections of the population,

Requests the International Commission of Jurists to investigate, examine, consider and report on the legal conditions in Africa and elsewhere with particular regard to the existence of the Rule of Law and the observation of fundamental human rights.

COMMITTEE II
Human Rights and Aspects of Criminal and Administrative Law

The Rule of Law is of universal validity and application as it embraces those institutions and principles of justice which are considered minimal to the assurance of human rights and the dignity of man.

Further as a preamble to these *Conclusions* it is decided to adopt the following text from the *Conclusions* of the Second Committee of the International Congress of Jurists, New Delhi, India, 1959:

"The Rule of Law depends not only on the provision of adequate safeguards against abuse of power by the Executive, but also on the existence of effective government capable of maintaining law and order and of ensuring adequate social and economic conditions of life for the society.

"The following propositions relating to the Executive and the Rule of Law are accordingly formulated on the basis of certain conditions which are either satisfied, or in the case of newly independent countries still struggling with difficult economic and social problems are in process of being satisfied. These conditions require the existence of an Executive invested with sufficient power and resources to discharge its functions with efficiency and integrity. They require the existence of a Legislature elected by democratic process and not subject, either in the manner of its election or otherwise, to manipulation by the Executive. They require the existence of an independent Judiciary which will discharge its duties fearlessly. They finally call for the earnest endeavour of government to achieve such social and economic conditions within a society as will ensure a reasonable standard of economic security, social welfare and education for the mass of the people."

1. Taking full cognizance of and incorporating herein by reference Clause III 3 (a) of the *Conclusions* of the First Committee of the above-mentioned International Congress of Jurists in New Delhi* it is recognised and agreed that legislation authorising administrative action by the Executive should not be discriminatory with respect to race, creed, sex or other such reasons and any such discriminatory provisions contained in legislation are considered contrary to the Rule of Law.

* "The Legislative must . . . not discriminate in its laws in respect of individuals, classes of persons, or minority groups on the ground of race, religion, sex or other such reasons not affording a proper basis for making a distinction between human beings, classes, or minorities."

2. While recognising that inquiry into the merits of the propriety of an individual administrative act by the Executive may in many cases not be appropriate for the ordinary courts, it is agreed that there should be available to the person aggrieved a right of access to:

(*a*) a hierarchy of administrative courts of independent jurisdiction; or

(*b*) where these do not exist, to an administrative tribunal subject to the overriding authority of the ordinary courts.

3. The minimum requirements for such administrative action and subsequent judicial review as recommended in paragraph 2 above are as follows:

(*a*) that the full reasons for the action of the Executive be made known to the person aggrieved; and

(*b*) that the aggrieved person shall be given a fair hearing; and

(*c*) that the grounds given by the Executive for its action shall not be regarded as conclusive but shall be objectively considered by the court.

4. It is desirable that, whenever reasonable in the prevailing circumstances, the action of the Executive shall be suspended while under review by the courts.

5. (i) No person of sound mind shall be deprived of his liberty except upon a charge of a specific criminal offence; further, except during a public emergency, preventive detention without trial is held to be contrary to the Rule of Law.

(ii) During a period of public emergency, legislation often authorises preventive detention of an individual if the Executive finds that public security so requires. Such legislation should provide the individual with safeguards against continuing arbitrary confinement by requiring a prompt administrative hearing and decision upon the need and justification for detention with a right to judicial review. It should be required that any declaration of public emergency by the Executive be reported to and subject to ratification by the Legislature. Moreover, both the declaration of public emergency and any consequent detention of individuals should be effective only for a specified and limited period of time (not exceeding six months).

(iii) Extension of the period of public emergency should be effected by the Legislature only after careful and deliberate consideration of the necessity therefor. Finally, during any period of public emergency the Executive should only take such measures as are reasonably justifiable for the purpose of dealing with the situation which exists during that period.

6. The courts and magistrates shall permit an accused person to be or to remain free pending trial except in the following cases which are deemed proper grounds for refusing bail:

(*a*) in the case of a very grave offence;

(*b*) if the accused is likely to interfere with witnesses or impede the course of justice;

(*c*) if the accused is likely to commit the same or other offences;

(*d*) if the accused may fail to appear for trial.

7. The power to grant bail is a judicial function which shall not be subject to control by the Executive. Although a court should hear and consider the views and representations of the Executive, the fact that

investigation of the case is being continued is not a sufficient ground for refusing bail. Bail should be commensurate with the economic means of the accused, and, whether by appeal or independent application, a higher court should have the power to release provisionally an accused person who has been denied bail by the lower court.

8. After conviction and pending review, the trial or appellate court should have discretionary power to admit the convicted person to bail subject to the grounds set forth in paragraph 6 above.

9. It is recommended that greater use be made of the summons requring appearance in court to answer a criminal charge in place of arrest and the consequent necessity for bail and provisional release.

COMMITTEE III

The Responsibility of the Judiciary and of the Bar for the Protection of the Rights of the Individual in Society

The Conference reaffirms the *Conclusions* reached by the Fourth Committee of the International Congress of Jurists, New Delhi, India, 1959, which are appended hereto; and having regard to the particular problems of emerging States, wishes to emphasise certain points in particular, and to add others.

1. In a free society practising the Rule of Law, it is essential that the absolute independence of the Judiciary be guaranteed. Members of the legal profession in any country have, over and above their ordinary duties as citizens, a special duty to seek ways and means of securing in their own country the maximum degree of independence for the Judiciary.

2. It is recognised that in different countries there are different ways of appointing, promoting and removing judges by means of action taken by the Executive and Legislative powers. It is not recommended that these powers should be abrogated where they have been universally accepted over a long period as working well—provided that they conform to the principles expressed in Clauses II, III, IV and V of the Report of the Fourth Committee at New Delhi.

3. In respect of any country in which the methods of appointing, promoting and removing judges are not yet fully settled, or do not ensure the independence of the Judiciary, it is recommended:

(a) that these powers should not be put into the hands of the Executive or the Legislative, but should be entrusted exclusively to an independent organ such as the Judicial Service Commission of Nigeria or the *Conseil supérieur de la magistrature* in the African French-speaking countries;

(b) that in any country in which the independence of the Judiciary is not already fully secured in accordance with these principles, they should be implemented immediately in respect of all judges, especially those having criminal jurisdiction.

4. It is recommended that all customary, traditional or local law should be administered by the ordinary courts of the land, and emphasised that for so long as that law is administered by special courts, all the principles enunciated here and at New Delhi, for safeguarding the Rule of Law, apply to those courts.

5. The practice whereby in certain territories judicial powers, especially in criminal matters, are exercised by persons who have no adequate legal

training or experience, or who as administrative officers are subject to the control of the Executive is one which falls short of the Rule of Law.

6. (*a*) To maintain the respect for the Rule of Law it is necessary that the legal profession should be free from any interference;

(*b*) In countries where an organised Bar exists, the lawyers themselves should have the right to control the admission to the profession and the discipline of the members according to rules established by law;

(*c*) In countries where an organised Bar does not exist, the power to discipline lawyers should be exercised by the Judiciary in consultation with senior practising lawyers and never by the Executive.

7. The Conference reaffirms Clause X of the *Conclusions* of the Fourth Committee at New Delhi, and recommends that all steps should be taken to ensure equal access to law for both rich and poor, especially by a provision for and an organisation of a system of Legal Aid in both criminal and civil matters.

8. The Conference expressly reaffirms the principle that retroactive legislation especially in criminal matters is inconsistent with the Rule of Law.

Appendix

**REPORT OF COMMITTEE IV
INTERNATIONAL CONGRESS OF JURISTS,
NEW DELHI, 1959**
The Judiciary and the Legal Profession under the Rule of Law

CLAUSE I

An independent Judiciary is an indispensable requisite of a free society under the Rule of Law. Such independence implies freedom from interference by the Executive or Legislative with the exercise of the judicial function, but does not mean that the judge is entitled to act in an arbitrary manner. His duty is to interpret the law and the fundamental principles and assumptions that underlie it. It is implicit in the concept of independence set out in the present paragraph that provision should be made for the adequate remuneration of the Judiciary and that a judge's right to the remuneration settled for his office should not during his term of office be altered to his disadvantage.

CLAUSE II

There are in different countries varying ways in which the Judiciary are appointed, re-appointed (where re-appointment arises) and promoted, involving the Legislative, Executive, the Judiciary itself, in some countries the representatives of the practising legal profession, or a combination of two or more of these bodies. The selection of judges by election and particularly by re-election, as in some countries, presents special risks to the independence of the Judiciary which are more likely to be avoided only where tradition has circumscribed by prior agreement the list of candidates and has limited political controversy. There are also potential dangers in exclusive appointment by the Legislative, Executive, or Judiciary, and where there is on the whole general satisfaction with calibre and independence of judges it will be found that either in law or in practice there is some degree of co-operation (or at least consultation) between the Judiciary and the authority actually making the appointment.

CLAUSE III

The principle of irremovability of the Judiciary, and their security of tenure until death or until a retiring age fixed by statute is reached, is an important safeguard of the Rule of Law. Although it is not impossible for a judge appointed for a fixed term to assert his independence, particularly if he is seeking re-appointment, he is subject to greater difficulties and pressure than a judge who enjoys security of tenure for his working life.

CLAUSE IV

The reconciliation of the principle of irremovability of the Judiciary with the possibility of removal in exceptional circumstances necessitates that the grounds for removal should be before a body of judicial character assuring at least the same safeguards to the judge as would be accorded to an accused person in a criminal trial.

CLAUSE V

The considerations set out in the preceding paragraph should apply to: (1) the ordinary civil and criminal Courts; (2) administrative Courts or constitutional Courts, not being subordinate to the ordinary Courts. The members of administrative tribunals, whether professional lawyers or laymen, as well as laymen exercising other judicial functions (juries, assessors, Justices of the Peace, etc.) should only be appointed and removable in accordance with the spirit of these considerations, in so far as they are applicable to their particular positions. All such persons have in any event the same duty of independence in the performance of their judicial function.

CLAUSE VI

It must be recognised that the Legislative has responsibility for fixing the general framework and laying down the principles of organisation of judicial business and that, subject to the limitations on delegations of legislative power which have been dealt with elsewhere, it may delegate part of this responsibility to the Executive. However, the exercise of such responsibility by the Legislative including any delegation to the Executive should not be employed as an indirect method of violating the independence of the Judiciary in the exercise of its judicial functions.

CLAUSE VII

It is essential to the maintenance of the Rule of Law that there should be an organised legal profession free to manage its own affairs. But it is recognised that there may be general supervision by the Courts and that there may be regulations governing the admission to and pursuit of the legal profession.

CLAUSE VIII

Subject to his professional obligation to accept assignments in appropriate circumstances, the lawyer should be free to accept any case which is offered to him.

CLAUSE IX

While there is some difference of emphasis between various countries as to the extent to which a lawyer may be under a duty to accept a case it is conceived that:

> 1. Wherever a man's life, liberty, property or reputation are at stake he should be free to obtain legal advice and representation; if this principle is to become effective, it follows that lawyers must be prepared frequently to defend persons associated with unpopular causes and minority views with which they themselves may be entirely out of sympathy;
> 2. Once a lawyer has accepted a brief he should not relinquish it to the detriment of his client without good and sufficient cause;
> 3. It is the duty of a lawyer which he should be able to discharge without fear of consequences to press upon the Court any argument of law or of fact which he may think proper for the due presentation of the case by him.

CLAUSE X

Equal access to law for the rich and poor alike is essential to the maintenance of the Rule of Law. It is, therefore, essential to provide adequate legal advice and representation to all those, threatened as to their life, liberty, property or reputation who are not able to pay for it. This may be carried out in different ways and is on the whole at present more comprehensively observed in regard to criminal as opposed to civil cases. It is necessary, however, to assert the full implications of the principle, in particular in so far as "adequate" means legal advice or representation by lawyers of the requisite standing and experience. This is a question which cannot be altogether dissociated from the question of adequate remuneration for the services rendered. The primary obligation rests on the legal profession to sponsor and use its best effort to ensure that adequate legal advice and representation are provided. An obligation also rests upon the State and the community to assist the legal profession in carrying out this responsibility.

Lagos, Nigeria
January 7, 1961

A Postscript to the African Conference on the Rule of Law

The first African Conference on the Rule of Law, held in Lagos, Nigeria, on January 3–7, 1961, had as its general theme "Government Action, State Security and Human Rights". This gathering is to be viewed not as an end in itself, but as an important first achievement in a long-range programme to promote the Rule of Law within the framework of specific African cultural traditions, political institutions and socio-economic realities.

The six objectives of the Conference were listed in *Newsletter* No. 9 (September, 1960) as follows:

(*a*) to discuss the major problems concerning the Bench and Bar in Africa, with an emphasis on the principles of the Rule of Law as elaborated by the International Congress of Jurists at New Delhi;

(*b*) to enable lawyers from areas of different cultural backgrounds and legal traditions in Africa to familiarise themselves with the varying viewpoints of their colleagues, and to examine possible common grounds for future African legal developments;

(*c*) to promote an exchange of experiences and opinions between African lawyers and prominent jurists from other continents on legal matters of current importance in newly independent States;

(*d*) to develop closer personal and organisational ties between the International Commission of Jurists and Bar Associations, the Judiciary, and legal study and research groups in Africa;

(*e*) to explore ways in which the International Commission of Jurists can assist in the training of future lawyers and in strengthening the independence and prestige of the Judiciary and Bar;

(*f*) to study the possibilities of establishing a long-range programme in Africa by the International Commission of Jurists.

The results of the Conference fulfilled these expectations in every respect. The contacts established among lawyers from various parts of Africa, the fruitful exchange of information which followed, the constructive plans for international co-operation amongst African lawyers and with the International Commission of Jurists, the proposals for long-range projects in the field of human rights, all reflected the success of this first gathering of members of the African legal profession.

The first of the above-cited objectives of the Conference emphasised the principles of the Rule of Law as elaborated by the International Congress of Jurists at New Delhi. The discussions in the plenary meetings and the three committees confirmed that the *Conclusions* of Delhi are generally accepted as a criterion of the Rule of Law in any orderly society. The awareness of their universal application underlay all deliberations of the Conference and was forcefully pointed out in the opening address of the Prime Minister of Nigeria, The Hon. Alhaji Sir Abubakar Tafawa Balewa: "The Rule of Law is not a Western idea, nor is it linked up with any economic or social system."

Recognising that the desire for justice and effective guarantees of human rights is not limited to a certain historical period but reflects rather the hopes of all humanity at all times, the Conference stressed that the application of the Delhi *Conclusions* not only benefits a free society but should be extended as of right "to the peoples of all countries, whether dependent or independent". The Conference formulated an important principle of strict responsibility for the meticulous observance of the Rule of Law between government authorities and dependent peoples. But, while imposing this unqualified obligation, the Conference left no doubt that "the object of the Rule of Law cannot be realised" unless the people have had an opportunity to adopt freely their Constitution and to elect a Legislature assuring democratic representation. In other words, there will be no full application of the Rule of Law in Africa until each country has attained political independence.

The success of the Conference was reflected in the resolutions prepared by the three committees and passed by the concluding plenary session together with a declaration to be known as the *Law of Lagos*. Beyond the substance of these documents, the positive results of the Conference can be measured by the atmosphere of genuine friendship and mutual understanding which developed between participants from all parts of the African Continent. Language difficulties still existing between French- and English-speaking lawyers proved to be no serious obstacle once these feelings prevailed.

This in itself was a major achievement of the Conference. Africa needs closer relations between its intellectuals to promote an active exchange of information and experience about its various legal systems at a time of growing demands for broad economic co-operation, for example, customs unions, commercial treaties, integration of communications. While the objective of facilitating the economic and social development of African countries is certainly desirable and necessary, the lawyers assembled in Lagos felt that a matter of primary concern is the search for a unity of principles and effective international protection in the field of human rights. This viewpoint was expressed in a motion which was incorporated in the *Law of Lagos* inviting the African Governments to study the possibility of an African Convention on Human Rights and of a court of appropriate jurisdiction that would entertain petitions for redress from persons aggrieved by the violation of their fundamental rights. Governments interested in such a Convention could refer to the Universal Declaration of Human Rights of 1948, to the European Convention on Human Rights of 1950, to the practice of the European Court of Strasbourg and to the preliminary work of a special commission set up in Latin America to prepare an Inter-American Convention on Human Rights. It is possible that this Lagos proposal will take some time to materialise—the above-cited examples offer useful lessons in patience and perseverance—but the prospect of agreeing in Africa on an integrated system for the protection of human rights with an adequate judicial enforcing machinery is certainly worth a major effort.

Another purpose which the Conference achieved was to make possible a frank and open debate of legal problems with the objective of reconciling opposing views rather than perpetuating existing differences. One of the responsibilities of the lawyer is to strive for solutions based on mutual understanding and good will; his labours cannot bear fruit in an atmosphere of antagonism and suspicion. Here, too, African jurists have set a fine example by the high level of their discussions and the respect for different views and attitudes as reflected in the legal philosophy of some of their colleagues and in the practice of some Governments.

The wish to promote understanding did not, however, weaken the awareness of sharp conflicts existing in parts of Africa between the legal forms and methods of the ruling authorities on the one hand and of the requirements of the Rule of Law on the other. The challenge is presented in some areas by political ideology and practice, in others by the existence of multi-racial communities which have not yet found a working basis for genuine co-operation based on an equality of opportunity; the latter presupposes the recognition of the rights of the majority as well as an effective protection of the no less precious rights of the minority. The Conference appreciated the concern shown by the International Commission of Jurists over such alarming developments in its recently published special study on *South Africa and the Rule of Law* and requested the Commission to extend its inquiries wherever the spirit of the Conference and the letter of its decisions appear to be violated.

The jurists who participated in the African Conference on the Rule of Law have by now returned to their homes. They have brought with them the satisfaction of having become acquainted with the problems and views of their African colleagues as well as with the experience of their friends from overseas. The International Commission of Jurists has achieved its primary objective—the opening of an international discussion which, taken up by existing associations of lawyers affiliated with the Commission and by its newly established National Sections, will contribute to the search for specific solutions of a question of vital importance for all new countries: the safeguarding of fundamental human rights in a politically independent society striving for social and economic advancement and combining, in the process, national unity as well as international co-operation.

19

THE CONFERENCE OF NEGRO WRITERS
AND ARTISTS
First Congress: Paris, September 19–22, 1956

RESOLUTION

Whereas the Conference has shown that there is a profound interest in the work undertaken during its sessions in regard to various Negro cultures which have often been ignored, under-estimated or sometimes destroyed;

Whereas there has been made evident the urgent necessity to rediscover the historical truth and revalue Negro cultures; these truths, often misrepresented and denied, being partly responsible for provoking a crisis in Negro culture and in the manner in which that culture relates to World culture;

We recommend that artists, writers, scholars, theologians, thinkers and technicians participate in the historic task of unearthing, rehabilitating and developing those cultures so as to facilitate their being integrated into the general body of World culture.

We Negro writers, artists and intellectuals of various political ideologies and religious creeds have felt a need to meet at this crucial stage in the evolution of mankind in order to examine objectively our several views on culture and to probe those cultures with a full consciousness of our responsibilities—first, before our own respective peoples, second, before colonial people and those living under conditions of racial oppression, and, third, before all free men of good will.

We deem it unworthy of genuine intellectuals to hesitate to take a stand regarding fundamental problems, for such hesitations serve injustice and error.

Jointly we have weighed our cultural heritages and have studied how they have been affected by social and general conditions of racialism and colonialism.

We maintain that the growth of culture is dependent upon the termination of such shameful practices in this twentieth century as colonialism, the oppression of weaker peoples and racialism.

We affirm that all peoples should be placed in a position where they can learn their own national cultural values (history, language, literature, etc.) and enjoy the benefits of education within the framework of their own culture.

This Conference regrets the involuntary absence of a delegation from South Africa.

This Conference is pleased to take due notice of recent advances made throughout the world, advances which imply a general abolition of the colonial system, as well as the final and universal liquidation of racialism.

This Conference invites all Negro intellectuals to unite their efforts in securing effective respect for the Rights of Man, whatever his colour may be, and for all peoples and all nations whatsoever.

This Conference urges Negro intellectuals and all justice-loving men to struggle to create the practical conditions for the revival and the growth of Negro cultures.

Paying tribute to the cultures of all lands and with due appreciation of their several contributions to the progress of Civilisation, the Conference urges all Negro intellectuals to defend, illustrate and publicise throughout the world the national values of their own peoples.

We Negro writers and artists proclaim our fellowship with all men and expect from them, for our people, a similar fellowship.

At the request of several members of Congress the Officers have undertaken the responsibility of setting up an International Association of Negro Men of Culture.

20

THE CONFERENCE OF NEGRO WRITERS AND ARTISTS
Second Congress: Rome, March 25–April 1, 1959

Preamble

The Negro Writers and Artists, meeting in Congress at Rome on the 25th, 26th, 27th, 28th, 29th, 30th and 31st March, 1959, welcome the process of decolonisation which has begun in the world on a large scale.

They consider that this movement should be extended and amplified and that, as the nineteenth century was the century of colonisation, so the twentieth century should be the century of general decolonisation.

They regard it as the imperative duty of the members of the S.A.C. to make themselves actively militant in all fields on behalf of this decolonisation, which is indispensable to the peace of the world and the development of culture.

They protest against all manifestations and all acts of violence, wherever they may happen, by means of which a retarded colonialism attempts to prevent the colonised peoples from regaining their freedom.

They reassert their conviction:

1. That political independence and economic liberation are the essential conditions for the cultural advance of the underdeveloped countries in general and the Negro-African countries in particular.

2. That every effort towards the regrouping of countries or nations artificially divided by imperialism, every realisation of fundamental solidarity and every determination towards unity are advantageous and profitable for restoring the equilibrium of the world and for the revitalisation of culture.

3. That every effort towards the personification and enrichment of national culture, and every effort to implant Negro men of culture in their own civilisation, constitute in fact, progress towards universalisation and are a contribution towards the civilisation of mankind.

The Congress, therefore, recommends the Negro Writers and Artists to regard it as their essential task and sacred mission to bring their cultural activity within the scope of the great movement for the liberation of their individual peoples, without losing sight of the solidarity which should unite all individuals and peoples who are struggling for the liquidation of colonisation and its consequences as well as all those who are fighting throughout the world for progress and liberty.

Resolution of the Commission on Literature

The Commission on Literature of the Second Congress of Negro Writers and Artists, after studying the Reports submitted to it, and after a general discussion of these Reports and of their conclusions, at its sessions of Thursday 26th, Friday 27th, Saturday 28th and Sunday 29th March, 1959, examined,

I. The state of vernacular literature in Negro Africa and the countries of African population, and the need to defend those oral literatures which constitute the real basis of Negro-African cultures and their ethics, as well as the legitimate expression of national or regional peculiarities in the various countries concerned.

This work of defence and development has already been undertaken, for example, for Ghana, Guinea and Haiti, where the sovereign Governments are encouraging the development of the autochthonous languages, either by financial assistance to existing institutions, or by including these languages in the school curriculum, or by publishing newspapers and reviews, etc., and by the creation of Drama Centres.

The Commission also examined,

II. The confrontation of these traditional cultures with the forms of Western culture, in the unhealthy, and most frequently barbarous context of colonisation.

This confrontation in most cases resulted in a dead stop and in *cultural degeneration*. It involved the countries of African population in a long period of silence and loss of personality.

This contact also brought about new structures within the traditional literature, to the extent that, for good or evil, every culture in our time is influenced by other cultures.

There is a need for the study of these new structures and for help in acquiring consciousness of them and thus ensuring the transition from oral literatures to the stage of written literature, without impairing the character and ethics of these literatures.

The Commission also examined,

III. The situation of the Negro writer in the modern world. Such a writer is most frequently cut off from his authentic public by the use of a language which, in its literary form, is inaccessible to the mass of Negro peoples.

Such a writer experiences serious difficulties in getting his work published, in the modern Western conditions in which he finds himself; his public is therefore most frequently a restricted one.

He may also suffer from another cause of disequilibrium in those cases where the use of his autochthonous language is imperative for him and where its creative possibilities are limited by the fact that this language is not in literary use.

Emphasis should nevertheless be laid on the progressive character of the use of the Western languages to the extent that they lead to economy of time in constructing the new Africa.

This observation should in no way lessen the obligation to develop the autochthonous languages.

In view of all the reasons and considerations set out above, the Commission on Literature calls the attention of the Delegates of the Second Congress of Negro Writers and Artists to the following projects which should be instituted in the various Negro States:

1. The institution in each independent country of a strict and rigorous plan for the fight against illiteracy, inspired both by the most modern techniques already in use, and the original peculiarities of the country in question.

2. An increase in the number of fundamentally decentralised popular libraries, and the use of films and sound-recordings.

3. The institution of African Cultural Research Centres; these Centres, which would be responsible for working out practical plans, would be in close contact with the International Organisations, and with other nations.

4. The translation into autochthonous languages, wherever possible, of representative works of Negro writers in the French, English, Portuguese, Spanish, etc., languages.

5. The exchange of translations between the various cultural areas (French, English, Spanish, Italian and Portuguese) of Africa and the other countries of African population. Negro writers should not necessarily adopt the contradictions between the various Western cultures emanating from the nations which have dominated the Negro world.

6. The creation of national organisations for aid to writers. Such organisations already exist in various forms in Ghana and Guinea.

7. The Commission proposes the creation of effective aid to young writers within the Society of African Culture itself.

8. The Commission recommends the Society of African Culture to arrange cultural meetings with the writers of all countries.

9. Finally, the Commission hopes that the Congress will call the attention of the Governments of Negro States to the need to support and encourage the creation of theatrical schools along the lines set out above.

The Commission on Literature hopes that Negro-African writers will work to define their common language, their common manner of using words and ideas and of reacting to them. The desire for an ordered language expressing coherent cultures is embodied, among other things, in work within a national reality from which the flagrant disorder specifically inherent in the colonial situation will be banished. This language, transcending the various languages used, transcending the legitimate forms of national cultures, will thus contribute towards strengthening the unity of the Negro peoples, and will furnish their writers with a working tool.

The Commission also finally recognises that this contribution to the progress of the Negro-African peoples cannot fail additionally to strengthen the universal brotherhood of mankind. The Commission had endeavoured to carry out its work bearing constantly in mind this brotherhood and the generosity of spirit which it implies.

Resolution of the Commission on Philosophy

Considering the dominant part played by philosophic reflection in the elaboration of culture,

Considering that until now the West has claimed a monopoly of philosophic reflection, so that philosophic enterprise no longer seems conceivable outside the framework of the categories forged by the West,

Considering that the philosophic effort of traditional Africa has always been reflected in vital attitudes and has never had purely conceptual aims,

The Commission declares:

1. That for the African philosopher, philosophy can never consist in reducing the African reality to Western systems;

2. That the African philosopher must base his inquiries upon the fundamental certainty that the Western philosophic approach is not the only possible one;

and therefore,

1. Urges that the African philosopher should learn from the traditions, tales, myths and proverbs of his people, so as to draw from them the laws of a true African wisdom complementary to the other forms of human wisdom and to bring out the specific categories of African thought.

2. Calls upon the African philosopher, faced by the totalitarian or egocentric philosophers of the West, to divest himself of a possible inferiority complex, which might prevent him from starting from his African *being* to judge the foreign contribution.

It calls upon the philosopher to transcend any attitude of withdrawal into himself and his traditions so as to bring out, in true communication with all philosophies, the true universal values.

It is highly desirable that the modern African philosopher should preserve the unitary vision of cosmic reality which characterises the wisdom of traditional Africa.

Synthesis by the Sub-Commission on Theology

We, African believers, of all forms of faith, meeting as the Theological Sub-Commission of the Second International Congress of Negro Writers and Artists,

I. Find:

1. That there is a difficult and heavy responsibility upon us, in the present crisis of human values; a difficult responsibility, since religion involves requirements which demand the whole man, whose profit is not material and does not immediately appear; a heavy responsibility, because our Negro-African culture is in danger of losing what makes it original, if the profoundly religious spirit which inspires it came to be extinguished.

2. That we have our proper cultural personality, which is the source of our originality.

3. That the fundamental values of that cultural personality which might allow a valid communication between the various confessions known to the Negro world, may be summed up as follows:

—a fundamental faith in a transcendental Force from which man draws his origin, upon which he depends and towards which he is drawn.

—the sense of a vital solidarity (*"solidarité"*), a French word which seems to us the least removed from the Fulah *neddaku*, the Bambara *maya*, the Madagascan *fihavanana*, and others, and which comprises a series of moral and social virtues, such as Ancestor worship, the veneration of the Elders, hospitality, the spirit of tolerance, etc.

—the vital union between spiritual and practical life.

4. That these fundamental values through which the African religious spirit finds expression, are undergoing a twofold crisis:

—by reason of their encounter with the modern world and with religions coming from elsewhere.

II. Declare:

1. That it is our duty to acquire and diffuse a better knowledge of our cultural patrimony which is profoundly penetrated by the religious spirit.

2. That we must be lucid in assessing what is obsolete and what is lasting in the expressions of our cultural heredity.

3. That we must lay our hearts and minds open to everything which is universal in the values of any culture or religious expression whatsoever, distinguishing in them what is universal and therefore valid for all men, from what is the proper expression of their own cultural heredity.

4. That we wish to establish communication between the different religions by which the Negro-African world lives, a communication which must not end in an insuperable opposition between one religion and another, but in a mutual enrichment which will enable each of them to express itself through Negro-African culture.

III. Motions.

1. We call upon all religious forces to preserve and enrich the religious spirit of the Negro world.

2. We ask all those who guide the destinies of our countries (politicians, artists and scientists), to give the religious spirit its proper place in Negro-African culture.

3. We invite the ministers of all religions to continue their efforts towards the comprehension of African culture and to make use of it in transmitting their message.

4. We call upon all the elect to assemble and make known our oral sacred literature.

5. We ask all foreign scientists who have the noble ambition of making us rediscover our religious traditions, while grateful to them for all that is positive in their contribution, to beware of passing too rapidly from hypothesis to assertion.

6. We decide to make greater use of *Présence Africaine* to make our work known.

7. We demand that we shall not be compelled, in the name of an unconditioned fidelity to Africa, and of technical progress erected into a supreme value, to renounce our religious convictions, thus forgetting the fact that no properly understood religion is in opposition to progress and denying the great African spirit of toleration.

Resolution on Technical Sciences and Medicine

It seems daring to refer to science in speaking of modern Africa, so distant is the memory of the Cultural Centres which were found all over ancient Africa.

We have not in effect shared in the scientific upsurge which began in Europe with the sixteenth century and gathered momentum in the nineteenth, so paralysed were we by the slave trade which not only drained Africa of more than a hundred million human beings, but also caused the destruction on the spot of whole populations and the flight of the survivors to the forest regions, a relatively effective place of refuge, but hardly propitious for the development of science.

The colonisation which succeeded the slave trade was no more favourable to us. Technique never develops except under the pressure of real needs and thanks to investment which is sometimes burdensome, African techniques, crystallised since the sixteenth century, could only evolve with difficulty in contact with more highly developed European techniques responding to priority requirements which are foreign to us.

At the same time, the obstacles which have limited the development of science in Africa are not all of an external character. There are internal obstacles (maintained and aggravated by colonisation) such as:

1. The initiatory form of scientific knowledge in old Africa. This form of spreading knowledge both dangerously limited the number of "those who know" (our wise men) and at the same time did not allow these "wise men," who before attaining full knowledge had already passed the most creative age, to give of their best.

2. The absence in the greater part of Africa of the writing which is necessary to sustain scientific reflection.

Report of the Commission on the Arts

Whereas:

The two points which received greatest attention of the Second Congress of Negro Artists and Writers under the headings of descriptions and spirit were:

1. The unity of thought indispensable to the equilibrium of the Black World, and

2. The overriding obligation imposed on all black artists to produce within their culture a liberation of all different forms of expression.

Whereas:

The Commission on the Arts finds that in the actual state of our knowledge, the work which has been done (mostly by Western specialists), and which is in the process of attempting to articulate general laws and the aesthetic principles of African art, does not yet yield more than hypotheses needing much further explanation!

Whereas:

The Society of African Culture is the sole existing medium on the international level for the mobilisation of the artistic production of black artists and writers, and has a unique possibility and responsibility for demonstrating before the world the richness and the value of the talent and competence of the new culture in the Negro world.

Whereas:

The Commission has understood the vital role of the cinema as a medium of communication, education, and indoctrination, which can be of extraordinary value to the native States of Africa (or of imminent harm, if delivered to remain by default, under alien domination);

Be it resolved that:

The Second International Congress of Negro Artists and Writers propose to the principal S.A.C. organisation the establishment of a team of Negro specialists who would be charged with making on-the-spot inventories of African sculpture to find out

(a) the general laws which have governed the elaboration of African sculpture and statuary;

(b) the spirit and the general laws governing the diverse expressions of Negro plastic art;

(c) the present condition of the painter and the sculptor in the

different artistic zones of the Negro world; the condition of the painter
and the sculptor in countries with populations of African descent;
African sources of these artistic zones; the influence of the African
plastic arts on Europe, and inversely, the influence of Western arts
on Negro-African art.

Motion by a Group of Marxists

We, African Marxists,

Recognise that the evolution of Societies, the steady improvement of
technique, recent discoveries, and the consequent emergence of new
economic links and new social relationships make the enrichment and
effective broadening of Marxism both possible and desirable.

The analyses of Western society worked out by Marx, although linked
to the interpretation of a specific system of production, namely capitalism,
enabled Marx to describe the feudal (pre-capitalist) forms of society, forms
whose equivalent can be found today in the regions which are commonly
called underdeveloped.

The economic situation with which Marx found himself faced at the
time when he was explaining the laws which govern society led him to
advocate certain forms of action.

It is nevertheless clear that in the particular case of underdeveloped
countries and, more precisely in the case of Africa, the original forms of
struggle take on specific dimensions; already at grips with colonialism,
African leaders must further take into account their need to promote a
programme of technical modernisation with the maximum speed and
efficiency.

African Marxists, in their reflections and in their practice, must look
strictly, not only at general economic problems, but also and especially at
the facts of economic underdevelopment and the cultural configurations
proper to their regions.

African Marxists must also draw inspiration from current experiments in
other underdeveloped countries which have already attained independence.

In consequence, considering that,

1. The cultural references in Marx's thought are nearly all drawn
from Western experience,

2. The economic situation of the Western proletariat cannot be
strictly identified with that of the underdeveloped people;

3. A doctrine is all the more universal so far as, on the one hand, it
takes into account all experience, historic, economic, etc., and the
diversity of the cultural genius of peoples, and on the other hand,
its application is controlled by a really representative authority,

We invite African Marxists to develop their doctrine on the basis of the
real history, aspirations and economic situation of their peoples and to
build and found it on the authority of their own culture.

21

THE ALL-AFRICAN TRADE UNION FEDERATION
Casablanca Charter: May 5–30, 1961

(EXTRACTS)

The representatives of the workers of Africa who have met together at the Casablanca Congress ... solemnly proclaim the INDEPENDENCE and UNITY of African Trade Unions and their common wish to respect and defend the fundamental principles of trade union action in Africa.

The workers of Africa, workmen and peasants, are engaged in an implacable struggle against colonialism, neo-colonialism, imperialism, feudalism and reaction.

They are fighting alongside all workers of the world in their common struggle against all forms of human exploitation. However, the conditions of the struggle are special.

Although capitalism has played a preponderant role in the evolution of western society, conversely, in our countries it is man who constitutes the most precious capital of all investible capital. Upon the strength of his arm depends the present and the future.

This truth implies new conceptions and work methods. ...

In modern Africa ... African trade unionism with its discipline and tangible sense, plays and will continue to play a more and more preponderant role ...

Unity and Solidarity

The unity of the workers is as indispensable as the independence of the trade unions. It is as an active force, united and undivided, that the workers can accomplish their mission of reform.

The unity of African workers is incompatible with trade union pluralism which saps this unity and shatters all militant actions.

In another sense, African trade unions could not collaborate with the workers' organisations which constitute communicating vessels for foreign directives or foreign influence. Those who persist in wanting to create an indifferent African trade union organisation as an instrument with which to serve foreign interests, must be unmasked and denounced as traitors to the African cause ...

Independence of Trade Unions

The independence of the trade unions entails notably:

The non-interference of governments and political parties in African trade union affairs.

The non-limitation of trade union methods of action, and above all the right to strike.

The non-interference of foreign organisations in the orientation, management and trade union action in Africa. African trade unionism must be the authentic expression of Africa and not the African version of the optics of a foreign trade union.

These principles of non-interference in the domain of trade unions must not be considered as a tactical position but as the intangible norms permitting the exercise of trade union freedom and the recognition of association rights . . .

International Relations

The Federation of All-African Trade Unions is an independent organisation which rejects all foreign interference in African trade union affairs.

It is composed of independent national trade union organisations which could not be affiliated to international trade union organisations.

Nevertheless, as a temporary measure, national trade union organisations belonging to central international trade unions at the time of the Congress are given a term of ten months in which to achieve disaffiliation.

The decisive phase which Africa is passing through at the moment is that of the workers, the peasants and all progressive forces in the continent and is characterised by the struggle against colonialism, neo-colonialism, imperialism, national reaction and underdevelopment.

An attitude of positive neutrality on the part of the workers is the only reply to these needs, of non-alignment and non-dependence with regard to the bloc-wrangling and international conflicts which divide the Great Powers.

Elsewhere the Pan-African centre will maintain brotherly and egalitarian relations with the workers of the world. All isolationism on the level of African struggle would in fact be a backward step and would be false. . . .

Thus the international relations of the Pan-African centre will be founded on free collaboration with all the workers of the world within the framework . . . fixed by this present Charter.

Role of African Trade Unionism in the Building of the New Africa

Colonialism has made all Africans exploited men. Also the workers and the peasants constitute the chief layer of African society, the most awakened and the most dynamic. Africa cannot do without them nor can she do anything against them.

Their role is first of all political: no worker is in a position to consider liberty as of no account, nor democracy as a sinecure; and they are the people principally involved . . .

. . . The role of African trade unionism is next economic and must analyse, explain and put into practice all actions on the economic plane to be taken with a view to freeing Africa from the ramifications of exploitation and inaugurating in particular the agrarian reform and industrialisation . . .

. . . Finally, African trade unionism must play a social role of the first order. If it alone holds the secret of the order and command for mobilisation it is because it alone holds the secret of how to educate the same masses. No method of instruction could replace trade unionism as an instrument of transformation of the mentality and habits of the African masses. . . .

22

THE ALL-AFRICAN PEOPLES CONFERENCE

I. STATUTES

A. Resolution on Establishment of a Permanent Organisation
Accra, December 5-13, 1958

Whereas the Imperialist Powers of Great Britain, France, Spain, Portugal, Belgium and the Union of South Africa have, between them, deprived various people of Africa of their freedom and liberty,

And whereas the leaders of political parties in Africa gathered in Accra between the 5th day of December, 1958 and the 13th day of December, 1958, are irrevocably resolved to wage a final assault upon the denial of freedom, liberty and fundamental human rights to people of Africa,

Be it resolved that the All-African Peoples Conference be established with a permanent secretariat in Accra with the following aims and objects:

(a) To promote understanding and unity among peoples of Africa.

(b) To accelerate the liberation of Africa from Imperialism and colonialism.

(c) To mobilise world opinion against the denial of political rights and fundamental human rights to Africans.

(d) To develop the feeling of one community among the peoples of Africa with the object to the emergence of a United States of Africa. And that the Conference Secretariat should be governed by the rules approved for that purpose at this Conference.

B. Constitution Adopted for Permanent Organisation
Accra, December 5-13, 1958

The members of Committee No. 5 were given the following terms of reference: "To consider the setting up of a Permanent Organisation".

In pursuance of this, the Committee decided on the following constitution as the basis for setting up a permanent organisation.

Name: The name of the Conference shall be the ALL-AFRICAN PEOPLES CONFERENCE.

Aims and Objects: The aims and objects of the Conference shall be as follows:

(a) To promote understanding and unity among peoples of Africa.

(b) To accelerate the liberation of Africa from imperialism and colonialism.

(c) To mobilise world opinion in support of African liberation and to formulate concrete means and methods to achieve that objective.

(d) To develop a feeling of one community among the peoples of Africa with the object of enhancing the emergence of a United States of Africa.

Secretariat: The Conference shall have a Permanent Secretariat and shall organise periodic conferences for the pursuit of the above aims and objects.

(a) The Conference shall establish and maintain sub-secretariats and agencies in various parts of Africa.

(b) The Permanent Secretariat of the Conference shall be located in Accra, Ghana.

Secretary-General: There shall be a Secretary-General. He shall hold office for three years subject to satisfactory work and conduct. At the end of his normal term of office he shall be eligible for reappointment. He shall be subject to the control and direction of the Working Committee.

Membership: Membership of the Conference shall be open to all African National Political Parties and National Federations of Labour that subscribe to the aims and objects of the Conference.

Frequency of Meetings: A Conference shall be summoned at least once every year to be held in such places as may be prescribed.

Voting: (a) Decisions at all meetings of the Conference, Heads of Delegations and Steering Committee shall be by vote of the *simple* and *not* absolute majority.

(b) Official delegates only shall have the right to vote.

(c) Each political party will have one vote to be signified by the Head of Delegation or his representative.

Language: All proceedings of the Conference, Steering Committee and meetings of Heads of Delegations shall be conducted in English and French.

Freedom Fund: (a) The funds of the Conference shall consist of donations from the Governments of Independent African States and the Governments of other African States.

(b) Member organisations should pay £10 a year. Organisations that cannot pay this fee may be exempted by the Executive Committee if their situations so justify.

(c) Member organisations are expected to give annual donations according to their ability to the Freedom Fund.

(d) Donations may also be received from organisations, institutions and individuals who are interested in the aims and objects of the Conference.

(e) No financial contributions will be accepted from foreign governments.

Committees:

Steering Committee: The Heads of Delegations to a conference shall elect a Conference Chairman and fourteen other members to form a Steering Committee for every particular Conference.

The organisation, control and proper conduct of the conference shall be in the hands of the Steering Committee.

Quorum shall be seven plus the chairman.

Working Committee: Three members from the Steering Committee shall be appointed to constitute a Working Committee to be stationed at the Permanent Secretariat to carry on the work of the Conference together with the Secretary-General. They shall hold the office for one year.

Preparatory Committee: The host Government in the territory where the

Conference is to be held shall set up a Preparatory Committee consisting of member organisations to make arrangements for the Conference.

Resolutions: (a) It will be the duty of every member party and union to use all its influence to ensure that the decisions of the Conference are carried out by the governments and organisations in their various territories.

(b) The Secretary-General shall be responsible for conveying the resolutions of the Conference to the appropriate authorities or bodies and taking such other steps as are required to put them into effect.

Constitutional Amendment: The Constitution may be amended by a simple majority of the Heads of Delegations at an Annual Conference, on the recommendation of the Steering Committee.

Amendments may be proposed by any member organisation.

It is hereby recommended that all the organisations which have participated in this conference as official delegations should be the Founder-Members of the proposed All-African Peoples Conference.

Chairman	—	Kojo Botsio, Ghana
Vice-Chairman	—	Bensalam, Algeria.
Joint Secretaries	{	Gikonyo Kiano Ernest Ouandie

C. Amended Constitution
Tunis, January 25-30, 1960

Article I. Name

The name of the Organisation shall be the All-African Peoples Conference.

Article II. Aims and Objects

The aims and objects of the Conference shall be as follows:

(a) To promote understanding and unity among the peoples of Africa.

(b) To develop a feeling of one community among the peoples of Africa.

(c) To accelerate the liberation of Africa from imperialism and colonialism.

(d) To mobilise world opinion in support of African liberation.

(e) To work for the emergence of a United States of Africa.

(f) To work for the economic, social and cultural development of Africa.

(g) To formulate concrete means and methods of achieving these objectives.

Article III. Membership

Membership of the Conference shall be open to all national political parties and national trade union congresses or equivalent bodies or organisations that subscribe to the aims and objects of the Conference.

Article IV. The Conference

(a) In the interpretation of this Constitution and in the determination of the programme and policy of the Organisation, the supreme authority shall be the Conference-in-Plenary.

(b) Representation at the Conference shall be of members affiliated under Article III.

(c) Each member organisation shall be represented by not more than five delegates.

(*d*) Observers may be invited from youth movements, women's associations and other friendly organisations at the discretion of the Steering Committee.

(*e*) Each affiliated organisation may submit proposals to the Secretary-General concerning the agenda and programme for a Conference not later than two months prior to the opening date of the Conference.

(*f*) The Conference shall endeavour to secure the widest possible measure of agreement among member organisations other than by simple majorities. However, when a vote is called for, the decision of the Conference shall be by simple majority, except in the case of proposals for the amendment of the Constitution or the expulsion of an organisation which shall require a majority of two-thirds of the votes cast. Each member organisation shall have only one vote.

(*g*) The Conference shall be convened once every year, and shall meet at such place and time as shall have been decided by the Conference-in-Plenary.

(*h*) Each Conference shall consider and decide upon:

(i) Reports on the activities of the Conference and the Steering Committee for the preceding year.

(ii) Proposals for the activities of the Organisation during the ensuing year.

(iii) Proposals for amendment of the Constitution of the Conference.

(iv) Reports from committees.

(*i*) The Standing Rules of Procedure for Conference shall be such as shall be laid down from time to time by the Steering Committee and shall be subject to approval by the Heads of Delegations.

(*j*) The expenses of delegates attending the Conference shall be borne by their respective member organisations.

Article V. Heads of Delegations

Heads of Delegations to a Conference shall be the governing body of the Conference when it is in session, and shall, among other functions:

(*a*) elect a Conference Chairman.

(*b*) determine the agenda for the Conference.

(*c*) appoint committees.

(*d*) consider financial reports and budgetary proposals.

Article VI. Steering Committee

(*a*) A Steering Committee shall be elected by the Heads of Delegations.

(*b*) The Steering Committee shall consist of twenty-two members.

(*c*) The Secretary-General shall be an ex-officio member of the Steering Committee.

(*d*) In the event of a member of the Steering Committee being unable to attend a meeting of the Committee, he may designate by written authority a substitute to attend in his place, and such designated substitute shall have all the rights and privileges of the Committee.

(*e*) The Steering Committee shall meet not less than twice in a year, and shall also meet at the written request of not less than eleven members thereof.

(*f*) The Steering Committee shall have authority to act on behalf of the Conference in accordance with the aims and objects of the Conference.

(*g*) The quorum for meetings of the Steering Committee shall be eleven members personally present.

(*h*) The Steering Committee shall elect one of its members as Chairman for each meeting.

Article VII. Finance

1 (*a*) The Secretary-General shall administer the funds of the Conference.

(*b*) An annual budget of the Conference, prepared by the Secretary-General, shall be approved by the Steering Committee at the beginning of each meeting of the Conference.

(*c*) The Steering Committee shall appoint the Treasurer and act on behalf of the Conference.

2. (*a*) The funds of the Conference shall consist of donations from the Governments of Independent African States and the Governments of other African States.

(*b*) Member organisations shall pay ten pounds (£10) a year to the Conference. Organisations which cannot afford this fee may be exempted by the Steering Committee if their circumstances so justify.

(*c*) Member organisations shall make annual donations to the Freedom Fund according to their ability.

(*d*) Donations may also be received from other African organisations, institutions and individuals who are interested in the aims and objects of the Conference.

(*e*) No financial or material contributions shall be accepted from sources other than those mentioned above.

(*f*) The Steering Committee shall prepare an annual budget based on the affiliation fees and donations collected and shall communicate it to the Heads of Delegations.

(*g*) The Steering Committee shall have the accounts of the Conference audited annually and shall submit the auditor's report to the Heads of Delegations.

Article VIII. Secretariat

(*a*) The Permanent Secretariat of the Conference shall be located in Accra, Ghana.

(*b*) The Permanent Secretariat shall be under the charge and control of a Secretary-General who shall be full time as soon as the Steering Committee shall so determine.

(*c*) The Secretary-General shall be appointed by the Heads of Delegations on a proposal of the Steering Committee.

(*d*) The Secretary-General shall hold office for three years and shall be eligible for reappointment on the expiration of his term of office.

(*e*) The Secretary-General may be removed from office by the Steering Committee by a two-thirds majority before the expiration of his term if the interests of the Conference so require.

(*f*) The Secretary-General shall be responsible to the Steering Committee for the efficient administration of the affairs of the Conference.

(*g*) He shall, in particular,

(i) collect material for discussion in Committees of the Conference.

(ii) issue publications authorised by the Conference or the Steering Committee.

(iii) notify member organisations of decisions of the Conference or the Steering Committee within one month thereof.

(iv) arrange with the Government and member organisations of the host country to set up a Preparatory Committee to make arrangements for each Conference.

(v) prepare a provisional agenda for each Conference and submit it to each member organisation at least one month prior to the Conference.

(vi) prepare the agenda for each meeting of the Steering Committee and circulate it to members not less than two weeks in advance of the meeting.

(vii) arrange for the execution of the decisions of the Conference, Heads of Delegations and the Steering Committee.

(viii) maintain contact with member organisations and the Governments of African countries.

(ix) visit various African countries from time to time to further the interests of the Conference and promote the attainment of its objectives.

(x) do all such necessary other things as shall be calculated to further the aims and objects of the Conference.

II. RESOLUTIONS ADOPTED BY THE ALL-AFRICAN PEOPLES CONFERENCE
Accra, December 5-13, 1958

1. Imperialism and Colonialism

1. Whereas the great bulk of the African Continent has been carved out arbitrarily to the detriment of the indigenous African peoples by European Imperialists, namely: Britain, France, Belgium, Spain, Italy and Portugal.

2. Whereas in this process of colonisation two groups of colonial territories have emerged to wit:

(a) Those territories where indigenous Africans are dominated by foreigners who have their seats of authority in foreign lands, for example, French West Africa, French Equatorial Africa, Nigeria, Sierra Leone, Gambia, Belgian Congo, Portuguese Guinea, Basutoland, Swaziland and Bechuanaland.

(b) Those where indigenous Africans are dominated and oppressed by foreigners who have settled permanently in Africa and who regard the position of Africa under their sway as belonging more to them than to the Africans, e.g. Kenya, Union of South Africa, Algeria, Rhodesia, Angola and Mozambique.

3. Whereas world opinion unequivocally condemns oppression and subjugation of one race by another in whatever shape or form.

4. Whereas all African peoples everywhere strongly deplore the economic exploitation of African peoples by Imperialist Countries thus reducing Africans to poverty in the midst of plenty.

5. Whereas All African Peoples vehemently resent the Militarisation of Africans and the use of African soldiers in a nefarious global game against their brethren as in Algeria, Kenya, South Africa, Cameroons, Ivory Coast, Rhodesia and in the Suez Canal invasion.

6. Whereas fundamental human rights, freedom of speech, freedom of association, freedom of movement, freedom of worship, freedom to live a full and abundant life as approved by the All-African Peoples Conference on 13th December, 1958, are denied to Africans through the activities of Imperialists.

7. Whereas denial of the franchise to Africans on the basis of race or

sex has been one of the principal instruments of colonial policy by Imperialists and their agents, thus making it feasible for a few white settlers to lord it over millions of indigenous Africans as in the proposed Central African Federation, Kenya, Union of South Africa, Algeria, Angola, Mozambique and the Cameroons.

8. Whereas Imperialists are now co-ordinating their activities by forming military and economic pacts such as NATO, European Common Market, Free Trade Area, Organisation for European Economic Co-operation, Common Organisation in Sahara for the purpose of strengthening their Imperialist activities in Africa and elsewhere,

Be it resolved and it is hereby resolved by the All-African Peoples Conference meeting in Accra 5th to 13th December, 1958, and comprising of over 300 delegates representing over 200 million Africans from all parts of Africa as follows:

1. That the All-African Peoples Conference vehemently condemns colonialism and imperialism in whatever shape or form these evils are perpetuated.

2. That the political and economic exploitation of Africans by Imperialist Europeans should cease forthwith.

3. That the use of African manpower in the nefarious game of power politics by Imperialists should be a thing of the past.

4. That Independent African States should pursue in their international policy principles which will expedite and accelerate the independence and sovereignty of all dependent and colonial African Territories.

5. That fundamental human rights be extended to all men and women in Africa and that the rights of indigenous Africans to the fullest use of their lands be respected and preserved.

6. The universal adult franchise be extended to all persons in Africa regardless of race or sex.

7. That Independent African States ensure that fundamental human rights and universal adult franchise are fully extended to everyone within their States as an example to Imperial Nations who abuse and ignore the extension of those rights to Africans.

8. That a permanent secretariat of the All-African Peoples Conference be set up to organise the All-African Conference on a firm basis.

9. That a human rights committee of the Conference be formed to examine complaints of abuse of human rights in every part of Africa and to take appropriate steps to ensure the enjoyment of the rights by everyone.

10. That the All-African Peoples Conference in Accra declares its full support to all fighters for freedom in Africa, to all those who resort to peaceful means of non-violence and civil disobedience as well as to all those who are compelled to retaliate against violence to attain national independence and freedom for the people. Where such retaliation becomes necessary, the Conference condemns all legislations which consider those who fight for their independence and freedom as ordinary criminals.

2. Frontiers, Boundaries and Federations

1. Whereas the great mass of African peoples are animated by a desire for unity;

Whereas the unity of Africa will be vital to the independence of its component units and essential to the security and general well-being of African peoples;

Whereas the existence of separate states in Africa is fraught with the dangers of exposure to imperialist intrigues and of resurgence of colonialism even after their attainment of independence, unless there is unity among them;

And whereas the ultimate objective of African nations is a Commonwealth of Free African States,

Be it resolved and it is hereby resolved by the All-African Peoples Conference that the Conference;

    (a) endorses Pan-Africanism and the desire for unity among African peoples;

    (b) declares that its ultimate objective is the evolution of a Commonwealth of Free African States;

    (c) calls upon the Independent States of Africa to lead the peoples of Africa towards the attainment of this objective; and

    (d) expresses the hope that the day will dawn when the first loyalty of African States will be to an African Commonwealth.

2. Whereas, as a first step towards the attainment of the broad objective of an African Commonwealth, the independent States of Africa should amalgamate themselves into groups on the basis of geographical contiguity, economic inter-dependence, linguistic and cultural affinity,

Whereas linguistic, religious and cultural divisions and national sovereignty should be subordinated to the overriding demands of Pan-African Unity where common geographical and economic considerations and national interests suggest the grouping of certain States;

Whereas amalgamation, federation or groupings should only take place between independent States governed by Africans;

Whereas each State should decide to which group it wishes to adhere by a referendum based on universal adult suffrage;

Whereas regional federations of groups should be regarded as a means to amend and should not be prejudicial to the ultimate objective of a Pan-African Commonwealth by hardening as separate entities and thereby impeding progress towards a continental Commonwealth;

Whereas the people of North Africa have taken the initiative towards a North African Federation and there is a strong desire in West Africa for a West African Grouping;

Whereas it is desirable that other groups should emerge in Africa provided they are not Federations visualised or constituted by colonial Powers against the wishes of the African people, since such Federations are a ready weapon in the hands of Colonial Governments and white settlers for the oppression of the African people;

And whereas countries which do not appear to fall naturally into any geographical group should after their attainment of independence decide by democratic processes whether to adhere to existing groups or to evolve different groups;

Be it resolved and it is hereby resolved by the All-African Peoples Conference that the Conference;

    (a) endorses the desire in various parts of Africa for regional grouping of States;

    (b) advocates that such groupings should be based on three principles, namely:

        (i) only independent States and countries governed by Africans should come together;

(ii) the establishment of groups should not be prejudicial to the ultimate objective of a Pan-African Commonwealth;

(iii) adherence to any group should be based on the wishes of the people ascertained by referendum on the basis of universal adult suffrage;

(c) recommends that countries which do not appear to fall naturally within any group should decide by similar means whether to adhere to any group or to evolve different groups.

3. Whereas artificial barriers and frontiers drawn by imperialists to divide African peoples operate to the detriment of Africans and should therefore be abolished or adjusted;

Whereas frontiers which cut across ethnic groups or divide peoples of the same stock are unnatural and are not conducive to peace or stability;

Whereas leaders of neighbouring countries should co-operate towards a permanent solution of such problems which accords with the best interests of the people affected and enhances the prospects of realisation of the ideal of a Pan-African Commonwealth of Free States;

Whereas the 20th February, 1959, will be an important date in the history of the Cameroons, when a special session of the United Nations General Assembly will discuss the question of unification and independence of the territory;

Be it resolved and it is hereby resolved by the All-African Peoples Conference that the Conference:

(a) denounces artificial frontiers drawn by imperialist Powers to divide the peoples of Africa, particularly those which cut across ethnic groups and divide people of the same stock;

(b) calls for the abolition or adjustment of such frontiers at an early date;

(c) calls upon the Independent States of Africa to support permanent solution to this problem founded upon the true wishes of the people;

(d) notes with satisfaction that a special session of the United Nations General Assembly will discuss the question of unification and independence of the Cameroons on the 20th February, 1959.

(e) invites all Africans to observe that date as Cameroons Day.

4. Whereas it is desirable that certain measures should be adopted by Independent African States and Dependent African countries which are in a position to do so towards achieving Pan-African unity;

Whereas firstly passports, travel certificates, etc., should be abolished in respect of bona-fide African tourists, visitors and students for the purpose of facilitating the Free movement of Africans from one territory to another and thereby promoting intercourse among Africans, provided that this is not used as an excuse by white settlers to indulge in mass movement of cheap labour;

Whereas secondly, it is desirable, for the purpose of promoting intercourse among Africans on a continental basis, that the English language should be taught in the Secondary Schools of French speaking territories and vice versa and that the histories of African nations should be taught in schools throughout Africa;

Whereas thirdly, it should be possible for Africans to enjoy reciprocal rights of citizenship at least in territories within the same regional group and not be subjected to discrimination on grounds of their country of origin, so that ultimately no African shall be considered an alien in any part of Africa;

Whereas fourthly, in order to promote inter-territorial co-operation certain forms of joint activity could be brought into being, such as a common West African Airline, intercommunications system, road and rail transport system, research and scientific institutions, and military organisations;

Whereas fifthly, regional conferences of political parties, trade unions, youth organisations, journalists and writers, women's organisations, etc., could be held regularly to promote singleness of purpose and community sense;

Whereas sixthly, Africans wherever they are in control could use radio services, the Press and other media of mass communication to promote the ideals of Pan-Africanism;

And whereas seventhly it is desirable that political parties throughout Africa should make provisions in their Constitutions and programmes for promoting African Solidarity;

Be it resolved and it is hereby resolved by the All-African Peoples Conference that the Conference;

(a) calls upon all States and countries in Africa which are in a position to do so implement the following programme forthwith;

(i) abolition of passports requirements and other travel restrictions for bona-fide African visitors, tourists and students;

(ii) reciprocal rights of citizenship for Africans from other territories;

(iii) reciprocal teaching of the English and French languages and the history of other African nations in the Secondary Schools of each territory;

(iv) organisation of inter-territorial enterprises;

(b) urges the organisation of regional Conferences respectively of political parties, trade unions, youth organisations, journalists and writers, women's organisations, etc.

(c) calls upon all Africans wherever they can to use the radio, the Press and other media of mass communication to promote the ideals of Pan-Africanism.

(d) urges political parties throughout Africa to provide in their Constitutions and programmes for the promotion of African Solidarity.

3. Racialism and Discriminating Laws and Practices

Whereas having heard shocking accounts of the brutal operation of racialism and discriminatory laws and denial of human rights on the continent of Africa from representatives of the participating organisations,

Whereas racialism is one of the outcomes of colonialism and the independence of States is a prerequisite for the end of discrimination,

Whereas Africans in the Union of South Africa, the Rhodesias, Nyasaland, Mozambique, Angola, Kenya, the Cameroons, Belgian Congo, Basutoland, South-West Africa and Kamerun are victims of a racialism that has reached alarming proportions;

Whereas racialism in Algeria has caused and is causing race extermination;

Whereas in a colonial country land belongs to a foreign Power;

Whereas the problem of land in a colonial territory represents the ugliest form of colonial rule that must be destroyed so that African authorities own the land;

Whereas the Universal Declaration of Human Rights is being flouted in Africa and the Africans are deprived of the rights of man;

Whereas the recognition of and respect for human dignity are the bases of a decent society;

Whereas those who practise racialism and discrimination are therefore out of step with the law;

Whereas colonial authorities do not respect international conventions;

Whereas democracy needs to be established immediately in Africa;

Whereas the colonial authorities have shown obstinate indifference towards resolutions adopted to set up a democracy;

Whereas the African must find concrete means of effectively reversing the situation;

Whereas Africa's destiny and political constitution must be forged by Africans themselves;

Be it resolved that this Conference registers its vehement protest against this ugly system;

Condemns the pernicious system of racialism and discriminating laws, especially as expressed in its extreme and most brutal forms in the Union of South Africa, Rhodesia, the Portuguese Territories of Angola, Mozambique, Principe and Sao Thome, where the indigenous populations exist under a régime of apartheid;

Condemns the lack of educational facilities and the denial of social benefits;

Condemns the denial of human democratic rights as enunciated in the Charter of the United Nations;

Condemns racial segregation, reserve systems and all other forms of racial discrimination and colour bar;

Condemns the use of forced labour in territories such as Angola, Mozambique, Belgian Congo, South and South-West Africa;

Condemns the political policies of territories like South Africa which base their minority rule of the majority upon apartheid's social doctrines;

Condemns the alienation of the African's best land for the use of European colonisers.

The All-African Peoples Conference declares that as long as the system of discrimination and racialism remains on this African continent it will arrest the development of the African peoples and stifle their self-expression;

Maintains that while discrimination continues to exist the problems facing Africa cannot be solved.

The All-African Peoples Conference calls upon the United Nations to reconstitute the Committee on the Racial Situation in the Union of South Africa;

If the United Nations should fail to reconstitute this committee this conference calls upon the Secretariat of the Independent States of Africa to set up such a Committee.

The All-African Peoples Conference declares that the struggle for the freedom of Africa is the task of the Africans themselves, and calls upon the workers, the peasants, and other sections of the toiling masses, together with the intellectuals, to unite their forces in common action for a final attack on discrimination and racialism;

Declares that political parties and leaders should recognise the need for a united front in the struggle for freedom and independence.

Convinced further that the overwhelming majority of the populations of the dependent territories have been made conscious of their rights under the Universal Declaration of Human Rights;

The All-African Peoples Conference recommends:

1. That the permanent Secretariat to be set up should urge any African independent States which conduct trade with South Africa to impose economic sanctions against the latter country as a protest against racial discrimination which the European minority are practising to the humiliation of the non-European majority. Such economic sanctions should include the boycott of South African goods.

2. That all African countries which supply South Africa with migrant labour should organise this reservoir of workers for its own use and thus withhold such labour from South African industry which has become the instrument of oppression. The permanent Secretariat should endeavour to give financial aid to any development plan that any country may have to initiate as a result of the diversion of its labour force.

3. That no African State should have any diplomatic relations with any country on our continent that practises race discrimination.

4. That April 15 should be set aside and called Africa Freedom Day, which all African countries and all friends of Africa throughout the world shall observe as a rallying point for the forces of freedom.

5. That the permanent Secretariat should set up a bureau of information. Such bureau should appoint correspondents in various African territories who will send factual news items relating to the Liberatory Movement to a central office for publication. The bureau should also be a depot from which liberatory journals in Africa will be circulated. This we believe will be not only a medium through which we shall get to know one another, but also through which we can co-ordinate our struggle.

6. That the Independent African States should form an "African Legion" consisting of volunteers who will be ready to protect the freedom of the African peoples.

7. That this Conference insists on immediate independence for all African territories in order to put an end to racial discrimination in the spirit of the United Nations Charter.

8. That this Conference rejects the claim of Portugal that its colonies constitute part of metropolitan Portugal, and demands immediate independence for countries in Africa under Portuguese rule.

9. That this Conference, considering that the future of the Mandated Territory of South-West Africa has been debated at the United Nations for twelve successive years, and that the Herero, Nama and other African inhabitants, who have been petitioning the United Nations during that time, still complain of the loss of their lands, and their humiliating subjection to the apartheid system, in this so-called sacred trust of civilisation; that this Conference calls on the Great Powers who entrusted the Mandate to South Africa, especially the United Kingdom, the United States, and France, together with other former members of the League of Nations, to

revoke the Mandate and take immediate steps to grant independence to South-West Africa.

10. This Conference regards as unacceptable and discreditable any plan that would allow the incorporation into the Union of South Africa's apartheid system of any African land or people whether belonging to the Mandated Territory of South-West Africa, or the British Protectorates of Bechuanaland, Basutoland and Swaziland.

11. That this Conference condemns the Central African Federation and all its discriminatory laws and practices which lead to social, cultural, economic and political racial consideration. Therefore calls upon the British Government to honour the Declaration of Human Rights as entrenched in the United Nations Charter and dissolve the Central African Federation in the benefit of all people.

12. That in respect of Kenya this Conference urges the British Government to end the present state of emergency in Kenya and the release of all political prisoners. Also that this Conference demands the abrogation of all discriminatory laws, the establishment of a common electoral roll based on adult suffrage with provision for one man one vote, and the insertion of laws in the Statute Books for the transfer of the lands and rights to the African people.

4. Tribalism, Religious Separatism and Traditional Institutions

Whereas we strongly oppose the imperialist tactics of utilising tribalism and religious separatism to perpetuate their colonial policies in Africa;

Whereas we are also convinced that tribalism and religious separatism are evil practices which constitute serious obstacles to

(i) the realisation of the unity of Africa;
(ii) the political evolution of Africa;
(iii) the rapid liberation of Africa;

Be it resolved that steps be taken by political, trade union, cultural and other organisations to educate the masses about the dangers of these evil practices and thereby mobilise the masses to fight these evils.

That in addition to any action taken by dependent countries, the independent countries shall

(a) allow their governments to pass laws and through propaganda and education, discourage tribalism and religious separatism;
(b) encourage their governments to give the dependent countries and their leaders effective aid in the fight to realise their common objectives rapidly.

Whereas the All-African Peoples Conference convened in Accra from the 5th December to the 13th December, 1958, realises that some of the African traditional institutions, especially chieftaincy, do not conform to the demands of democracy.

And whereas some of these institutions actually support colonialism and constitute the organs of corruption, exploitation and repression which strangle the dignity, personality and the will of the African to emancipate himself.

Be it resolved that those African traditional institutions whether political, social or economic which have clearly shown their reactionary character and their sordid support for colonialism be condemned.

That all conscientious peoples of Africa and all African political leaders be invited to intensify and reinforce their educational and propaganda activities with the aim of annihilating those institutions which are incompatible with our objectives of national liberations.

And that governments of independent countries be called upon to suppress or modify these institutions.

III. RESOLUTIONS ADOPTED BY THE ALL-AFRICAN PEOPLES CONFERENCE

Tunis, January 25-30, 1960

General Resolution

The Second Conference of African Peoples assembled at Tunis from 25th to 30th January, 1960, confirming the declarations and resolutions adopted at the first conference of African peoples held at Accra in December, 1958:

Salutes the heroic people of Africa struggling for liberty, dignity and independence;

Bows before the martyrs fallen in the course of the glorious struggle against the forces of slavery and colonialist oppression;

Notes with satisfaction the progress, across the whole of Africa, of the historic movement towards liberation, and emphasises joyfully the fact of the African peoples becoming conscious of their personality and their strength;

Records with similar satisfaction the accession to independence in the course of the year 1960 of the peoples of Cameroon, of Togo, of Nigeria, of Somalia and of the Congo; likewise the prospects of independence opening before other peoples on the African continent;

Considering nevertheless the holding under foreign oppression of more than twenty African countries, without any prospect of a solution, despite the clearly expressed will of all the African peoples to attain their independence;

Considering the desperate efforts of white colonists to consolidate their racial domination in the regions of South Africa, the federation imposed on Rhodesia and Nyasaland, Kenya, and the obstinate wish of South Africa to incorporate South-West Africa and the protectorates of Basutoland, Swaziland and Bechuanaland into the Union, hence to place all these countries under perpetual white domination;

Indignant at the savage and inhuman repression exerted by foreign imperialism on the Africans struggling to obtain their liberty, and at the inhuman racial discriminatory measures applied against Africans by the South African Government and the colonialists of East and Central Africa, and at the ignoble policy of deportation, torture and genocide pursued by France in North Africa to destroy the courage and dignity of our Algerian brothers, and by other colonial Powers in other African countries;

Considering the essential part played by the heroic resistance movement and by the sacrifice of the Algerian people in the struggle against imperialism and colonialism in Africa;

Considering the criminal obstinacy of France in proceeding with her nuclear tests in the African Sahara, thus adding to the list of her foul deeds, defying the unanimous reproof of the African peoples and international opinion, and exposing all these peoples to the most serious dangers;

Considering further the manoeuvres of the imperialists at the heart of the international organisations, aiming to establish in Africa regional, racial or linguistic divisions, in order to hinder Africans from becoming aware of the common interests uniting them all;

Considering the existence of the French Community, a new form of imperialist domination, and the present attempts of the French Government to impose upon countries associated with this community and on the threshold of independence, bonds of a kind which would deprive them of true national sovereignty;

The Conference

Demands the immediate and unconditional accession to independence of all the African peoples, and the total evacuation of the foreign forces of aggression and oppression stationed in Africa;

Proclaims the absolute necessity, in order to resist the imperialist coalition more effectively and rapidly free all the dependent peoples from foreign oppression, of co-ordinating and uniting the forces of all the Africans, and recommends the African States not to neglect any form of co-operation in the interest of all the African peoples;

Denounces vigorously the policy of racial discrimination applied by colonialist and race-conscious minorities in South and East and Central Africa, and demands the abolition of racial domination in South Africa, the suppression of the Federation of Nyasaland and Rhodesia, and the immediate independence of these countries;

Proclaims equality of rights for all the citizens of the free countries of Africa and the close association of the masses for the building up and administration of a free and prosperous Africa;

Calls on the peoples of Africa to intensify the struggle for independence, and insists on the urgent obligation on the independent nations of Africa to assure them of the necessary aid and support;

Recommends therefore the speedy setting up of an organisation designed to co-ordinate the aid and solidarity of all the independent countries with regard to helping African peoples engaged in the struggle, and in particular the sending, at the request of the G.P.R.A., of African volunteers to Algeria, the collection of funds and African information;

Affirms the will of the African countries to live in harmony with all the countries of the world, and recommends the African Governments to be active in liquidating the neo-colonialist groups, particularly any foreign military establishments on their soil;

Considering moreover the important social and economic "enclaves" created by the imperialist countries in Africa in the industrial and agricultural sectors, by the establishment of special monetary, financial, technical and social institutions entirely controlled by themselves;

Observing that these foreign "enclaves" result in the exploitation of the human, vegetable and mineral resources of Africa, and that they have been installed in the service of foreign economic systems;

Observing further that the existence of these "enclaves" enables the imperialist countries to bind the economy of certain African countries very stringently in the domains of customs, finance, trade, currency, etc.;

Considering on the other hand, that the imperialists are aiming at the organisation of all these new institutions of domination with each African people taken separately, while they are themselves co-ordinating strictly their action in order to present a united front against the efforts of economic liberation on the part of Africa;

The Conference
Affirms the absolute necessity of turning the economy of the African countries to the profit of its peoples, and of acting with unity in the economic field, as in the political and cultural fields;

Proposes therefore the creation by all the Independent African States, of common organisations for the conduct of finance and commerce, and of centres of social and economic research, for the purpose of studying the forms of technical assistance to Africa and of training the technicians whom Africa needs to ensure her economic development and her social progress;

Proclaims finally the irrevocable character of the movement towards African independence, liberty and unity;

The Conference
Sends out a resounding call to all the peoples of Africa to redouble their watchfulness, so that the African continent shall henceforth be a land propitious to the blossoming of liberty, dignity and well-being.

Economic and Social Resolution

Considering the underdeveloped state of African economies which is a result of the colonial system and foreign domination;

Considering the tendency of the colonialist countries to substitute economic for political domination and thus rob the newly won independence of African States of its true content;

Considering also the departmentalisation and lack of harmony existing in the African economies and the inadequacy of technical cadres and finance;

Considering that economic growth and development constitute the surest guarantee of the freedom of the African Continent;

Considering that foreign Powers sometimes use their economic aid as a means of endeavouring to divide the African territories and isolate the Independent States from territories that are still under colonial rule;

The Conference
Affirms that independence is a prerequisite to all economic development.

Declares that the peoples of Africa are determined to work for the economic development and liberation of Africa, for the benefit and under the control of the masses.

Recommends to the Independent African States:

1. The intensification of their efforts to wrest their respective countries from economic dependence on the imperialist countries.

2. The refusal to enter into any undertaking with foreign Powers which may either directly or indirectly prejudice the movement for the liberation and unity of the African continent.

3. The development of the co-operative system and the harnessing of the essential resources of their territories in the interests of the masses, to ensure social justice and raise the living standard of their peoples.

4. The promotion of industrialisation, the direction of effort towards agrarian reform, and the modernisation of agriculture in order to make Africa's economy independent.

5. The encouragement of joint enterprises and inter-African companies in order to achieve the maximum result from the development of the resources of Africa in the interests of the peoples, and move along the path of African unity.

6. The removal of customs barriers between the Independent African States.

7. The progressive liberalisation of commercial exchanges and the con-clusion of multilateral payments agreements, with a view to developing economic exchanges and the consequent setting up of an African Common Market, the formation of an African Transport Company (Land, Air and Sea) to promote exchanges among the African territories.

8. Regular meetings between Economic and Finance Ministers with a view to co-ordinating their economic policies.

9. The setting up of an African Investment Bank to promote develop-ment projects.

10. The creation of an African Institute for Research and Training of the various cadres.

11. The Conference decides that its Secretariat should edit a popular review on social and economic studies.

Resolution on African Unity

Considering the present state of Africa, where colonialism, after desperate efforts, is retreating over the entire continent;

Considering that the nations which were yesterday still under foreign domination are now acquiring independence, and that the time has come for the African peoples to apply themselves in all clarity and without weakness to the task of constructing their unity;

Considering the artificial character of the divisions imposed by force on the continent;

Considering that national independence draws its strength from the building-up of a constructive inter-dependence, as a means of discouraging the imperialists;

Considering that the division of Africa into various spheres of influence provides the imperialist States with a means of maintaining their pressure;

Since the community of struggle against colonialism and the poverty of our peoples imposes on us the formation of social policies strictly turned towards the improvement of living conditions for the African masses;

Since the great idea of Pan-Africanism constitutes a new element in the national consciousness of African peoples;

After analysing the idea of unity which uplifts the African peoples, decides to mobilise the African masses around this idea and to make its realisation the fundamental objective of their action and their thought;

The Conference

Renews its enthusiastic support for the recommendations adopted by the Conference of Independent African States held at Accra on the 28th April, 1958, likewise by the first Conference of African Peoples held at Accra in December, 1958; recommends particularly the application of the points concerning teaching in schools and universities of general knowledge about the whole of Africa, elimination of falsehoods concerning the history of Africa due to foreign and colonialist influences, standardisation (or equivalent recognition) of diplomats, the teaching and serious study of African languages, the teaching of African civilisation and culture.

With a view to rapid implementation, the Conference recommends the following decisions:

1. The granting by the Independent States of bursaries to students of different regions of Africa in order to deepen human and cultural contacts. The Secretariat of the Conference shall be informed of decisions taken on this matter by the Independent States.

2. The exchange of agricultural experts in order to compare and extend beneficial techniques and experiments to their respective national economies.

3. The organisation within the framework of national broadcasting of African cultural, musical and folklore programmes, in order to become better acquainted, on a continental scale, with the personality of the different regions of Africa.

4. The promotion of exchanges between African States, of teachers and of students.

5. The organisation of sporting and cultural events, likewise art exhibitions, between African States.

6. The organisation, as early as possible, of an African Youth Festival; acting upon the invitation made to the Conference by the Democratic Party of Guinea which invites the Conference to hold the first Festival of African Youth at Conakry in 1961.

7. Asks the Conference to take the initiative in calling together in 1960 all the student and youth movements of Africa, with a view to setting up a co-ordinating organisation between these various movements.

Asks that at such a conference, all the youth and students' movements of Africa, wherever their headquarters is situated, may be represented.

8. Recommends the Independent African States to turn their attention to the fact that inter-African and inter-continental systems of transport are strictly dependent on the old colonial Powers.

9. Recommends the setting up of regional organisations to study the specific problems of different parts of the continent.

10. Recommends in this regard, that frequent regional conferences should be held.

11. Recommends strongly to the Independent African States to facilitate movements of citizens by abolishing visas.

12. Recommends the immediate setting up of a central solidarity fund, to give aid to refugees fleeing from their countries on account of colonialism.

13. Records with satisfaction the will for unity amongst African Trades Unions, and in this respect recommends the following resolution.

14. Demands emphatically the setting up alongside the General Secretariat, of bodies instructed to see to the realisation in concrete terms of its different recommendations.

Resolution on the Unity of African Trades Union Organisations

The Second Conference of African Peoples gathered at Tunis on the 25th to 30th January, 1960.

Fully conscious of the particular and decisive part to be played by the working class in the struggle of African peoples for the total liberation and the unity of the Continent, for democracy and social progress:

Considering the unanimous will of the workers of Africa to pursue the struggle against underdevelopment in order to create economic prosperity and install a régime of democracy, liberty and social justice,

Considering the urgent necessity of reinforcing trade unionism so as to allow it to play its decisive part in the economic and social battle,

Considering the resolution adopted on 9th November, 1959, by the Steering Committee of the Conference of African Peoples and inviting the workers of Africa to realise their unity in the interest of the struggle for independence and the affirmation of the African personality,

Considering that there is no contradiction between the aspirations of African workers, and that trade union unity will permit them to lead speedily to victory the combat for national independence and liberation from all forms of exploitation,

Appeals to the Governments of all the independent countries of Africa and to all the democratic and popular forces of Africa to recognise the existence of trade union rights.

Hails and supports unreservedly the convocation in mid-May 1960 at Casablanca of an African Trade Union Congress, in the service of the African cause, open to all the authentic national trade unions who are sincerely working for the political and social emancipation of the labouring masses.

The Conference fully supports the efforts towards unity of the workers of Africa and of their trade union organisations.

It invites them forthwith to redouble their ardour and to work with a view to assuring a resounding success for the Casablanca Conference, which should mark a decisive step in the realisation of the unity of the African Trade Union movement.

Resolution on Algeria

The Second All-African Peoples Conference, which met at Tunis from 25th to 30th January, 1960, proceeded to a full study of the situation in Algeria.

It salutes the progress made by the Algerian People in the war of independence under the direction of the National Front of Liberation and the Provisional Government of the Algerian Republic and pays respectful and fraternal homage to the brave combatants of the Army of National Liberation and the whole Algerian People who have put themselves in the forefront of the struggle against colonialism.

The Conference considered with indignation the monstrous crimes committed each day in Algeria by the French army of aggression which have brought to this African country the worst atrocities of Nazism.

It bows to the innumerable martyrs in the cause of Algerian independence, and, in particular, turns its thought towards the million and a half Algerians deported to concentration camps and towards the prisoners and internees who are suffering in colonialist gaols.

The Second All-African Peoples Conference recalling the resolution of the Steering Committee of October, 1959, concerning Algeria, noting the recognition by France of the right of the people of Algeria to self-determination,

Firmly supports the attitude of the Provisional Government of the Republic of Algeria, which appointed five delegates, now detained in France, with a view to opening discussions with the French Government on the conditions of application of self-determination, including the conditions of a cease-fire,

Regrets that the French Government had refused these discussions, and denounces its policy of delay and manoeuvres designed to prolong war of aggression against the Algerian people.

Denounces and condemns more particularly the scheme to partition Algeria and affirms the principles of the indivisibility and integrity of Algerian territory.

The Second All-African Peoples Conference has analysed the recent events in Algeria marked by the entry into open battle of the army and the extremists against the central authorities.

These events illustrate the stagnation of French politics and the surrender of power in France.

The Conference expresses its grave concern at the unleashing of the uncontrollable extreme colonialist forces directed by irresponsible elements.

This situation will lead to the exacerbation of the war and an increase in the suffering of the Algerian people and constitutes a grave threat of extension of the conflict in North Africa and danger to world peace.

In consequence, the Conference calls for vigilance by all the peoples of Africa who must close their ranks to deliver in 1960 a decisive blow for African Independence.

It has decided to recommend immediately:

1. To the Independent African States Governments who have not yet done so to recognise the Provisional Government of the Algerian Republic.

2. To all the African Independent Governments the inclusion in their budget of regular financial contribution in favour of struggling Algeria.

3. Also the Conference demands the withdrawal from Algeria of tens of thousands of soldiers from Black Africa maintained by France with complicity of the Governments of their countries and urges the Independent States and the African Peoples to do all they can to put an end to this odious tragedy amongst African brothers organised by French colonialism.

4. Recommends the creation of a corps of African Volunteers for the war of the Independence of Algeria and requests the African Independent States to facilitate the achievement of this enterprise.

5. Given the spontaneous aggravation of the situation in Algeria the Conference makes her pressing appeal to the UNITED NATIONS to impose peace and recognition of Algerian independence.

Message from the Second All-African Peoples Conference to the President of the United States and the American Congress

The Second All-African Peoples Conference which met at Tunis from the 25th to 30th January, 1960, having studied the Algerian problem at a time when the situation in Algeria is worsening, notes once again that the support given to France in its colonial policies by the U.S.A. has serious prejudicial effects for the African peoples.

In Algeria American arms are used by the French to kill Algerians. American financial and economic aid enable France to prolong the war. Diplomatic support by the United States which was again accorded to

France at the last Session of the United Nations General Assembly encourages her to delay a just and peaceful solution which the Algerian people have sought for the last five years.

The African people solemnly ask you to cease these policies which prejudice the friendship and understanding among our peoples as well as the cause of peace on the Continent and in the world.

Resolution on South Africa

The Second All-African Peoples Conference, having examined the situation in South Africa which has only worsened, urges the African peoples and Trade Unions as well as the Governments of the Independent African States to organise a boycott of goods from South Africa and South-West Africa.

Instructs the Secretariat of the Conference to take all effective measures for the practical application of this decision.

Resolution on the Cameroon

The Second All-African Peoples Conference, meeting at Tunis from 25th to 30th January, 1960.

Hails the attainment of Independence of the Cameroon, an outcome of the Cameroon People's struggle.

Deplores the present situation in this African country.

Requests the withdrawal of French troops to be effected immediately and that democratic freedom be restored and respected.

Recommends to the African Independent States to use their good offices in order to help the Cameroon People to find a quick and adequate solution to the present political crisis.

Resolution on the Community

The Second All-African Peoples Conference, meeting at Tunis from the 25th to 30th January, 1960, has been widely informed of the intended situation to the populations in some member States of the French Community, particularly to those of the Chad, of the Niger, of the Ivory Coast and of the Mauritania.

Bows in memory to all those who have fallen in these countries as a result of blows of the French colonialism.

Hails the courage of patriots who are struggling against odd régimes imposed owing to electoral trickery.

It requests:

(a) The restoration of trade unionism and democratic freedoms,

(b) The cessation of prosecutions and liberation of citizens arbitrarily detained,

(c) Holding of free and democratic elections in order to form Assemblies and true Governments emanated from their people.

Resolution on Congo

The Second All-African Peoples Conference notes with satisfaction the forthcoming accession of the Congo under Belgian domination to independence.

Supports the nationalist leaders calling for free and democratic elections before the proclamation of independence.

Resolution on Ruanda-Urundi

The Second All-African Peoples Conference having examined the situation in the Ruanda-Urundi, vigorously condemns the acts of barbarities committed against the people of Ruanda-Urundi, requests the Belgian Government to lift immediately the state of emergency proclaimed three months ago,

Denounces the withholding by the British imperialists of the right of asylum to the Banyaruanda refugees in Uganda.

Resolution on Portuguese Colonies

Having examined the situation created in African countries under Portuguese domination which are still undergoing a régime of forced labour and where the indigenous peoples are subjected to an unbridled exploitation,

The Conference

Condemns the colonial policies of Portugal and denounces the systematic repression which strangles the national Movements, as well as the preparations for war by the Portuguese Government in Angola,

Reaffirms the right of the people to national independence and urges the African Independent States and all the peoples of Africa to give them their unconditional support.

Demands the immediate liberation of all political prisoners in Angola, Mozambique, so-called Portuguese Guinea, Sao Tome and Cape Vert.

Appeals to member Organisations of the Conference to organise a day of solidarity during 1960, in favour of the peoples under Portuguese domination.

Appeals to the Special Committee of the UN established to study the question of non-self-governing territories, to pose the problem of decolonisation and independence of these territories.

Is preoccupied with the fact that Portugal is intensifying the repression.

Resolution on Kenya

Considering the attitude and desire of the Kenya White settlers to continue white supremacy and domination in Kenya which is mainly an African Country and bearing in mind their (Europeans') attitude towards the Africans' great desire for the immediate release of their national leader, Mr. Jomo Kenyatta, now detained without reasonable cause, the Kenya delegation urges the Second All-African Peoples Conference to do all it can to:

1. Demand from the British Government an immediate independence for the peoples of Kenya through an electoral system based on democratic principles of one man one vote on universal adult suffrage.

2. Demand an immediate release of Mr. Jomo Kenyatta, the Kenya African National leader, to come out of detention and lead his people.

3. Demand the immediate restoration to the Africans of Kenya of their legitimate land which has for long remained in the hands of European Settlers, without the consent of the Africans who continue to suffer from poverty and hunger.

Resolution on Tanganyika

Whereas this Conference notes the Imperialist trick of using pigmentation as an excuse to perpetuate colonialism in East and Central Africa;

Whereas this Conference notes the use of European economic privilege in the so-called multiracial countries to perpetuate and prolong colonialism in East and Central Africa;

1. This Conference welcomes the declaration of Responsible Government in Tanganyika and urges the British Government to grant complete internal self-government to be followed by the granting of complete self-government in the shortest possible period.

2. This Conference calls upon the British Government to implement universal adult suffrage on the basis of one man one vote during the forthcoming General Elections in Tanganyika.

Resolution on Zanzibar

Convinced that self-rule is the birthright of the people of Zanzibar and taking into consideration the unanimous demand of all the people of the country, and the dangerous state of frustration engendered by the further continuation of colonial rule on a people capable of looking after themselves;

Convinced that unity is essential for the liberation of Zanzibar and that division only serves the interests of imperialism, and that any such local divisions in any country have serious effect on the work of this Conference which is dedicated to bringing about Unity and Freedom to the whole continent of Africa;

Convinced that education is an essential factor in the liberation and development of Africa, and impressed by the education aid granted by some Independent African States to various African countries in the way of scholarships and the establishment of educational institutions in Africa.

This Conference:

1. Urges the British Government to grant self-government to Zanzibar this year.

2. Condemns all such organisations in Zanzibar or outside it which allow themselves to be made tools of colonialism by fomenting or perpetuating inter-racial, inter-tribal, inter-religious or inter-communal differences; and calls upon all political parties and trade unions of Zanzibar to form a United front for the liberation of their country.

3. Appeals to all African States, which are in a position to do so, to grant educational facilities through scholarships and the establishment of educational institutions in the African countries which stand in need of such aid.

Resolution on South-West Africa

The Second All-African Peoples Conference condemns emphatically the application of the vicious and oppressive policy of apartheid in the international Territory of South-West Africa and the exploitation of the people of that Territory by the Government of the Union of South Africa and the Administration of South-West Africa.

Calls upon the Government of the Union of South Africa to abolish all discriminatory laws, regulations and practices in South-West Africa.

Calls upon the African States to refer the violations of the Mandate and the Acts of Aggression and despoliation of the People of this International Territory of South-West Africa to the Security Council for immediate action.

Calls upon the African members of the United Nations to take action to secure the compulsory Jurisdiction of the International Court of Justice and its judgment on the compatibility of the policy of apartheid which is being enforced there with the *sacred trust of civilisation* accepted by the Government of the Union of South Africa under the Mandate Agreement for South-West Africa.

Calls upon all Governments and Organisations in Member States of the United Nations to embark on the boycott of all goods produced in the Union of South Africa under the Mandate Agreement for South African defiance of the United Nations resolutions on the International Territory of South-West Africa.

Resolution on Somaliland

The Conference after a careful survey of the situation in Somaliland artificially divided,

Denounces the colonial repression which is dealt with in this country.

Hails and supports the struggle of the people of Somaliland for independence and unity in order to give birth to a bigger Somaliland.

Requests the immediate liberation of detained patriots.

Resolution Relating to Northern Rhodesia, Southern Rhodesia and Nyasaland

The Second All-African Peoples Conference held in Tunis from 25th to 29th January, 1960, deplores the continued existence of the Federation of Rhodesia and Nyasaland in spite of the overwhelming opposition of the entire African population to the imposition of the Federation against their wishes.

Further, the All-African Peoples Conference notes with disgust the mass arrests of Africans, including women, in Nyasaland and the mass detentions and rustications of African nationalists in Nyasaland, Southern Rhodesia and Northern Rhodesia on account of their expression and demand of fundamental human rights and self-determination.

This Conference is abhorred by the persistence of the British Government in supporting the continued oppression and domination of Africans by the few irresponsible settlers; by the illegal and brutal beatings of African demonstrators in Nyasaland, Northern Rhodesia and Southern Rhodesia during Mr. Macmillan's visit.

By the refusal of the British Government to accept the report of the Devlin Commission which openly stated that Africans in Nyasaland were opposed to Federation and cleared Dr. Hastings Kamuzu Banda on charges of inciting violence.

The Conference is appalled by the appointment of the Monckton Commission to recommend the perpetuation of the settler-governed Federation and not to break it up in accordance with the wishes of the Africans. This Conference, therefore, resolves and demands:

1. That the British Government breaks up the Federation of Nyasaland and Northern Rhodesia and grants complete independence to Nyasaland and Northern Rhodesia and a democratic Government based on one man one vote to Southern Rhodesia.

2. The release of Dr. Banda, James Chikerama and all other political detainees, and the ending of the state of emergency and laws embodying Nyasaland, Northern Rhodesia and Southern Rhodesia.

3. The Conference recommends and supports the boycotting of the Monckton Commission by Africans in Nyasaland, Northern Rhodesia and Southern Rhodesia.

4. Condemns the use of African soldiers from neighbouring territories against freedom fighters in the Federation.

5. Conference appeals to all Independent African States to put the question of the Central African Federation before the forthcoming session of the United Nations and proclaims its unflinching solidarity with the African people of Northern Rhodesia, Southern Rhodesia and Nyasaland in their fight against imperialism and colonialism.

IV. RESOLUTIONS ADOPTED BY THE ALL-AFRICAN PEOPLES CONFERENCE
Cairo, March 23-31, 1961

Resolution on the Liberation of Dependent Countries

The Third Conference of African Peoples meeting at Cairo from 25th to 31st March, 1961, confirming the declarations and resolutions adopted at the First and Second All-African Peoples Conferences held respectively at Accra in December 1958 and in Tunis in January 1960, salutes the heroic Freedom Fighters of Africa struggling to wage the final onslaught on Imperialism in Algeria, Angola, Basutoland, Bechuanaland, Cape Verde Islands, Kenya, Mozambique, Nyasaland, Northern Rhodesia, Portuguese Guinea, Ruanda-Urundi, Southern Rhodesia, South-West Africa, Swaziland, S. Tome and Principe Islands, Uganda, South Africa, Zanzibar and other colonial territories.

Convinced that the time has come for intensifying the struggle against Imperialism;

Aware of the fact that Imperialists and Colonialists in their desperate bid to hold their unjustified possessions in Africa, have become more ruthless in their oppression of African freedom fighters;

Noting with concern that many African freedom fighters are forced to carry on their struggle against Imperialism outside their own countries;

Endorsing the necessity in some respects to resort to force in order to liquidate colonialism;

Aware of the fact that imperialists pour money into Africa in order to promote puppets as well as foster disunity to thwart the struggle towards the true liberation of Africa;

Disturbed by the disastrous effects which imperialistic propaganda through the radio and the Press have on the unity of freedom fighters;

Contemptuous of the role of the negative United Nations in the struggle for African Liberation;

Convinced of the vital role that Independent African States are destined to play in the final liquidation of imperialism and colonialism;

The All-African Peoples Conference

Welcomes the creation of an African Freedom Fund and the willingness of Independent African States to contribute to this Fund;

Recommends the creation of an effective machinery forthwith to consolidate and administer this Fund, namely an All-Africa Freedom Fund

Committee consisting of three members elected by the Steering Committee among the representatives from the Independent African States and three from the representatives from the dependent African countries with the Secretary-General as the Executive Officer. And that this committee shall meet at least once every three months to study the financial needs of all the African territories struggling for freedom;

Urges the establishment of a Free-Africa Radio Station under the direction of the All-African Peoples Conference in an independent African country which is strategically placed to carry out an effective campaign to help African freedom fighters in various colonial territories;

Condemns all those who, under the guise of nationalism, act as agents of colonialism and imperialism;

Calls upon all the African freedom fighters to close their ranks and wage a common onslaught on imperialism and colonialism;

Demands the immediate withdrawal of all colonial governments from Africa;

Urges all African freedom fighters whether fighting with violent or non-violent means to intensify their struggle to the maximum in order to bring about the speedy liquidation of imperialism and colonialism from Africa;

Calls upon all the freedom-loving peoples of the world to condemn imperialism and offer their unflinching support to the African freedom fighters;

And proclaims the necessary solidarity of the African Peoples' Liberation Movements with all the forces of liberty and emancipation throughout the world.

Resolution on Algeria

After having studied the latest developments of the situation in Algeria, the Third All-African Peoples Conference meeting in Cairo from 25th to 31st March, 1961, greets the zealous struggle of the Algerian people.

Considering that self determination is the only means of allowing the Algerian people to realise democratically their independence in sovereignty and territorial integrity;

Considering that it is the strengthening of the Algerian people supported by all the forces of African, Asian and democratic independence which has led the French Government to accept the proposition of G.P.R.A. of 16th January, 1961;

Considering that the manoeuvres and the pretensions of French colonialism tend to the partitioning of the Sahara from the national Algerian territory and its integration to France, and constitute a serious danger for African independence and unity and a direct menace for international peace;

The Conference

1. Refers to the resolution on Algeria, adopted by the Second All-African Peoples Conference held in Tunis in January, 1960.

2. Decides to give unanimous support to the Provisional Government of the Republic of Algeria in its decision of beginning negotiations with the French Government concerning the putting into effect of the principle of self determination of the Algerian people.

3. To recommend to African States to increase their political, diplomatic and material support in the present phase in view of allowing the Algerian people to realise their full and complete sovereignty and to respect the integrity of the integration of the Algerian national territory.

4. To give total support to the stand of the G.P.R.A. in connection with the Algerian Sahara as being an integral part of national Algerian territory and raising the sovereignty of the Algerian people.

Resolution on Nyasaland and Rhodesia

Whereas the undemocratic imposition by British imperialists of a Central African Federation on the nine million Africans of Northern Rhodesia, Southern Rhodesia and Nyasaland has resulted in a barbaric, savage and outrageous domination of the Africans by colonialists led by Roy Welensky;

Whereas it is the inherent right of the Africans of Central Africa to choose their own Government and mode of life;

Whereas the existence of British rule over Central Africa is nothing but an accident of history;

Whereas the recent tendencies in Britain and among the governing Party as regards Northern Rhodesia, Southern Rhodesia and Nyasaland are contrary to the spirit of the recent expulsion of South Africa from the Commonwealth;

Whereas the recent constitutional changes in Northern Rhodesia and Southern Rhodesia fall far short of the aspirations of the people and are a ghostly reflection of barbaric intentions of the British Government over the African people of Central Africa;

Whereas the continued detention and imprisonment of African nationalists by colonialists and imperialists is contrary to democratic principles;

It is resolved therefore that this Conference

(a) Condemns the present constitutional changes in Northern Rhodesia and Southern Rhodesia and demands the immediate granting of independence to the two Rhodesias on the principle of one man one vote;

(b) Demands the immediate and unconditional dissolution of the Central African Federation and the consequent independence of the Central African territories of Nyasaland, Northern Rhodesia and Southern Rhodesia; who by their right will decide their political future;

(c) Calls upon all Commonwealth countries to eject the imposed Central African Federation from the Commonwealth as it is in fact a pocket edition of the apartheid policies of the Union of South Africa;

(d) Calls upon all African and Commonwealth countries not to fraternise with the imposed Central African Federation through diplomatic exchanges, trade relations, touristic or other socio-cultural exchanges;

(e) Demands the immediate release of all political prisoners and detainees in Nyasaland and the two Rhodesias such as George Nuandolo, Chikerama and Masuki Chipembere whose only crime is their dedication to the struggle against imperialism and colonialism;

(f) Calls upon the All-African Peoples Conference and the Independent African States to redouble their aid and support to the Africans of Central Africa against British imperialism;

(g) Calls upon all African Independent States to see to it that:

(i) No Independent African State should export nor import anything to or from this Federation;

(ii) Federal airlines should not be allowed to use African Independent States' territorial air space nor be accorded landing facilities;

(iii) That Afro-Asian States should raise the issue of Central African Federation at the forthcoming United Nations General Assembly;

(h) Appeals to the freedom-loving countries of the world to condemn British imperialism in Nyasaland and the Rhodesias as vigorously as possible.

Resolution on South-West Africa

The Third All-African Peoples Conference emphatically condemns the Government of the Union of South Africa and its policies in South-West Africa,

Demands that the South African Administration quits the territory of South-West Africa forthwith,

Energetically calls on the United Nations to act against South Africa with uncompromising firmness and utmost immediacy,

Calls on the African Independent States to take the initiative in S.-W. Africa by actively backing the entrance of the Committee on S.W.A. into S.W.A.,

Calls on the African States to press for and impose sanctions on South Africa, economic, diplomatic and otherwise,

Calls on all freedom-loving countries of the world to condemn British UN policy towards the South-West Africa issue.

Resolution on the Three High Commission Territories

1. Considering that the High Commission Territories were under the protection of the British Imperialists through the will and the contention of the Peoples of the protectorates some ninety years ago,

2. Considering that the British Imperialists ruled the aforesaid territories by proclamations which were never and are still not appreciated by the Peoples of these countries,

3. Considering also that Britain through her District Resident Commissioners stationed at different places within the protectorates has managed and succeeded to divide the peoples of these territories, particularly those of Bechuanaland, by creating different tribal chiefs and emphasising the importance of minor and important differences existing in the language at the different parts of the protectorate,

4. Considering that Swaziland has been divided into portions:

(a) So called Crown land.

(b) Land for sale and division into farms for the Union Boer farmers,

5. Considering that Britain has successfully managed to impose colour bar and discrimination in all its forms into the protectorates but failed to embark on economic development of these so called protectorates,

6. Considering that the independence of the protectorates will accelerate the freedom and the independence of the Union of South Africa,

7. Considering also the repercussions that will be born out of the expulsion and withdrawal of South Africa from the Commonwealth and the advocated and envisaged expulsion of South Africa from the United Nations,

This Conference

1. Recommends to the Independent States of Africa to grant scholarships to the youth of the protectorates for training in administrative, secretarial and technical work, and otherwise in order to prepare them for the take over,

2. Calls upon the Independent States to help the organisations in the protectorates, aspiring for freedom and independence and basing their struggle on the standing principles of the A.A.P.C. and true African nationalism to rally their people to independence,

3. Demands that Britain grants unconditional independence to the peoples of the protectorates immediately.

Resolution on Angola

The Third All-African Peoples Conference after examining the present situation in Angola, a situation essentially characterised by the state of popular rebellion on one hand, and by the intensification of the barbarian repression of the Portuguese on the other hand, greets the Angolian Patriots who, since the events of last February, fight courageously against the Portuguese Colonialists.

The Conference, convinced that the people of Angola are ready at any moment to assume national sovereignty, condemns all manoeuvres tending to allow imperialists and neo-colonialists intervention in Angola, in particular the propagation of the divisions between the people, the territorial disintegration of the country or the instoration of a Government of stooges.

It recommends:

1. That the Afro-Asian countries members of the UN engage all their efforts in view of obliging Portugal to apply the resolutions of the General Assembly of 14th December, 1960, concerning liquidation of colonialism.

2. That the Independent African States reconsider their position concerning diplomatic and commercial relations with Portugal.

3. That the African States remain vigilant before an eventual intervention of UN in Angola by guarding themselves to take the position which will place them in a situation where they will have to sanction the imperialist manoeuvres.

Resolution on Mozambique:

The Third All-African Peoples Conference expresses its indignation on the conditions of existence of the People of Mozambique which the Portuguese Colonialists have compelled to forced labour, to the deportation to the mines of South Africa and to an inhuman and degrading exploitation.

It recommends specially that concrete measures be taken immediately in view of supporting the liberation movements directed by the patriots of this country.

Special Motion

The Third All-African Peoples Conference having learned with indignation that on the one day of February 5, 1961, 3,000 Angolese were massacred at Luanda by the forces of repression, decides to make February 5th the day of solidarity with all the people and patriots who fight the Portuguese barbarian colonialism.

Resolution on Portuguese Guinea and the Islands of Cape Verde

The Third All-African Peoples Conference, having closely studied the report concerning the condition of the people of "Portuguese" Guinea and the islands of Cape Verde,

1. Strongly proclaims the inalienable right of the people of "Portuguese" Guinea and the islands of Cape Verde to national independence and the attainment of their freedom by all possible means;

2. Denounces the conspiracies of Portuguese colonialism directed at establishing a new form of colonial domination in these countries in collaboration with some African traitors and the support of American imperialists and West Germans;

3. Condemns the relations between the Government of Senegal and the Portuguese Government, which have been denounced for being contrary to the interests and the cause of freedom of the people of Portuguese Guinea and the islands of Cape Verde;

4. Appeals to these two African peoples to establish unity, either between them (around one party) or with the peoples of other Portuguese colonies, for the speedy and total liquidation of colonial domination.

Resolution on Kenya

This Third All-African Peoples Conference meeting in Cairo, being concerned with the true independence of all countries in Africa, vehemently deplores the obdurate attitude of the British imperialists in Kenya and their continued refusal to the immediate and unconditional release of Kenya's National leader, Jomo Kenyatta.

1. Release of Jomo Kenyatta:

The Conference being convinced that Kenyatta is the only leader who can and will bring unity, peace and stability to Kenya; and taking note of the pledge made by Kenya nationalists to stand firm and that without Kenyatta's immediate and unconditional release and leadership they would not participate in the Government; endorses this stand and calls on all Kenya leaders to work energetically and positively for Kenyatta's immediate and unconditional release to come and lead his people in unity to complete independence.

The Conference condemns the refusal of the British Government to release Kenyatta as being both provocative and calculated to precipitate a crisis and political chaos wherein only the interests of the imperialists could be advanced. The Conference, therefore, supports the struggle of the peoples of Kenya for the immediate release of Kenyatta in the knowledge that right will triumph over imperialism and injustice.

2. Unity and Independence:

The Conference recognises that unity among nationalists is the most effective weapon in the struggle against colonialists and imperialists and calls on all Kenya people in the spirit of the recent Lodwar Conference to establish such unity and not to allow personality conflicts and selfishness to frustrate this endeavour to achieve total independence in 1961.

3. Military Bases:

The Conference condemns the British Government's action of setting up military bases in Kenya and looks upon this as an act of hostility and aggression on African soil constituting tangible instruments of the cold war and, therefore, supports the Kenya people in their determination to remove these symbols of imperialism in Kenya.

4. Cold War:

The Conference being conscious of danger of the cold war and neo-colonialist tactics and being concerned about the manifestations of cold war manoeuvres in Kenya and elsewhere in Africa, calls upon the people of Kenya to eradicate these manifestations and to constantly safeguard themselves against this danger.

Resolution on South Africa

1. The Third All-African Peoples Conference,

Noting with concern that the vicious economic exploitation, brutal political oppression and savage social degradation of the oppressed majority of the people of South Africa by the colonial Government of South Africa and by colonial imperialist interests continues unabated;

Noting, also, with dismay the sinister determination of the colonial Government of South Africa and imperialist interests to prevent at all cost the takeover by governments of the majority;

Noting further, with jubilation the virtual expulsion of the colonial government of South Africa from membership of the Commonwealth,

The Conference resolves as follows:

(a) Condemns all foreign and colonial investors who continue to allow the investors and landed industrial and commercial interests to be used for the exploitation, oppression and degradation of the indigenous people and other oppressed minorities for the prevention of a peaceful takeover by the people of South Africa;

(b) Deplores and deprecates investment and landed industrial and commercial interests by outsiders, because by so doing they become parties in the exploitation, oppression and degradation of the people of South Africa;

(c) Urges that no members of the Commonwealth Prime Ministers' Conference should have any practical relations with South Africa as formerly exercised before the withdrawal of South Africa from the Commonwealth;

(d) Calls on the Afro-Asian Group in the United Nations to press for the earliest expulsion of South Africa from that organisation.

2. The Conference further resolved as follows:

Appeals to all Independent African States and other freedom-loving countries of the world to:

(i) Sever diplomatic relations with South Africa;

(ii) Close all their ports to South African vessels and any other vessels registered in terms of the laws of that country;

(iii) Prevent their own ships from entering South African ports;

(iv) Boycott South African goods;

(v) Refuse landing and passage facilities to all aircraft belonging to the South African Government and companies registered under the laws of that country;

(vi) Appeals to PAFMECA and other African territories to endeavour to prevent and halt labour supply from reaching the mines and factories of the Union;

(vii) Urges the Trade Union Movement and workers in Africa and throughout the world to refuse to handle cargo to and from South Africa;

(ix) Welcomes the move for barring South Africa from the Federation of International Football Associations, and urges the formation of the All-African Sports Federation.

Resolution on Ruanda-Urundi

1. Considering that the problem of Ruanda-Urundi is closely linked to that of the Congo and that no happy solution to the Congo question can be reached so long as the Belgian imperialists remain in Ruanda-Urundi,

2. Considering that the Belgian imperialists have conducted a policy of repression as a result of which thousands of nationalists are imprisoned and basely persecuted, while tens of thousands of patriots were forced to seek refuge in neighbouring countries,

3. Considering that the Belgian Government, disregarding the UN resolutions, has created military bases in Ruanda-Urundi which contribute a serious threat to Africa in general and to the Congo in particular, and has likewise installed two puppet governments thus balkanising the territory under trusteeship,

The Conference:
Condemns the military bases created by Belgian imperialists in Ruanda-Urundi;

Condemns the creation of puppet Governments and the division of the territory into entities that cannot survive, as well as the imperialist manoeuvres to federate Ruanda-Urundi with secessionist Katanga;

Demands the immediate withdrawal of Belgian troops and the liquidation of their military bases, the general and unconditional amnesty of all political prisoners and the return of the refugees;

The organisation and control of legislative elections in Ruanda-Urundi by the UN and the installation of democratic institutions;

The creation of African troops to re-establish and maintain order during the formation of a national police force;

The unconditional removal of Belgian trusteeship and the access of Ruanda-Urundi to complete independence.

Resolution on Neo-Colonialism

The Third All-African Peoples Conference meeting in Cairo from the 25th to the 31st of March, 1961, having carefully reviewed the current situation in Africa,

Considers that neo-colonialism, which is the survival of the colonial system in spite of formal recognition of political independence in emerging countries which become the victims of an indirect and subtle form of domination by political, economic, social, military or technical means, is the greatest threat to African countries that have newly won their independence or those approaching this status.

Emphasises the examples of the Congo, the French Community, the Federation of Rhodesia and Nyasaland, which indicate that the colonial system and international imperialism, realising their failure in facing the development of revolutionary movements in Africa, make use of many means to safeguard the essential of their economic and military power.

When the recognition of national independence becomes inevitable, they try to deprive these countries of their essence of real independence. This is done by imposing unequal economic, military and technical conventions; by creating puppet governments following false elections, or by inventing some so-called constitutional formulae of multi-national co-existence intended only to hide the racial discrimination favouring settlers.

Whenever such machinations appear insufficient to hamper the combativity and determination of popular liberation movements, dying colonialism tries, under the cover of neo-colonialism or through the guided intervention of the United Nations, the balkanisation of newly independent States or the systematic division of the political or syndical vivid forces, and in desperate cases, like in the Congo, colonialism goes as far as plots, repressive measures by army and police, and murder in cold blood.

Conscious that neo-colonialism manifests itself through economic and political intervention, intimidation and blackmail in order to prevent African States from directing their political, social and economic policies towards the exploitation of their natural wealth for the benefit of their peoples,

Considers that such countries as the United States, Federal Germany, Israel, Britain, Belgium, Holland, South Africa and France are the main perpetrators of neo-colonialism.

Manifestations of Neo-Colonialism

This Conference denounces the following manifestations of neo-colonialism in Africa:

(a) Puppet governments represented by stooges and even fabricated elections, based on some chiefs, reactionary elements, anti-popular politicians, big bourgeois compradors or corrupted civil or military functionaries.

(b) Regrouping of States, before or after independence, by an imperial Power in federations or communities linked to that imperial Power.

(c) Balkanisation as a deliberate political fragmentation of States by creation of artificial entities, such as, for example, the case of Katanga, Mauritania, Buganda, etc.

(d) The economic entrenchment of the colonial Power before independence and the continuity of economic dependence after formal recognition of National sovereignty.

(e) Integration into colonial economic blocks which maintain the under-developed character of African economy.

(f) Economic infiltration by a foreign Power after independence, through capital investments, loans and monetary aids or technical experts of unequal concessions, particularly those extending for long periods.

(g) Direct monetary dependence, as in those emergent independent States whose finances remain in the hands of and directly controlled by colonial Powers.

(h) Military bases sometimes introduced as scientific research stations or training schools, introduced either before independence or as a condition for independence.

Agents of Neo-Colonialism

The Conference exposes the following active agents of neo-colonialism:

(a) Colonial embassies and missions serving as nerve centres of espionage and pressure points on the local African Governments directly or through their civil or military technicians.

(b) So-called foreign and United Nations technical assistants who ill-advise and sabotage national political, economical, educational and social development.

(c) Military personnel in armed forces and police, as officers or advisers who serve, above all, the colonial interests directly, or through local officers who remain loyal to their former masters.

(d) The representatives from imperialist and colonial countries under the cover of religion, Moral Re-armament, cultural, Trade Union and Youth or Philanthropic Organisations.

(e) The malicious propaganda by radio, Press, literature controlled by imperial and colonial countries, as well as in some independent African countries where Press and radio are still owned by imperialist Powers.

(f) Puppet Governments in Africa being used by imperialists in the furtherance of neo-colonialism, such as the use of their good offices by the neo-colonial Powers to undermine the sovereignty and aspirations of other African States.

Means of Fighting Neo-Colonialism

The Conference, whose very reason of existence is the mobilisation of African masses for the liberation of Africa, is firmly convinced that it is by intensifying this mobilisation that Africa will find the most efficient way to fight neo-colonialism and to extract the last roots of imperialism.

It is the duty of popular, political, syndical, youth and women's organisations not only to inspire and to wage the struggle against neo-colonialism but also, and above all, to be vigilant, to control the correct application of the general outline and to denounce all those who attempt to deviate it from its real objectives.

The Conference realises that the struggle against neo-colonialism must be associated with the struggle against all forms of opportunism which is the mask of the accomplices of imperialism.

It is therefore by the awakening of the conscience of the masses by the establishment of landmarks of real liberation, that the masses will be freed from the power of certain slogans and formulas that only serve as a camouflage for colonialism.

That is why the Conference:

(a) Condemns the balkanisation of emerging States, whether dependent or independent, as a way to perpetuate neo-colonialism in Africa (Congo, Mauritania, Northern Rhodesia, Buganda, etc.);

(b) Condemns the federations and communities created before independence under the patronage of colonial States;

(c) Invites all Independent African States to give aid and assistance to liberate the African countries still under foreign domination.

(d) Urges all Independent African States which still retain foreign military and para-military bases to liquidate these bases as soon as possible.

(e) Reaffirms its determination to continue to mobilise popular mass opinion to denounce enemies of true independence and agents of neo-colonialism, camouflaged in all possible forms;

(f) Denounces aid with expressed or unexpressed strings attached;

(g) Urges the Independent African States to intensify their efforts for the creation of an effective form of co-operation among the African States in the Economic, Social and Cultural domains, in order to frustrate neo-colonialism;

(h) Deplores the attitude of some Independent African States who, under the guise of neutrality, are passive even on vital matters affecting the whole of Africa, and who, by their passive activities in fact promote the cause of neo-colonialism;

(i) Calls for the immediate launching of the All-African Trade Union Federation as an effective means of counteracting neo-colonialism.

Resolution on the United Nations

Considering that the increasing number of Independent African States and the increasing importance of the African Continent in world affairs demands a revision of the Charter of the United Nations, so as to give our continent appropriate representation on the Security Council, and other bodies of the UN;

Considering that the UN's actions in the Congo have clearly proved the ineffectiveness of its present set-up to implement the resolutions of the Security Council, and its subjection to imperialist Powers;

Considering that the United Nations has therefore become an instrument of neo-colonialism under whose cloak colonial Powers re-enter independent countries;

The Conference calls upon the Independent African States and other freedom-loving States to demand the reorganisation of the general secretariat and the revision of the United Nations Charter to conform with the present world situation.

Resolution on the Congo

The Third All-African Peoples Conference, having studied the situation in the Congo;

Bows before the fighters who fell in the course of the glorious struggle against reactionary, enslavement and colonialist oppression forces;

Expresses its particular indignation at the savage assassination of Mr. Patrice Lumumba, permanent member of our Conference and Prime Minister of the Legitimate Government of the Congo Republic;

The Conference, conscious of the dramatic situation of the Congo;

Considering that this situation was created by the imperialists helped by a handful of opportunists, in the sole aim of destroying the Congolese nation and thus ensuring the continuation of the colonialist régime in the country;

Noting that, by the meeting of puppets at Tananarive (Malagasy), the imperialists are attempting to apply their classical method of "Divide and Rule";

Considering that the United Nations is directly responsible for all that goes on in the Congo and for the serious and regrettable deterioration of the situation;

Considering that this situation, should it persist, might degenerate into an inter-African or world conflict due to the slowness of the United Nations;

Considering that the Congolese crisis should come to an end;

Supports the resolutions of the Addis-Ababa and Casablanca Conferences and of the meeting of the All-African Peoples Conference Steering Committee at Dar-es-Salaam;

Demands the immediate implementation of all the Security Council resolutions in order to:

> (a) stop imperialistic military intervention in the Congo and expel Belgian, French, British, German and other mercenaries in the service of puppets in the Congo,
>
> (b) to restore law and order by the normal functioning of national institutions, namely the Parliament;

Considers that the only legitimate Government of the indivisible Republic of the Congo is that presided over by Mr. Gizenga, and calls upon the African States to recognise this Government and establish effective diplomatic relations with it;

Denounces the machination of the United Nations aiming at considering the puppet governments serving imperialism as the representatives of the Congolese people;

Warns against the procrastination of the United Nations and believes that the resolutions of the Security Council should be applied at once to restore unity and legality in the Congo;

Calls upon the Independent African States to endeavour for the implementation of the resolutions of the Security Council as soon as possible;

Demands the immediate punishment of those responsible for the vubu, Mobutu, Tshombe, Kalondji;

Denounces the role played by General Kettani in the degradation of the situation in the Congo and demands the dismissal of Dag Hammarskjoeld equally responsible for the murder of Lumumba;

Proclaims that Patrice Lumumba is the "Hero of Africa";

Condemns the economic blockade organised by the Mobutu gangs exposing millions of inhabitants to famine and diseases;

Asks the United Nations to urgently take the necessary measures that will allow provinces actually under the control of the legal Government to obtain their normal provisions;

Appeals to neighbouring countries to facilitate the transit of victuals and medicines destined to the population of the Congo;

Launches a strong appeal to the people and States of Africa to help, by every possible means, the brother people of the Congo to continue their struggle for the liberation and unification of their territory.

Resolution on the Kameroun

The Third All-African Peoples Conference;

Considering that there exists in the Kameroun strong French, British and West-German military bases, in conformity with the agreement signed between the Kameroun Government and these Powers,

Considering that a popular consultation was organised in this country in the presence of a foreign army and at the moment when all democratic freedoms were suppressed and when the population did not express itself freely,

Condemns the agreements signed between Mr. Philips and the French Government eliminating national sovereignty and practically converting this territory into a French department in Africa;

Strongly stands against the bombardment of numerous regions in the

Kameroun by the French artillery and the repeated executions of Kameroonese people struggling for independence;

Strongly protests against the arbitrary division into two parts, not only of the Kameroun as a whole but of West-Kameroun;

Hails the results of the plebiscite held on February 11th and 12th this year as a victory of the Kameroonese people and the fruit of many years of struggle for a true unity and independence;

Regrets that numerous frauds were organised by the British imperialists to prevent the Kameroun from regaining its political entity;

Requests all Independent African States to consider the gravity of the situation in the Kameroun and to support the following propositions which answer the profound aspirations of the people of the Kameroun both in the UN and outside it:

    1. The immediate and complete withdrawal of French and British military troops and technicians in the Kameroun.

    2. The abrogation of French, British and other agreements.

    3. The restoration and respect of democratic and syndical freedoms and the liberation of political prisoners in the two zones.

    4. The immediate and complete Africanisation of management posts;

Invites all the popular forces of Africa to support the Kameroonese people in their just struggle for true unity and independence.

Resolution on Reorganisation of Structures and Liquidation of Remnants of Imperialism

The Third All-African Peoples Conference,

Considering that political, economic, cultural and social institutions in African countries have been deflected from their objectives by the colonisers with a view to securing their domination,

Considering also that colonial domination has hindered the normal development of African countries,

Considering that as a result, the African has been robbed of his personality and been made the victim of oppression, exploitation and plunder,

Considering the persistent influence of colonial domination on human mentality, and on the organisation of political structures in countries,

Considering that independence can not become effective without the liquidation of the remnants of colonial régimes and the reorganisation of administrative, judicial, economic and social structures,

Calls on all African Independent countries to proceed without delay to the full decolonisation of all structures in order to satisfy the peoples' aspirations for justice, dignity and the full exercising of their responsibilities;

Invites political parties and Trade Union organisations in each African country to mobilise themselves to bring about the reorganisation of these structures.

A. At Political Level:

By suppressing all institutions of a discriminatory character, preserved by the colonialists for the sole object of serving their own interests: reactionary institutions supported by the colonialists.

By reorganising the judiciary and administration.

B. At Economic Level:

The Conference demands the modification of structures in such a way as to effectively subordinate the economy of the countries to the needs of national interests, by exercising control over exports, imports and investments, guaranteeing a harmonious control of production with a view to the steady improvement of the living conditions of the people.

By introducing agrarian reforms.

By creating currencies and national banks, free from the domination of colonial Powers.

By establishing internal commercial links and lines of communication permitting profitable co-operation.

C. At Cultural and Social Level:

The Conference demands the reorganisation of Education in such a way as to remove from curricula all ideas tending to give the African a sense of inferiority, and to re-establish authentic history;

The organisation of youth in such a way that its activities embrace sports, popular artistic education and national construction.

Resolution on Economic Unity

The Third All-African Peoples Conference notes with satisfaction the intensification of the struggle of the African peoples for the achievement of their political independence with a view to decolonising the political, economic and social structures of Africa.

The Conference records with interest the progress made in some African States leading to a complete liquidation of colonialism and the remnants by a radical change in the economic and social structures imposed by colonialism so as to exploit the resources and riches of the African peoples.

The Conference notes that this progress was achieved as a result of the close economic co-operation between the African States in the development of air transport, the creation of indigenous monetary zones, etc., and commercial exchanges. It was possible because of the new changing world situation which has opened to the Independent African States not only new markets but also new perspectives for ensuring a more and more harmonious and effective development of the African economy.

Considering that Political Independence is given full meaning by economic independence, the Conference calls upon the Independent countries to orientate themselves firmly towards a democratisation of the political and social structures which alone can accelerate the achievement of the material and moral conditions of the African peoples by a rational and equitable repartition of their resources in the interest of the masses by an appropriate planning of the national economy.

With a view to accelerating this process of development and the attainment in the shortest possible time of an economic and social equilibrium in Africa, the Conference calls for:

1. Firstly and as soon as possible an Inter-State African Transport Company (Land, Sea and Air) to facilitate travelling and exchanges between the African States.

2. The creation of an African Bank for investment to facilitate the realisation of development projects.

3. The signing of multilateral customs and foreign exchange agree-

ments in order to develop economic exchanges which would easily lead to the creation of a common African Market.

On the social level the Conference calls for:

1. Respect for the democratic right of Trade Unions necessary for the development of a constructive and independent trade union movement.

2. The creation of a Council of States, Supra-National, which can control and examine cases involving the violation of the democratic rights of workers.

On the cultural level, the Conference demands:

1. The creation of a common research institute to promote a true and authentic African culture.

2. The creation of a large Academy to be called the Academy of African Solidarity, the offer of scholarships and an increase in cultural exchanges as regards teachers, students, doctors, engineers, specialists in agronomy, sports and especially the youth.

Resolutions on African Unity and Solidarity

The Third All-African Peoples Conference,

Considering that this unity must emanate from the freely expressed will of African peoples,

Considering that all African States and organisations have the duty to display a real unanimous will to unite,

Considering that economic unity is indispensable for the viability of any political organisation,

Considering that imperialism, colonialism and neo-colonialism act directly or indirectly to divide the African States, create real obstacles to the realisation of African Unity and the affirmation of African personality,

Recommends all Governments of Independent African States to create:

1. An African Consultative Assembly composed of members representing the parliaments of Independent States, having a Permanent Secretariat and holding periodical sessions in order to formulate a common policy of African States.

2. A Council of African States entrusted with the study and implementation of the recommendations of the Consultative Assembly especially as regards foreign policy.

3. A Commission of African Experts to elaborate a common economic policy in order to promote and consolidate African political unity, provided that the basis of such an economic community is founded upon the co-ordination of development plans in each State with a view to transforming and unifying the present structures.

4. A Commission of African Commanders entrusted with the study, definition and organisation of an African joint defence in order to contribute to the total liberation of the African dependent countries or to the consolidation and protection of African countries subjected to foreign pressures.

5. A Cultural Commission to formulate an African policy in the field of education and cultural exchanges.

This policy must aim at fighting illiteracy, the creation of common institutions of education and the development of all values of the African culture.

The Conference calls upon Trade Unions, Youth, Farmers' and Women's Organisations to hold:

1. An African Trade Unions Conference with a view to creating an All Trade Unions Federation.

2. An African Youth Conference and the organisation of a festival with a view to creating a unified African Youth Movement.

3. An African Women's Associations Conference with a view to creating a unified organisation of African Women.

4. An African Farmers' Associations Conference with a view to creating a unified Movement of African Farmers.

The Conference calls upon the Steering Committee to take all the necessary measures towards the creation of an African Press Agency and an African Information Centre.

Considering that effective and efficient African solidarity will speed up the movement towards the liberation and unity of Africa and will consolidate the independence of sovereign African States, the Conference recommends the African States and organisations to grant:

1. Political support to all genuine national movements struggling for the achievement of independence, political democracy and social justice in their countries.

2. Material support by financing a Solidarity Fund managed by the African Peoples Conference.

The Conference invites its General Secretariat to establish contacts and hold constant consultations with the organs of the Afro-Asian Peoples Solidarity Conference for the realisation of our common objectives.

23

THE IDEA OF AN AFRICAN PERSONALITY
Extracts from Dr. Edward W. Blyden's Presidential
*Address to the Liberia College, 1881**

Those who have lived in civilised communities, where there are different races, know the disparaging views which are entertained of the Negroes by their neighbours, and often, alas, by themselves. The standard of all physical and intellectual excellence in the present civilisation being the white complexion, whatever deviates from that favoured colour is proportionately depreciated until the black, which is the opposite, becomes not only the most unpopular but the most unprofitable colour.

Black men, and especially black women, in such communities, experience the greatest imaginable inconvenience. They never feel at home. In the depth of their being they always feel themselves strangers, and the only escape from this feeling is to escape from themselves, and this feeling of self-depreciation is not diminished, as I have intimated above, by the books they read.

Women, especially, are fond of reading novels and light literature; and it is in these writings that flippant and eulogistic reference is constantly made to the superior physical and mental characteristics of the Caucasian race, which by contrast, suggests the inferiority of other races, especially of that race which is furthest removed from it in appearance.

It is painful in America to see the efforts which are made by the Negroes to secure outward conformity to the appearance of the dominant race. This is by no means surprising; but what is surprising is that, under the circumstances, any Negro has retained a particle of self-respect.

Now, in Africa, where the colour of the majority is black, the fashion in personal matters is naturally suggested by the personal characteristics of the race, and we are free from the necessity of submitting to the use of 'Incongruous feathers awkwardly stuck on'.

Still we are held in bondage by our indiscriminate and injudicious use of foreign literature, and we strive to advance by the methods of a foreign race. In the effort, we struggle with the odds against us. We fight at the disadvantage which David would have experienced in Saul's armour. The African must advance by methods of his own. He must possess a power distinct from that of the European. It had been proved that he knows how to take advantage of European culture and that he can be benefited by it. Their proof was perhaps necessary, but it is not sufficient. We must show that we are able to go alone, to carve out our own way. We must not be satisfied that, in this nation, European influence shapes our

* *Latitude* (Afrikawa Society, July–Sept., 1960, London).
263

polity, makes our laws, rules in our tribunals and impregnates our social atmosphere.

We must not suppose that the Anglo-Saxon methods are final, that there is nothing for us to find out for our own guidance, and that we have nothing to teach to the world. There is inspiration for us also. We must study our brethren in the interior who know better than we do the laws of growth for the race. We see among them the rudiments of that which, with fair-play and opportunity will develop into important and effective agencies for our work. We look too much to foreigners and are dazzled almost to blindness by their exploits, so as to fancy that they have exhausted the possibilities of humanity. Doctor Alexander Winchell, a professor in one of the American universities, who has lately written a book, in the name of the science in which he reproduces all the old slanders against the Negro, and writes of the African home as if Livingstone, Basil, Stanley and Cameron had never written, mentions it as one of the evidences of Negro inferiority, that in 'Liberia he is indifferent to the benefits of civilisation' whose theories are to degrade him in the scale of humanity, and of which such 'socialists' as Dr. Winchell are the exponents and representative elements. We recommend all Africans to treat such 'benefits' with even more decided indifference. Those of us who have travelled in foreign countries and who witness the general results of European influence along this coast have many reasons for misgivings and reserves and anxieties about European civilisation for this country.

Things which have been of great advantage to Europe may work ruin to us and there is often such a striking resemblance, or such a close connection between the hurtful and beneficial, that we are not always able to discriminate.

It will be our aim to increase the amount of purely disciplinary agencies, and to reduce to its minimum the amount of those distracting influences to which I have referred as hindering the proper growth of the race. The true principle of mental culture is perhaps this: *to preserve an accurate balance between the studies which carry the mind out of itself, and those which recall it home again. When we receive impressions from without we must bring from our own consciousness the idea that gives them shape; we must mould them by our own individuality.* [My Italics, C. L.] Now, in looking over the whole world I see no place where this sort of culture for the Negro can be better secured than in Africa; where he may, with less interruption from surrounding influences, find out his place and his work, develop his peculiar gifts and powers; and for the training of Negro youth upon the basis of their own idiosyncracies, with a sense of race individuality, self-respect, and liberty.

It is true that culture is one, and the general effects of true culture are the same, but the native capacities of mankind differ, and their work and destiny differs, so that the road by which one man may attain to the highest efficiency is not that which would conduce to success of another. The special road which has led to the success and elevation of the Anglo-Saxon, is not that which would lead to the success and elevation of the Negro.

It will be our aim to introduce into our curriculum also the Arabic, and some of the principal native languages, by means of which we may have intelligent intercourse with the millions accessible to us in the interior, and learn more of our own country. We have young men who are experts in the geography and customs of foreign countries; who can tell all about the proceedings of foreign statesmen in countries thousands of miles away; can talk glibly of London, Berlin, Paris and Washington, know all about Gladstone, Bismarck, Gambetta and Mayes but who knows anything about Musahdu, Medina, Kankan or Sego, only a few hundred miles from us?

Who can tell the doings of Fanfi-doreh, Ihahuna Sissi or Fahquequeh or Cimoro of Bopora, only a few steps from us? Now as Negroes, allied in blood and race to these people, this is disgraceful, and as a nation, if we intend to grow and prosper in this country, it is impolitic, it is short-sighted, it is unpatriotic; but it has required time for us to grow up to these ideas, to understand our position in this country.

It is the complaint of the intelligent Negro in America that the white people pay no attention to his suggestions or his writings; but this is only because he has nothing new to say. *Let us depend on it that the emotions and thoughts which are natural to us command the curiosity and respect of others far more than the showy display of any mere acquisitions which we have derived from them, and which they know depend more upon our memory than upon any real capacity.* What we must follow is all that concerns our individual growth. Let us do our own work and we shall be strong and worthy of respect; try to do the work of others and we shall be weak and contemptible.

There is magnetism in original action, in self-trust, which others cannot resist. The time is past when we can be content with putting forth elaborate arguments to prove our equality with foreign races. Those who doubt our capacity are more likely to be convinced of their error by the exhibition, on our part, of those qualities of energy and enterprise which will enable us to occupy the extensive field before us for our own advantage and the advantage of humanity, for the purpose of civilisation, of science, of good government and progress generally, than by any more abstract argument about the equality of races. The suspicions disparaging to us will be dissipated only by the exhibition of the indisputable realities of a lofty manhood as they may be illustrated in successful efforts to build up a nation, to wrest from nature her secrets, to lead the van of progress in this country and to regenerate a continent.

24

STATEMENT ON AFRICAN AFFAIRS*
The Hon. Obafemi Awolowo, Lagos, June 28, 1961

From the beginning of recorded history, the black man has been the most conspicuous butt of all manner of inhuman treatment. In the palaces of the Arabian Potentates—both in the Middle East and in North Africa—he was degraded and enslaved. When the so-called 'Dark Continent of Africa' was discovered, the European marauders hunted him down like a common beast, captured him, and sold him into slavery in the Americas and the West Indies. The era of trading in, and of enforcing the services of black slaves, was terminated only to be replaced by the European Powers which initiated it with a legalised form of political and economic enslavement of the entire black peoples of the Continent of Africa. The scramble for Africa as well as the permanent settlement of Europeans in certain parts of Africa was motivated wholly and solely, and without any redeeming feature, by the political, economic and military self-interests of the European powers which engaged in that unholy adventure. . . .

Today, for most parts of Black Africa, the inhuman, humiliating and degrading position delineated above remains more or less the same . . . barring a handful of countries on the Continent, Africa is still as ever under Western imperialist bondage.

In the prevailing circumstances, we have to make a choice from three mutually exclusive alternatives. We may take the line of least resistance and allow the Western imperialists to continue to hold us in thrall; or by our complacency and by falling prey to the sweet advances of Western imperialists, we may give cause (albeit unwittingly) for the forces of extremism to gather strength and subsequently erupt, with disastrous consequences for all of us; or we may see wisdom in *purposeful unity* to the ends (a) that all the countries of Africa shall, at the earliest possible time, be truly free and sovereign; and (b) that the black man shall be absolute and undisputed master in his own home, and shall enjoy unaffected and unpatronising equality with the other races of the world.

The first alternative does not merit any consideration. All African nationalists are determined that Africa shall be free. Incomplete or diminished sovereignty is more insidious than open subjection. In the one case the imperialist continues to perpetrate his mischiefs behind the scenes, using the indigenous rulers as catspaws and thereby escaping the just condemnation of the world. In the other, because he is directly

---

* This is an extensive summary of the text of a Press Statement issued by Mr. Awolowo, Leader of the Opposition in Nigeria, and leader of the Action Group.

responsible for the consequences of his doings and misdoings, he is more circumspect in his actions in order to avoid the odium of adverse world opinion.

The second alternative is out of the question. Africa has been too late in the race for progress. It cannot afford to behave like the mythical Phoenix in the confident belief that by burning and destroying itself a more glorious Africa would arise from the ashes of the dead.

The only choice open to us is the third alternative. It is in respect of this that I have some definite proposals to make.

Before I make these proposals, it will, I think, be helpful, if I first of all adumbrate the aims which, in my considered view, we must set out to achieve as well as the principles or considerations by which our thoughts and actions must be guided in the pursuit of our declared objectives.

The aims and objects of all sincere African nationalists should be:

1. To win without delay complete freedom and sovereignty for all those African States which are at present only nominally independent; (a) by the abrogation of any military or defence pact or ties as well as of all rights and privileges appurtenant to such pact or ties; and (b) by the elimination of undue economic or technical dependence on *any single* alien country.

2. To set a target date or dates in the very near future for the complete liberation of all colonial territories wherever they may be on the Continent of Africa.

3. The immediate termination of the existence of any military base in any part of Africa and the evacuation of all occupation troops on the Continent whether they are attached to specific military bases or not.

4. The immediate extermination of apartheid in South Africa.

5. The outlawry of any form of discrimination or segregation against the black peoples in particular and Africans in general, in Africa and in other parts of the world.

6. To uphold and defend the dignity of the African (particularly the black African), and the sovereignty of any Independent African State against derogation or violation from any quarter whatsoever.

7. To promote and establish a community of interests among all the peoples of Africa, and to this end to work assiduously for the realisation of the ideal of a political union or a confederacy (whichever is practicable in the prevailing circumstances) among all African States.

8. As a first practical step towards the emergence of an All-Africa political union, to take immediate steps to divide the Continent into Zones.

9. To influence the immediate introduction in each Zone of a customs and monetary union as well as economic, technical, cultural and other forms of essential co-operation, and to foster an early emergence of a political union among the independent countries situate within each Zone.

10. Non-involvement of all African countries in the present East-West power politics and struggles as well as non-partisanship in the Arab-Israeli dispute and conflict.

Having set out the aims and objects, what then are the principles by which we ought to be guided in pursuing these aims and objects?

In certain parts of the world today and in spite of their vaunted civilisation, the colour of the skin still counts for very much—far more than a man's personality, his character and the calibre of his brain. The fairer the skin, the greater the respect and the better the treatment he receives and can evoke. The colour of his skin, in spite of his intellectual equality with his white-skinned fellow-Americans, has militated against the Negroes' holding any top post in the public life of the United States today. In Egypt the darker-skinned Egyptians, contemptuously called the Felahin, are a depressed majority in that ancient land. They do not enjoy social and political equality with their fairer-skinned fellow Egyptians. The Mullatoes, in certain parts of the world, assume an air of superiority over their darker-skinned brothers and sisters, and are in any case placed on a higher pedestal by their white progenitors. Even in South Africa, Kenya, Central African Federation and in some other parts of the world, the fairer-skinned Asians and Arabs enjoy far better and more humane treatment than the black peoples. *The first principle which I, therefore, advocate is that, in the present context of the world, the black man qua the colour of his skin is confronted with certain knotty and intractable problems which are peculiar to him.*

No nation or group of people in the world today can successfully solve their more important problems in isolation. 'Two heads are better than one', says an old adage. But for the two heads to be better than one, they must be sympathetically attuned and harmoniously united in tackling the problems which confront one or both of them. *The second principle, therefore, is that the best interests of Africa lie only in co-operation between any African nation or group of African nations on the one hand, with any other nation of the world on the other, which is genuinely in sympathy with the aspirations of Africa as summed up in the aims and objects already stated above.*

There are six continents in the world—Europe, Asia, North America, South America, Australia and Africa. Of these, the most despised, through the ages, is Africa. It is only on our Continent that naked colonialism or neo-colonialism in various guises is still firmly in the saddle. There are probably some 200 million negroes in the world. Of these about 170 million are on the Continent of Africa. It is clear from these facts that the battle for the final destruction of colonialism or neo-colonialism, and for respect for the Negro peoples wherever they may be in the world, will be fought and won only in Africa. *The third principle which I am urging, therefore, is that all the countries and peoples on the Continent owe it a duty to Mother Africa to plan and work in concert until the aims and objects before-mentioned have been fully achieved.*

Now to my proposals.

I advocate the immediate setting up of an *ORGANISATION FOR AFRICAN COMMUNITY.* The membership of the Organisation should be confined to African Political Parties or Nationalist Movements. In other words, Governments as such would not be eligible for membership. The reasons for confining membership to political parties or nationalist movements are simple. Governments are bound by international law and usage which nationalist movements are not obliged to observe. Sometime ago, the All-African People's Congress resolved to recruit Africans and send them as volunteers to fight on the side of the Algerian nationalists. If either the Casablanca Powers or the Monrovia Powers were to pass a similar resolution, it would be interpreted by France as a declaration of war, or at all events as an unfriendly act. Furthermore, by confining membership to political parties or national movements, it will be possible to admit into the Organisation:

(a) the African Nationalist Movements in South Africa, Central African Federation, Kenya, and other dependent African territories;

(b) all the political parties in a country with a two-party or multi-party system; and

(c) the nationalist movements in Egypt—if they are separable from those in Syria.

Before any nationalist party or movement is admitted into the Organisation, it must avow its unshaken faith in every one of the aims which I have outlined above. Any party or movement which finds itself unable to adopt the aims, in their entirety, would not qualify for admission.

The Organisation should have a permanent secretariat which should be well staffed; and it would draw its funds from the following sources: (*a*) subscriptions from member-movements; (*b*) donations from individual Africans and from well-wishers; and (*c*) grants or subventions from Governments controlled by political parties or nationalist movements which are members of the Organisation.

The aims of the Organisation would be those which I have before stated, and any additional ones which those who agree to launch the Organisation may consider necessary.

The functions of the Organisation would be primarily to devise ways and means of accomplishing these aims, and secondarily to tackle such problems as may from time to time affect the whole or any part of Africa. The Organisation would have its own media of mass communication and propaganda, and would control all such instruments as are essential for the attainment of its objects; but generally it would operate through its adherents in all parts of Africa, employing, for the effectuation of its purposes, any methods which the prevailing circumstances in any part of Africa dictate.

The political union of Africa is an ideal which is not only worth working for but also one which can be realised. The present trends in the world indicate that the larger the population, and the more expansive the territory, of a State, the greater the chances of its more effective and more rapid development. Africa with a population of 200 millions and an area of $11\frac{1}{2}$ million square miles (the Sahara Desert covers $3\frac{1}{2}$ millions of the area), if united, would compare more than favourably with (i) Russia: Population—200 millions: Area—8,598,678 square miles; (ii) China: Population—650 millions: Area—3,876,956 square miles; (iii) USA: Population—160 millions: Area—2,974,725 square miles; and (iv) India: Population—450 millions: Area—1,709,500 square miles.

But the problem of uniting under one Government and under one leadership a Continent which lacks the racial, cultural and linguistic homogeneity of USA, the centuries-old cultural and national unity of China and (to a great extent) of India, and the ideological orientation and cohesion of Russia, must not be underestimated. The distinguishing factors which I have just mentioned are complicated by the fact that Africa has internal stresses and strains, divisions and conflicts, inherent in its political, economic and cultural evolution. But the problem, I believe, could be minimised if the Continent is divided into Zones, and each Zone is organised on the lines of Nos. 8 and 9 of the aims already stated.

In this connection, I must confess to my inability to venture concrete suggestions which will embrace the whole of Africa. But I have this much to say. The Sahara Desert is a natural line of demarcation between the Northern and Southern parts of Africa. It is my considered view that the countries of North Africa (with a population of about 40 millions) should, as a first step, constitute a Zone. As for the other territories south of the Sahara, I do not hesitate to repeat what my Party has been consistently advocating, namely that certain countries of West Africa (with a population of more than 90 millions) should constitute another Zone.

When at a Press Conference in Ghana I had said, in answer to a question, that if I were the Prime Minister of Nigeria I would see to it that Nigeria joined the Ghana-Guinea-Mali Union, I was accused, by the spokesman of the Federal Government, of having fallen under the magic spell of Dr. Nkrumah, and of departing from the Action Group party line. In view of this misplaced criticism, I quote the following relevant passages from the Action Group Policy Paper on West African Union which was published in 1959:

'A powerful and progressive West African Union would exercise such influence on the Continent of Africa as would accelerate the achievement of freedom for all other African peoples on the Continent. It would also be an inspiration to all negroes outside Africa, and a place to which they can look up to with pride.

'From the above, it is clear that a West African Union in one form or the other is a stark necessity in our time. The countries expected to be included in the Union are: Senegal (now Mali and Senegal), French Sudan, Gambia, the Republic of Guinea, Ivory Coast, Upper Volta, Dahomey, Niger, the four territories of French Equatorial Africa, the two Cameroons, Ghana, Liberia, Nigeria, Portuguese Guinea, Sierra Leone, Spanish Guinea and the Congo.

'The declared aim of Ghana and Guinea to form a Union which they intend as nucleus of a West African Federation is, therefore, a good idea, even though the Action Group may disagree with some of the details and procedure.

'Whilst the Action Group believes that the character of a West African Union is yet to be determined, it will nevertheless propose that the procedure to be adopted in realising this aim should recognise four stages as follows:

(*a*) the exploratory stage, when political leaders of the countries concerned should meet to know one another and discuss matters of common interest;
(*b*) the co-ordinating stage when there should be established agencies of inter-territorial economic, cultural and other forms of essential co-operation;
(*c*) the stage of a form of confederacy; and finally
(*d*) the stage of a form of Union or federation the character of which should be determined by events and time.

'There can be no doubt that from the history of other peoples desiring to come together, a West African Union may sound very unrealistic. But, others have come together to create the USA and the USSR. With the will we in West Africa can prove to the world that we can achieve our noble objective.'

It will be seen from the above quotation that my advocacy for Nigeria joining a Ghana-Guinea-Mali Union is in accordance with the settled, declared and longstanding policy of the Action Group, and that the stage now reached by the Ghana-Guinea-Mali Union, with Upper Volta recently added, is one of confederacy which accords with the third stage in the procedure for a West African Union suggested by the Action Group.

If I were the Prime Minister of Nigeria, I would strive to do much better than merely joining the Ghana-Guinea-Mali-Upper Volta Union. I would direct my energies in this field to the early political integration of all the countries which are mentioned in the Action Group Policy Paper, and would leave no stone unturned in fostering the political union of all the States in Africa.

As to how many Zones into which the remaining parts of Africa should be divided—this is a matter which must be left for consideration and settlement by the OAC (Organisation for African Community). In this regard, however, one important point must be emphasised. It is a grave error of judgment for anyone to imagine that there is a ready answer or an easy solution to the all-important problem of attaining the ideal of an All-African Political Union. There is no disagreement at all, among African nationalists, as to the soundness of this ideal. But as to the methods of attaining the ideal, there will, until the ideal is realised, always be as many points of view as there are groups of people (African and non-African) who ever give careful and considered thoughts to the issues involved.

More explicitly, therefore, in order that it may achieve its aims and objects with a despatch which the pressing needs and the deep yearnings and aspirations of Africa demand, the OAC must first and last be a revolutionary body. It must openly advocate the overthrow of all white rule in Africa, whether such rule is by white settlers or by white colonial Powers. To this end, it must also openly encourage and assist by all means at its disposal, every African nationalist movement which is working for the overthrow of such rule.

Any member-movement of the Organisation, whether it is the party in power in any country or not, which is proved to be disloyal to any of the aims and objects of the Organisation, should be expelled and ostracised. Where a political party or nationalist movement is expelled, it would be the duty of the OAC to do all in its power, through its adherents and agencies, to weaken and if possible eradicate the followership and influence of such a party or movement in its home base and anywhere else in Africa.

25

THE FUTURE OF PAN-AFRICANISM

Extracts from an Address by the Rt. Hon. Dr. Nnamdi Azikiwe, Governor-General of Nigeria, delivered in London to the Committee of African Organisations on August 12, 1961

I think that Pan-Africanism should be concretised either in the form of regional States or one Continental State, whichever is feasible, allowing this to be done voluntarily without upsetting the total sovereignty of the States concerned. If this barrier is hurdled, I suggest that the African States concerned should sign and ratify conventions, among others which I shall dilate upon, guaranteeing fundamental human rights among their citizens, social security among their workers, and collective security among their populations.

Above all, I will suggest that African States should now, as an earnest of their sincere belief in Pan-Africanism, declare a doctrine of non-intervention in the Continent of Africa, making it clear that the establishment of the continued existence of any colonial territory in Africa, by any non-African State, shall be regarded as an unfriendly act of aggression against the African States collectively. . . .

Not being a seer, I can only prophesy that the nature of this political union may be continental or regional, but the fact remains that Pan-Africanism is destined to be feasible either in the immediate or distant future.

Whether the unity of African States is possible or not depends upon the ability of African leaders to resolve the problems created by the social intercourse of the inhabitants of Africa. As I said earlier on, these are mainly anthropological, sociological, and ideological, and they affect not only the individual Africans themselves but also their societies. It is my candid opinon that if pursued in the right spirit, most of these problems can be effectively adjusted for the emergence of a fertile soil that will be favourable for the evolution of some sort of association of African States.

Pan-Africanism in action has proved the existence of deep-seated fears which exist in the minds of certain African leaders in some African States. The Principles of Monrovia demonstrate the nature of these fears, to wit: the right of African States to equality of sovereignty irrespective of size and population; the right of each African State to self-determination and existence; the right of any African State to federate or confederate with another African State; respect for the principle of non-interference in the internal and domestic affairs of African States *inter se*; and the inviolability of the territorial integrity of each African State. These are well known accepted principles of International Law.

The proposal to integrate Togo and Ghana has been a source of anxiety to the Ghanaian, Togolese and other friends of Pan-Africanism. The claim of Morocco to sovereignty over Mauritania is a denial of the right to self-determination to the Mauritanians according to those who believe in Mauritania. The refusal of Sudan to attend the Monrovia Conference because Mauritania was invited shows the nature of the cleavage between the Casablanca and Monrovia Powers. The walking-out of the Morocco delegation from the International Labour Conference when the Republic of Mauritania was admitted into its membership, is another pointer. The fact that the Casablanca Powers support the claim of Algeria to self-determination, on the one hand, and, on the other, deny the right of Mauritania to self-determination, indicates the gravity of these problems.

If the issues mentioned in the preceding paragraphs are secondary, it is essential that we examine also the primary ones. First, the inhabitants of the African continent are not racially homogeneous. In North Africa, the majority of the population belong to the Mediterranean group of the Caucasoid race. In Africa south of the Sahara, the majority are Negroid, with the exception of a small minority of European settlers in southern Africa who are either members of the Alpine or Nordic groups of the Caucasoids. The co-existence of these racial groups has created a social problem in Africa as the *apartheid* and *Mau Mau* have shown.

Secondly, the existence of various linguistic groups in Africa has intensified the problem of communication and human understanding. Whilst those who live on the fringe of the Mediterranean are Hamitic-speaking, the Africans of the west are mainly Sudanic-speaking. The indigenous central and southern Africans are Bantu-speaking. The inhabitants of eastern Africa are partially Sudanic, Bantu, Hamitic and Semitic. The small European elements in southern Africa speak either English or Afrikaans. Emerging out of this milieu is the fact that to millions of Africans either English or Arabic or Swahili or Hausa is the *lingua franca*, whilst the rest have to manage as best they can.

Thirdly, the impact of various cultures on African society has created basic problems of social unity. One example is the activities of the Pan-Arab League which seeks to unite under one fold all the Arab-speaking peoples not only of Africa but also of the Middle East. Another example is the attempt being made in certain quarters to create an Islamic Confederation which will cut across racial, linguistic and cultural lines. Then there is the move to interpret Pan-Africanism purely in terms of race and to restrict its membership and activities to the Negroids and thereby exclude other races who live in Africa who are not black.

These three problems are real. The practice of racial segregation and discrimination is a disturbing factor in society, as the examples of the United States, the Union of South Africa and the Central African Federation have shown. The official use or recognition of any particular language to the detriment of others has not made for harmonious human relations and the experiences of India, Pakistan, Ceylon, and the USSR are a great lesson. My conclusion is that parochialism in the realms of race, language, culture or religion has often led to social disintegration.

Therefore, it constitutes a social and psychological barrier which must be hurdled if Pan-Africanism is to become a reality.

If the anthropological problems are basic, then the sociological are complex since they affect the economic, political and constitutional aspects of the lives of those concerned. Economically, the existence of tariff walls and barriers has tended to alienate rather than draw closer the relations of those who should be good neighbours. High competitive markets have led to cut-throat methods of bargaining and distribution. The use of separate currencies as legal tender has accentuated social differences. With separate road, railway, aviation and communications systems, Africans have become estranged to one another.

The political issues are even confounding. Granted that political union is desirable, the question arises whether it should be in the form of a federation or a confederation. If the former, should it be a tight or a loose one? In any case sovereignty must be surrendered in part or in whole, in which case, it will be desirable to know whether it is intended to surrender internal or external sovereignty or both? In this context, we cannot overlook the struggle for hegemony as indeed has been the case in the last few years. Hand in glove with the struggle for hegemony goes the manoeuvre for the control of the armed forces for the effective implementation of policy.

The constitutional implications of Pan-Africanism present to its builders a challenge to create a heaven on earth for African humanity. Therefore, the powers of the executive must be clearly defined, bearing in mind that in most of the progressive States of the world, Heads of States exercise powers formally and Heads of Governments formulate policy and do the actual governing. Nevertheless, the vogue is to accept the supremacy of the legislature, as a forum for airing the views of the electorate and strengthening the hands of the executive.

Pan-Africanists must also guarantee the independence of the judiciary, not necessarily by stratifying judges as a select and privileged elite but by ensuring that they shall perform their functions without fear or favour and at the same time be responsible to the people for their actions and behaviour. To obtain maximum efficiency in the machinery of administration, the civil service must be insulated from partisan politics. As for the people themselves, their fundamental rights must be guaranteed and entrenched in any document or instrument creating any association of African States.

African Leviathan

With such a background, the future of Pan-Africanism can be tackled optimistically. I have never disguised my belief that African States can unite for the achievement of certain political objectives; but in spite of my optimism, I have never hidden my fears that the barriers to be overcome are many and variegated. As I see it, there is bound to arise an African leviathan in the form of a political organisation or association or union or concert of States. Such a leviathan may be formed on a continental basis, in which case, we may have, say, an association of African States. It may be formed also on a regionalised basis, in which case we may have the emergence of a union of North African States or West African States or Central African States or East African States or South African States. It is not impossible for such a leviathan to be formed on any other basis that may be distinct from a continental or regional one.

Once such a leviathan has become a reality, it will be necessary for the nature of form of its Government to be known. Three main forms are known to students of government; unitary, federal and confederate. If it is to be unitarian, then it will be highly centralised with some devolution of its internal sovereignty to its local government units. If it is to be federal, then it will be necessary to decide whether the internal sovereignty of the federal government shall be explicitly defined, whilst allocating to it the exclusive exercise of external sovereignty, but reserving residuary powers to its co-ordinate units, as is the case of Nigeria, or vice versa, as is the case of Canada, or a mixture of both systems, as is the case of India. If it is to be a confederate form of government, then both the external and internal sovereignties of the individual members of the confederation shall remain intact, subject to whatever aspect of same may be surrendered for the smooth operation of the confederated States. Ghana-Guinea-Mali Union is an example of this.

Howbeit, such a leviathan on becoming a *fait accompli* must be accepted as a concert of African States. In the light of what has happened in Europe and America, I am of the opinion that a concert of African States, as envisaged, must be properly organised and must have organs of administration. It should be organised to enable top level decisions to be made probably by Heads of States or Heads of Governments or their representatives. A Parliament of African States will have to meet periodically for general discussion of the problems confronting the African concert. Naturally, it should be organised on the basis of the United Nations Assembly. To settle disputes amicably, among African States, a Pan-African Court of International Justice will necessarily be set up and it should interpret the laws of members of the concert in addition to the accepted principles of International Law. A Pan-African Secretariat, manned co-operatively by nationals of the concert will be responsible for the administration of the day-to-day affairs of this African leviathan.

Having established what, for want of a definite name, I have preferred to term a concert of African States, the need to safeguard its unity and to guarantee the fundamental rights of the citizens of the States forming the concert becomes apparent. It is essential that the unity of the concert should be safeguarded because of the problems of Pan Africanism which hitherto have been discussed *in extenso*. Not only that, each State-Member of the concert must seriously devise ways and means of raising living standards of their inhabitants, to make the union worthwhile. Whilst doing this, they must realise that the continent of Africa, which has suffered degradation for centuries can also set an example of how to restore the dignity of man in Africa.

Convention on Economic Co-operation

In the case of the former, I suggest that members of the concert should promulgate a Convention on Economic Co-operation which should be signed, ratified and enforced by all its signatories and accessories. This convention should declare a customs union between all its signatories to enable their inhabitants to break down all tariff walls and barriers which separated them. When the Republics of Ghana and Upper Volta removed customs barriers between the two countries recently, it was a forward step towards African unity. Economic integration of this nature is destined to crystallise a spirit of oneness and thus quicken the pace towards political integration.

Another economic factor which can bring political unity nearer is the establishment of a common market. It is my considered view that this should be one of the stipulations in a convention designed to encourage economic co-operation among African States. A common currency should be used as legal tender in any concert of African States. Both Ghana and Nigeria made inexcusable mistakes when they virtually destroyed the uniting influence of the West African currency on their attainment of independence; but this mistake can be rectified now and thus help to revamp the economies of not only Sierra Leone and the Gambia, but those of other countries which may be willing to join such a concert.

The Convention on Economic Co-operation should not only enforce a common currency in its territories of jurisdiction, but it should ensure the creation of régimes which should make possible a regional road authority, a trans-African railway system, a Pan-African airways, and a telecommunications authority. If the West African States would establish a regional road authority, movement of individuals and goods in their respective countries would quicken and solidarity of views would be cemented. If their railway, aviation and telecommunication systems are organised on a uniform basis, the economic integration of these territories would be a foregone conclusion.

Convention on Collective Security

In order to make secure the safety of the properties and persons who live in the territories of this concert of African States, I suggest that the members of the concert should also promulgate an African Convention on Collective Security. This should make provision for the following: a multilateral pact of mutual defence which shall stipulate that an attack on any member of the concert shall be construed to be an attack on the concert jointly and severally; an African High Command, consisting of the General Staff of each member of the concert, whose function shall be to determine military strategy, tactics and logistics so as to safeguard the territorial integrity of the concert.

In connection with this Convention on Collective Security in Africa, the concert should postulate a doctrine of non-intervention in Africa, on the same lines as the Monroe Doctrine in the western hemisphere. This doctrine should make it clear that the establishment or the continued existence of any colonial territory in the Continent of Africa, by any European or American or Asian or Australian power shall be regarded not only as an unfriendly act, but as an act of aggression against the concert of African States. This is one concrete way of making it impossible for certain nations who have been forced to surrender their colonial swag in Africa, to seek by devious methods to continue their insidious game.

Then, there should be incorporated in such a convention a Pan-African Declaration of Neutralism. This declaration should define what neutralism means. It should explain that it is coterminous with non-alignment and that it means an independent policy which should not oblige members of the concert either to inherit the prejudices of other nations or to join forces directly or indirectly with any bloc of nations against any other bloc in any war, or to act in such a way and manner as to give the impression that any particular bloc or group of nations is right or wrong in its approach to the solution of international problems.

Convention on Human Rights

Finally, the concert of African States should promulgate an African Convention on Human Rights as an earnest of their belief in the rule of law, democracy as a way of life, respect for individual freedom, and respect for human dignity. This convention on human rights should declare categorically the faith of the States-Members of the concert of Africa in freedom under the law. It should be unequivocal in declaring the right of Africans to life, liberty and the pursuit of happiness. It should define in detail all the fundamental liberties of the citizen which shall neither be abridged nor denied to the African, excepting under due process of law; and it should make it clear that the African has an inalienable right to free speech, free Press, freedom of assembly, freedom of association, freedom of movement, freedom from discrimination, freedom from want, freedom from inhuman treatment, freedom from slavery or forced labour, and freedom of conscience and worship.

That is how I see the future of this African leviathan. From its roots which take us to the days of the Anti-Slavery Society and the American Colonization Society to the partition of Africa by the Berlin Conference of 1885, Africa has been evolving from a so-called 'dark continent' to a continent of light. From the days when Edward Wilmot Blyden dreamt of an African personality to the time when Marcus Aurelius Garvey preached his sermons on 'back to Africa', and Casely Hayford, duBois, Aggrey, Kenyatta, Javabu, Padmore, and other prophets of Pan-Africanism dreamt dreams and saw visions of a new Africa, the Continent has experienced a great awakening. . . .

An African federation or confederation, either on a regional or continental basis, has many blessings for the Continent of Africa and its inhabitants. Politically, it will raise the prestige of African States in the councils of the world; it will make Africa a bastion of democracy, and it will revive the stature of man by guaranteeing to African citizens the fundamental rights of man. From a military point of view, such a concert of States will protect the people of Africa not only from external aggression and internal commotion, but also it would safeguard the whole of Africa by a system of collective security. Economically, by abrogating discriminatory tariffs, we create a free trade area over the entire Continent and thereby expand the economy of all African countries involved, thereby raising living standards and ensuring economic security for African workers. Socially, it will restore the dignity of the human being in Africa.

The Challenge

In conclusion, it is my firm belief that an African leviathan must emerge ultimately: it may be in the form of an association of African States or in the form of a concert of African States; but my main point is that so long as the form of government is clearly understood and an efficient machinery for organisation and administration is devised, backed by multilateral conventions which would enhance the standard of living of Africans, safeguard their existence by collective security, and guarantee to them freedom under the law in addition to the fundamental human rights, the dream of Pan-Africanism is destined to come true.

Finally, one of the leading Africanists of all times, Edward Wilmot Blyden said: 'It is really high time that a unity of spirit should pervade the people of the world for the regeneration of a Continent so long despoiled by the unity or consent of these same people. Thinking Negroes should ask themselves what part they will take in this magnificent work of reclaiming a Continent—their own Continent. In what way will they illustrate their participation in the unity of spirit which pervades the people of their fatherland?'

That was Dr. Blyden preaching Pan-Africanism in the nineteenth century. On our part, what shall we do? History will chronicle the choice made by us in the twentieth century.

REFERENCES

Frequent references are made to the following periodicals, and miscellanies:

Africa South: Originally published in Cape Town, but removed to London in 1960. Publication was suspended in London in December, 1961.

Black Orpheus: Ministry of Education. W. Nigeria Government, Ibadan, Nigeria.

Ghana Today: A fortnightly review issued by Ghana High Commissioner's Office, London.

Présence Africaine: 42, Rue Descartes, Paris, 5e.

Race: Journal of the Institute of Race Relations, 6 Duke of York Street, London, S.W.1. Published by Oxford University Press.

Race Relations: Journal of the South African Institute of Race Relations, P.O. Box 97, Johannesburg.

The Phylon Quarterly: The Atlanta University Review of Race and Culture, Georgia, U.S.A.

West Africa: 2 Hind Court, London, E.C.2.

1. *Crisis*, February, 1919 (N.A.A.C.P., New York).
2. G. Shepperson, *Notes on Negro American Influences on the Emergence of African Nationalism* (*Journal of African History*, Vol. 1, No. 2. Cambridge University Press, 1960).
3. Arthur P. Davies, *The Alien-and-Exile Theme in Countee Cullen's Racial Poems* (*Phylon*, Vol. XIV, 1953).
4. Davies, *op. cit.*
5. Harold R. Isaacs, *Five Writers and Their African Ancestors* (*Phylon*, Third Quarter, 1960). This is a most valuable attempt to understand the relationship between Negro writers and Africa.
6. James Ivy, in *The Semantics of being Negro in the Americas* (*Présence Africaine*, Vol. XXIV–XXV, 1959), gives a useful outline of the meaning and associations of "Negro."
7. Harold R. Isaacs, *The American Negro and Africa: Some Notes* (*Phylon*, Vol. XX, No. 3, 1959).
8. Warner, Junker and Adams, *Color and Human Nature* (Washington, 1941). Sutherland, *Color, Class and Personality* (Washington, 1942).
9. Ras Khan, *The Poetry of Dr. R. E. G. Armattoe* (*Présence Africaine*, February-March, 1957).
10. Langston Hughes, *The Langston Hughes Reader* (Braziller, New York, 1958); *Selected Poems* (Knop F. New York, 1959); *Tambourines to Glory* (John Day, New York, 1958).
11. Olumbe Bassir (Ed), *An Anthology of West African Verse* (Ibadan, 1957).
12. Samuel Allen's translation in *Africa as Seen by Negroes* (*Présence Africaine*, 1958).
13. Miriam Koshland's translation in *Black Orpheus*, 1958.
14. Shepperson, *op. cit.*
15. *The Aims and Methods of a Liberal Education for Africans*, Inaugural Address as President of Liberia College, Monrovia, January 5, 1881. Quoted by Edward Blyden in *Christianity, Islam, the Negro Race* (London 1887) pp. 82-107.
16. A. Césaire, *Culture and Colonisation* (*Présence Africaine*, Nos. 8, 9, 10, 1956).

17. G. Shepperson and T. Price, *Independent African* (The University Press, Edinburgh, 1958).
18. Joseph Booth, *Africa for the African* (1897?).
19. Shepperson and Price, *op.cit.*
20. Shepperson and Price, *op. cit.*
21. Shepperson and Price, *op. cit.*
22. W. E. B. duBois, *Dusk of Dawn*, New York, 1940.
23. Shepperson and Price, *op. cit.*
24. W. E. B. duBois, *Soul of Black Folks* (1903). *The Negro* (1915). *Dark Princess* (1927). *Color and Democracy* (1945), (London, 1946). *The World and Africa* (1946). *In Battle for Peace* (1952). *Black Reconstruction* (1955).
25. J. Garvey, *Philosophy and Opinions* (New York, 1923).
26. Horace R. Clayton and St. Clair Drake, *Black Metropolis* (New York, 1945): James Weldon Johnson, *Black Manhattan* (New York): J. A. Rogers, *World's Great Men of Colour* (New York, 1946): Elliot M. Rudwick: *W. E. B. duBois* (University of Pennsylvania Press, 1960).
27. Harold R. Isaacs, *DuBois and Africa* (*Race* Vol. 2. November, 1960). This is a valuable critical study of duBois.
28. *New York Times*, March 5, 1959.
29. P. K. Isaka Seme, *The Regeneration of Africa* (Colombia University Press, 1906).
30. Sol Plaatje, *Native Life in South Africa* (1912).
31. D. D. T. Jabavu, *The Black Problem* (1921): *The Segregation Fallacy* (1928).
32. Dr. A. B. Xuma, *Reconstituting the Union of South Africa* (Johannesburg, 1932).
33. Monica Hunter, *Reaction to Conquest* (Oxford University Press, 1936)
34. Dr. Nnamdi Azikiwe, *Renascent Africa* (Lagos, 1937). *Nigeria in World Politics* (Lagos, 1959). *Zik Speaks* (Cambridge University Press, 1960). *The Future of Pan-Africanism* (Nigeria Information Service, London, 1961).
35. Bishop Alexander Walters, *My Life and Work*.
36. Shepperson and Price, *op. cit.*
37. Shepperson and Price, *op. cit.*
38. Shepperson and Price, *op. cit.*
39. Shepperson and Price, *op. cit.*
40. *New York Evening Globe Mail*, quoted by G. Padmore, *Pan-Africanism or Communism* (Dobson, London, 1956).
41. G. Padmore, *op. cit.*
42. C. L. R. James, *The Black Jacobins;* (Secker and Warburg, London, 1938).
43. C. Legum, *Bandung, Cairo and Accra* (The African Bureau, London, 1958), gives a brief account of this break with the Comintern.
44. Jomo Kenyatta, *Facing Mount Kenya* (Secker and Warburg, London, 1953). His book is dedicated "To Moigoi and Wamboi and all the dispossessed youth of Africa . . . for perpetuation of communism with ancestral spirits through the fight for African freedom, and in the firm faith that the dead, the living and the unborn will write to rebuild the destroyed shrines."
45. Padmore, *op. cit.*
46. N. Azikiwe, *The Atlantic Charter and British West Africa*. This was published in Lagos in 1943 by a group of West African editors claiming the right of self-determination under Clause III of the Atlantic Charter.
47. A. Toynbee, *The Ultimate Choice* (*Race*, Vol. 2, 2). *Note:* I do not agree with Prof. Toynbee's views on all aspects of this question. I consider the weakness of his argument derives from his failure to distinguish between race-consciousness and racialism. (C. L.)
48. Parliamentary Debates, Federation of Nigeria (Lagos, August 11, 1959).
49. *Eastern Nigeria Today* (Enugu, May, 1961).
50. David Diop, *Les Temps du Martyr* (Ed. Bassir. *op. cit.*).
51. C. Legum, *Congo Disaster* (Penguin, London, 1961).
52. Paul Robeson, quoted by Vernon McKay in *The Concept of Pan-Africanism* (*Race Relations Journal*, Vol. XXVII, No. 3. Institute of Race Relations, Johannesburg, 1960).

53. Jean-Paul Sartre, *Orphée Noir* in Senghor's *Anthologie de la Nouvelle Poésie Négre et Malgache* (Presses Universitaires de France, Paris, 1948).
54. Aimé Césaire, *Four Poems* (translated by Miriam Koshland) (*Black Orpheus*, January, 1948).
55. C. Legum, *Bandung, Cairo and Accra, op. cit.*
56. A. G. Nasser, *The Philosophy of Revolution* (Cairo, 1953).
57. *Egyptian Gazette* (Special Conference Issue), Cairo, January 1, 1958.
58. Padmore, *op. cit.*
59. Padmore, *op. cit.* This resolution stands as quoted by him.
60. C. Legum, *Bandung, Cairo and Accra, op. cit.*
    C. Legum, *Accra Diary* (*Africa South*, Vol. 1, No. 2, 1958). K. Nkrumah, *I Speak of Freedom* (Heinemann, London, 1961); Praeger, New York, 1961).
61. Catherine Hoskyns, *Pan-Africanism at Accra* (*Africa South*, Cape Town, Vol. 3, No. 3, 1959).
62. K. Nkrumah, *op. cit.*
63. N. Azikiwe, *The Future of Pan-Africanism, op. cit.*
64. C. Legum, *Congo Disaster, op. cit.*
65. Hella Pick, *The Brazzaville Twelve and How They Came To Be* (*Africa Report*, Vol. 6, No. 5, New York, 1961).
    Philippe Decraene, *Le Panafricanisme* (Presse Universitaires de France, Paris, 1959).
    Thomas Hodgkin and Ruth Schachter, *French-Speaking West Africa in Transition* (*International Conciliation*, Carnegie Endowment for International Peace, 1960).
66. *Fraternité*, the Ivory Coast government organ, described the Brazzaville decisions as the birth of a new bloc embracing the ideas of its President, M. Houphouet-Boigny.
67. Margaret Roberts, *Summary at Casablanca* (*Africa South*, Vol. 5, No. 3, London, 1961).
68. Interview with Hella Pick, *The Guardian*, Manchester, May 15, 1961.
69. *West Africa*, London, May 6, 1961.
70. K. Nkrumah, *op. cit.*
71. K. Nkrumah, *op. cit.*
72. *Awo, The Autobiography of Chief Obafemi Awolowo* (Cambridge University Press, 1961).
73. *Sunday Post*, Lagos, September 10, 1961.
74. Statement at a Press Conference in London, August 23, 1961.
75. D. K. Chisiza, *Realities of African Independence* (*The Africa Publications Trust*, London, 1961).
76. L. Radovanović, *From Bandung to Belgrade* (Yugoslavia Information Service, 1961).
77. *Sunday Post*, Lagos, September 10, 1961.
78. For a discussion on these and other aspects of non-alignment see *Neutralism*, The Washington Center of Foreign Policy Research, 1961.
79. Chisiza, *op. cit.*
80. *The Times*, London, October 16, 1961.
81. *Ghana Today*, London, April 26, 1961.
82. *West Africa*, London, June 27, 1961.
83. Sékou Touré, *The Political Action of the Democratic Party of Guinea*. Vol. III (Conakry, 1960).
84. Modeiba Keita, translation of an address in French at Chatham House, London, May 17, 1961 (*International Affairs*, Vol. 37, No. 4).
85. Peter Partner, *A Short Political Guide to the Arab World* (Pall Mall, London, 1960); (Praeger, New York, 1960).
86. William Sands, *Prospects for a United Maghreb* (*The Arab Middle East and Muslim Africa*, Thames & Hudson, London, 1961).
87. Dr. M. S. Agwani, *Political and Economic Challenges in the Maghreb* (Indian Council for Africa, New Delhi, 1960).

88. Habib Bourguiba. *The Victory Speech* (delivered to the Sixth Neo-Destour Party Congress, Sousse, March 2, 1959).
89. *Afrique Action* (Tunis, October 17, 1960).
90. Ben Barka, *The Unity of the Maghreb* (*Africa South*, Vol. 5, No. 2, London, 1961).
91. Peter Kilner, *The Sudan since Independence* (London, 1961). J. S. R. Duncan, *The Making of the Modern Sudan* (Blackwood, London, 1959).
92. I. M. Lewis, *A Pastoral Democracy* (Oxford University Press, 1961).
93. E. Sylvia Pankhurst, *Eritrea on the Eve* (1952). G. V. Trevaskis, *Modern Eritrea* (Oxford University Press, 1960).
94. Clyde Sanger, *The Guardian*, Manchester, October 24, 1960.
95. Donald Rothchild, *Toward Unity in Africa* (Public Affairs Press, Washington, 1961).
96. *Report of the Commission on Closer Union of the Dependencies in Eastern and Central Africa*, Cmd. 3234 (London, 1929). *Statement of the Conclusions of H.M.G. in the U.K. as regards Closer Union in East Africa*, Cmd. 3574 (London, 1931). *East African Royal Commission Report*, Cmd. 9475 (London, 1955). Bernard Chidzero, *Tanganyika* (Oxford University Press, 1961).
97. *Drum*, Johannesburg, January, 1961.
98. *Ghana Today*, London, July 5, 1961. I. Wallerstein, *Background to Paga* (*West Africa*, London, July 29 and August 5, 1961).
99. Ghana News Agency, October 25, 1961.
100. Philippe Decraene, *West African Unity* (*Africa South*, London, Vol. 4, No. 2, 1960).
101. Hodgkin and Schachter, *op. cit.*
102. Catherine Hoskyns, *African Unions and Politics* (*West Africa*, London, September 3 and 10, 1960). Thomas Hodgkin, *Nationalism in Colonial Africa* (Muller, London, 1956).
103. Gogo Nzeribe, *The Ghanaian Worker*, Accra, November 7, 1959.
104. *Free Trade Unions in the Fight for African Freedom* (I.C.F.T.U.–A.F.R.O. Publication, Brussels, 1961).
105. Tom Mboya, speaking at the second I.C.F.T.U.–A.F.R.O. Conference, Lagos, 1959.
106. Resolutions of second I.C.F.T.U.–A.F.R.O. Conference, 1959.
107. *One Africa*, Ghana T.U.C., January, 1961.
108. *Joint Declaration on behalf of the Ghana T.U.C. and the Kenya Federation of Labour*, Nairobi, November 21, 1960.
109. *Free Trade Unions in the Fight for African Freedom* (I.C.F.T.U.–A.F.R.O. Publication, 1961).
110. *The African Trade Unions*, Press statement by Julius K. Nyerere, Dar-es-Salaam, December, 1960.
111. *The I.C.F.T.U. and Pan-Africanism*, Press release, Brussels, June 15, 1961.
112. I.C.F.T.U. Radio Service, Brussels, June 8, 1961.
113. *West Africa*, London, June 10, 1961.
114. *A.F.L.–C.I.O. Free Trade Union News*, New York, June, 1961.
115. *West Africa*, London, June 10, 1961.
116. *The African Worker*, S.A.C.T.U., Johannesburg, September 1, 1961.
117. Leopold Senghor (Ed.), *Anthologie de la Nouvelle Poésie Négre et Malgache*, translated by Samuel Allen (Presses Universitaires de France, Paris, 1948).
118. John Reed, The Relevance of Nègritude (*Central African Examiner*, Salisbury, June, 1961).
119. Janheinz Jahn, *Aimé Césaire* (*Black Orpheus*, 1958).
120. *Nègritude* (*Black Orpheus*, 1958).
121. J.-P. Sartre, *Orphée Noir*, *op. cit.*
122. Allen, *op. cit.*
123. E. Mphahlele, *Down Second Avenue* (Faber, London, 1959).
124. *Encounter* (London, March, 1961).

125. George Lamming, *In the Castle of My Skin* (Michael Joseph, London, 1953). *The Emigrants* (Michael Joseph, London, 1954). *Of Age and Innocence* (Michael Joseph, London, 1958). *The Pleasures of Exile* (Michael Joseph, London, 1961).
126. Alioun Diop, *Opening Address to First Congress of Negro Writers and Artists* (*Présence Africaine*, Nos. 8, 9, 10, 1956).
127. Richard Wright, *Native Son* (New York, 1940). *12 Million Black Voices* (New York, 1942). *Black Boy* (New York, 1945). *Black Power* (his journey to Ghana) (Dobson, London, 1956). *The Color Curtain* (his impressions of the Bandung Conference) (Dobson, London, 1956). *The God That Failed* (Ed. by R. H. S. Crossman, Hamish Hamilton, London, 1950).
128. Richard Wright, *Tradition and Industrialization* (*Présence Africaine*, Nos. 8, 9, 10, 1956).
129. Jacques Rabemananjara, who returned to Madagascar after nearly 15 years' exile in Paris, includes among his published works *Sur les Marches du Soir* and *Les Dieux Malgaches*, Paris.
130. Jacques Rabemananjara, *Europe and ourselves* (*Présence Africaine*, Nos. 8, 9, 10, 1956).
131. Davidson Nicol, *The Soft Pink Palms* (*Présence Africaine*, Nos. 8, 9, 10, 1956).
132. John A. Davies, *Discussion at the First Congress of Negro Writers and Artists* (*Présence Africaine*, Nos. 8, 9, 10, 1956).
133. A. Césaire, *Culture and Colonisation* (*Présence Africaine*, Nos. 8, 9, 10, 1956).
134. L. Senghor, *Discussion at the First Congress of Negro Writers and Artists* (*Présence Africaine*, Nos. 8, 9, 10, 1956).
135. Alioun Diop, *op. cit.*
136. Michael Dei-Aneng, *Wayward Lines from Africa* (London, 1946).
137. Janheinz Jahn, *Muntu* (Faber, London, 1961).
138. A. Césaire, *The Man of Culture and His Responsibilities* (*Présence Africaine*, Nos. 24, 25, 1959).
139. Senghor, *op. cit.*
140. Sékou Touré, quoted by Césaire in *The Political Thought of Sékou Touré* (*Présence Africaine*, No. 29, 1960).
141. A. Césaire, *Letter to Maurice Thorez* (*Présence Africaine*, 1956).
142. Richard Wright, *op. cit.*
143. Harold R. Isaacs, *A Reporter at Large* (*The New Yorker*, May 13, 1961).
144. Statement by Mr. Julius Nyerere to the Second Conference of Independent African States, 1961.
145. For a valuable discussion on the practices of the "non-aligned", see Ernest W. Lefever, *Nehru, Nasser, Nkrumah on Neutralism* in *Neutralism, op. cit.*
146. *The Times*, London, May 15, 1961.
147. Speech in Bamako, August 22, 1961.
148. Address to Belgrade Conference, 1961.
149. *The Guardian*, Manchester, August 23, 1961.
150. N. Azikiwe, *Nigeria in World Politics, op. cit.*
151. Address to the Belgrade Conference, September, 1961.
152. Address to The Royal Institute of International Affairs, London, June 7, 1961.
153. Address to the Belgrade Conference, 1961.
154. Address to the Belgrade Conference, 1961.
155. Address to the Belgrade Conference, 1961.
156. Address to the Belgrade Conference, 1961.
157. *The Times*, London, May 15, 1961.
158. Sékou Touré, *Africa Speaks* (Van Nostrand, Princeton, N.J., 1961).
159. *Africa Digest*, London, October, 1961.
160. *The Washington Star*, December 9, 1961.
161. Quoted by Douglas G. Anglin in *The Canadian Journal of Economics and Political Science*, May, 1958.
162. Address to The Royal Institute of International Affairs, London, June 7, 1961.
163. Interview with William Attwood, *Look*, New York, June 25, 1957.

164. K. Nkrumah, *African Prospect* (Accra, 1961).
165. Address to the Belgrade Conference, 1961.
166. Address to the Belgrade Conference, 1961.
167. Speech on the ninth anniversary of the Egyptian Revolution, July 22, 1961.
168. Address to the Belgrade Conference, 1961.
169. Address to the Belgrade Conference, 1961.
170. Statement in Ghana Parliament, July 4, 1961.
171. K. Nkrumah, *Ghana's Policy at Home and Abroad* (Accra, 1957).
172. Ghana–Soviet communique signed by President Dr. Nkrumah and Premier Khruschev, July 25, 1961.
173. Address to the First All-African People's Conference, 1958.
174. Interview with William Attwood, *Look*, New York, June 25, 1957.
175. Address to the Belgrade Conference, 1961.
176. Sékou Touré, *Africa Speaks, op. cit.*
177. Address to The Royal Institute of International Affairs, London, June 7, 1961.
178. *The New York Times*, September 16, 1961.
179. Address to the Belgrade Conference, 1961.
180. Chisiza, *African Realities, op. cit.*
181. Address to The Royal Institute of International Affairs, London, May 17, 1961.
182. S. Olympio, *Africa Speaks, op. cit.*
183. *The Washington Star*, March 9, 1961.
184. Jacques Rabemananjara, *Variations on the Guinean Theme* (*Présence Africaine*, Vol. 1, No. 29, 1960).
185. Sékou Touré, *L'Expérience Guinéenne* (*Présence Africaine*, 1959).
186. *International Affairs*, London, October, 1961.
187. Césaire, *The Political Thought of Sékou Touré, op. cit.*
188. K. Nkrumah, *I Speak of Freedom, op. cit.*
189. T. Mboya, *Vision of Africa, Africa Speaks, op. cit.*
190. A. Diop, *Opening speech at the Second Congress of Negro Writers and Artists*, Rome, 1960.
191. Statement to General Assembly of the United Nations, April 5, 1958.
192. Statement to the Belgrade Conference, 1961.
193. Statement to First Conference of Independent African States (Accra, April, 1958).
194. Address to the Ghana National Assembly, May 30, 1961.
195. *New York Times*, October 27, 1961.
196. Sékou Touré, *Africa's Destiny* (*Africa Speaks, op. cit.*).
197. Address to The Royal Institute of International Affairs, London, June 7, 1961.
198. Memorandum on East African Federation for P.A.F.M.E.C.A., Dar-es-Salaam, January, 1961.
199. Address to Second Conference of Independent African States, Addis Ababa, 1960.
200. N. Azikiwe, *The Future of Pan-Africanism, op. cit.*
201. *Ghana Today*, London, April 26, 1961.
202. Interview with the author, December, 1960.
203. Foreword to *Nigeria: The Prospects For Democracy* by Chief H. O. Davies (Weidenfeld & Nicholson, London, 1961).
204. Awolowo, *Awo, op. cit.*
205. J. Nyerere, *The African and Democracy* (*Africa Speaks, op. cit.*).
206. Quoted by Césaire, *The Political Thought of Sékou Touré, op. cit.*
207. Abubaker Tafawa Balewa, *op. cit.*
208. J. Nyerere, *The African and Democracy* (*Africa Speaks, op. cit.*).
209. Sékou Touré, Address to P.D.G. Conference, Conakry, September 14, 1959.
210. Nyerere, *op. cit.*
211. Olympio, *op. cit.*
212. T. Mboya, *Vision of Africa* (*Africa Speaks, op. cit.*).

213. Chisiza, *op. cit.*
214. Chief H. O. Davies, *Nigeria: The Prospects for Democracy, op. cit.*
215. Interview with the author, December, 1960.
216. Awolowo, *Awo, op. cit.*
217. N. Azikiwe, *Nigeria in World Politics*, London, 1959.
218. Address to The Royal Institute of International Affairs, London, May 17, 1961.
219. Address to P.D.G. Congress, Conakry, September 14, 1959.
220. Address at C.P.P. Tenth Anniversary, Accra, June 12, 1949.
221. Address to P.D.G. Congress, Conakry, September 14, 1959.
222. Speech in Ghana Parliament on the motion for Approval of the Government's Revised Constitutional Proposals, November 12, 1956.
223. Dr. T. O. Elias, *Reflections on the Law of Lagos* (Journal of the International Commission of Jurists, Vol. III, No. 1, Geneva, 1961).
224. Gabriel d'Arboussier, *The Significance of the Lagos Conference* (Journal of the International Commission of Jurists, Vol. III, No. 1, Geneva, 1961).
225. Quoted by Césaire, *The Political Thought of Sékou Touré, op. cit.*
226. Senghor, *The African Path to Socialism* (*Venture*, Fabian Commonwealth Bureau, London, November, 1961).
227. Address at the tenth anniversary of the C.P.P., Accra, June 12, 1949.
228. Quoted by Senghor, *Venture, op. cit.*
229. *The Arab Review*, Vol. II, No. 16, 1961.
230. Quoted by Hodgkin, *A Note on the Language of African Nationalism* (St. Anthony's Papers, No. 10, Chatto & Windus, London, 1961).
231. Senghor, *Venture, op. cit.*

INDEX

Abbas, Ferhat, 192
Abboud, General Ibrahim, 113, 115, 201
Abdoulage, Diallo, 84
Abidjan, 50, 78
Abidjan-Niger, Rly, 78
Abrahams, Peter, 31, 104
Abubakar, *see* Balewa
Academy of African Solidarity, 261
Accra, 63, 66, 79, 90, 183; Bureau of
African Affairs, 31; AAPO Con-
ference (1958), *see under* All-African
Peoples' Organisation; AATUF in-
augurated, 83–4; Conference of
Independent African States (1958),
see under Conferences; ICFTU Con-
ference (1957), 82; UAS meeting
(1961), 183; WFTU Conference
(1961), 87
Action Group (Nigeria), 57–8, 266 n,
270
Addis Ababa, 72 (*see also* Conferences
of Independent African States, 1960)
Adjei, AKO, 46–7; on balkanisation,
120; statement at Addis Ababa,
170–1
Adoula, Cyrille, 87
Africa for the Africans (Booth), 22
'Africa for the Africans' slogan, 22–3,
38, 44
Africa Freedom Day, 142, 234
Africa Freedom Fund, 154, 247
African Charter, *see* Casablanca
Charter
African Christian Union, 22
African Colonial Enterprise (Thorne's)
26 n
African Commonwealth, proposal for,
230
African Consultative Assembly, pro-
posed (1961), 187
African Development Fund, 171
African Legion, 234
African Methodist Episcopal Zion
Church, 24, 27–8
African National Congress, 27, 34

'African Personality,' concept of, 20–22,
38, 83, 111, 117–18, 139, 141, 163,
277; Address on, 263–5
African Times and Orient Review, 41
African Trade Union Confederation, 91
African Transport Co., 239
African Unity, concept of, 170, 261
Afrique Equatorial Française (AEF),
77–80, 121
Afrique Occidentale Française (AOF),
77–9
Afro-Asian Solidarity Movement, 40,
262
AFRO Regional Organisation, 85, 86
Agbebi, Majola, 20
Aggrey, 277
Ahidjo, Ahmadou, 181, 201
Airlines, 79, 159, 232, 250, 276
Akintola, Chief S. L., 31
Algeria, 48 n., 50, 67, 83, 106; AAPC
resolutions on, 228, 232, 236–7,
241–2, 248; appeal to U.S. on.,
242; Casablanca resolution on, 191;
Independent African States reso-
lutions on, 139, 142, 149–51, 165–6,
196, 199; National Liberation Front
(FLN), 42, 43, 49, 67; Provisional
Govt., 46, 51, 53, 60 n., 112, 116,
152, 165, 196; trade unions, 85, 87,
89; war in, 36, 42, 61, 68, 142, 180
All-African Peoples' Organisation
(AAPO), 42–4, 48, 49, 53, 72;
constitution of, 223–8; first conference (Accra, Dec. 1958), 42–4,
81, 82, 223–36; second conference
(Tunis, 1960), 42–3, 73, 81, 84,
236–47; third conference (Cairo,
1961), 42, 43, 247–62
All-African Trade Union Federation
(AATUF), 81–91, 221–2
Allen, Stanley, 94
Ali, Duse Mohammed, 41
Almoravid Empire, 68
American Colonisation Society, 26 n.,
277

PRAEGER PAPERBACKS

PAN-AFRICANISM
A Short Political Guide

by COLIN LEGUM

Pan-Africanism is the most important cultural, political, and emotional force on the contemporary scene. It pervades, permeates, and influences all other concepts—such as Negritude, Western forms of democracy, socialism, and Communism. It is meaningful to all African leaders—and it means something different to each of them.

Colin Legum describes the origins and growth of this movement, interprets its basic ideas, and analyzes its impact on Africans since its transplantation in 1958. In an attempt to isolate the emotional reactions and drives that have produced its ideas, he probes the story of the experiences of a widely dispersed people, those of African stock who had lost independence and freedom and, in regaining them, have reasserted their dignity—that majestic, magical concept in the vocabulary of Pan-Africanists and the mainspring of all their actions.

An extensive appendix that contains the manifestoes and statements of the movement and its leaders—here assembled for the first time—adds greatly to the documentary value of the book.

THE AUTHOR: Colin Legum has been involved in African affairs since the late 1930's. He was a leader of the Johannesburg City Council and helped to found the Africa Bureau in London in 1952. Alone or with others, he has written five books on the African scene—among them the massive and comprehensive *Africa—A Handbook to the Continent*. Since 1949, Mr. Legum has been the Commonwealth Correspondent of *The Observer*.

A complete catalog of Praeger Paperbacks currently in print will be sent at your request.

FREDERICK A. PRAEGER, *Publisher*
64 University Place, New York 3, N.Y.